W9-BRY-524

EXITING YOUR BUSINESS, PROTECTING YOUR WEALTH

Exiting Your Business, Protecting Your Wealth

A Strategic Guide for Owners and Their Advisors

John M. Leonetti

WILEY

John Wiley & Sons, Inc.

This book is printed on acid-free paper. ∞

Copyright © 2008 by John M. Leonetti. All rights reserved.

Published by John Wiley & Sons, Inc., Hoboken, New Jersey.
Published simultaneously in Canada.

No part of this publication may be reproduced, stored in a retrieval system, or transmitted in any form or by any means, electronic, mechanical, photocopying, recording, scanning, or otherwise, except as permitted under Section 107 or 108 of the 1976 United States Copyright Act, without either the prior written permission of the Publisher, or authorization through payment of the appropriate per-copy fee to the Copyright Clearance Center, Inc., 222 Rosewood Drive, Danvers, MA 01923, 978-750-8400, fax 978-646-8600, or on the web at www.copyright.com. Requests to the Publisher for permission should be addressed to the Permissions Department, John Wiley & Sons, Inc., 111 River Street, Hoboken, NJ 07030, 201-748-6011, fax 201-748-6008, or online at http://www.wiley.com/go/permissions.

Limit of Liability/Disclaimer of Warranty: While the publisher and author have used their best efforts in preparing this book, they make no representations or warranties with respect to the accuracy or completeness of the contents of this book and specifically disclaim any implied warranties of merchantability or fitness for a particular purpose. No warranty may be created or extended by sales representatives or written sales materials. The advice and strategies contained herein may not be suitable for your situation. You should consult with a professional where appropriate. Neither the publisher nor author shall be liable for any loss of profit or any other commercial damages, including but not limited to special, incidental, consequential, or other damages.

For general information on our other products and services, or technical support, please contact our Customer Care Department within the United States at 800-762-2974, outside the United States at 317-572-3993 or fax 317-572-4002.

Wiley also publishes its books in a variety of electronic formats. Some content that appears in print may not be available in electronic books.

For more information about Wiley products, visit our Web site at http://www.wiley.com.

Library of Congress Cataloging-in-Publication Data

Leonetti, John M., 1970-
    Exiting your business, protecting your wealth: a strategic guide for owners and their advisors/John M. Leonetti.
        p.   cm.
    Includes index.
    ISBN 978-0-470-37618-8 (cloth)
1. Sale of business enterprises.   2. Business enterprises--Finance.   3. Business planning.
4. Tax planning.   I. Title.
HD1393.25.L46 2008
658.1'64--dc22

                                                            2008017694

Printed in the United States of America
10 9 8 7 6 5 4 3 2 1

This book is dedicated to every business owner who struck out on their own, to control their own destiny, and to build wealth so that future generations would have the opportunities that were not available to them.

At the top of this list is my father, Mario (and my mother who supported his decisions).

Understanding how to protect the illiquid business wealth that is trapped in your privately-held business is the purpose of this book. Behind that purpose is the graceful liberation of the business owner from their business after a lifetime of hard work, dedication, and sacrifice. Change is a necessary part of this process and this book is written to assist in learning how to best understand and apply the concepts necessary to implement those changes.

And, to the advisors that serve these business owners: This book will assist you in your efforts to provide creative solutions for the exit strategy plans that protect your business owner clients' wealth and empower you to be the trusted advisor that they need you to be.

CONTENTS

PREFACE

This is a book for business owners who are looking to maximize their business investment while also achieving their personal goals.

Across the United States, millions of business owners and entrepreneurs are approaching retirement age and have a need to protect the wealth they have built in their businesses. This Baby Boomer generation of business owners faces a number of obstacles in developing and executing an exit strategy that suits their needs. This book is written for those who run private businesses and are now preparing themselves for an exit. Its aim is to help these business owners to understand their options for exiting as well as their mental and financial readiness for that exit. Unfortunately, too few business owners know the options that exist for exiting their business or how to apply them to their personal situation.

For 15 years, this author has had a number of roles:

- Business owner in a family business
- Financial advisor with two of the largest firms in the world
- Legal advisor
- Business consultant
- Merger and acquisitions associate
- Exit strategies consultant to business owners
- Paid speaker
- Adjunct professor
- Author
- Mentor
- Training coach to the private finance/exit strategies community
- Most notably in the context of this book, an exiting business owner

The path that brought me to where I am today has opened my eyes to many areas of exit strategies that continue to disappoint me. First and foremost is the fact that business owners who had the courage to build a successful business can reach the end of their careers, be worth many millions of dollars, be respected by those they do business with, and still receive advice in a fragmented manner that tends to emphasize the way that the advisor gets paid, rather than providing holistic and comprehensive advice which focuses on that owner's true goals. A highly fragmented marketplace of advisors makes it very difficult for exiting business owners to navigate the numerous choices for an exit, to design the optimal exit and to assemble the optimal team. The step-by-step system in this book brings order to the complex exit strategy planning process allowing an exiting owner to better identify and organize the resources that they need.

Because 70% of private business owners report that their business is their primary source of income, a successful exit strategy is critical to owners who want to retire. Also, as you will see, only a small percentage of businesses (20%) successfully sell to an outside buyer. If we apply this low percentage of successful sales against the total number of businesses in the United States today, we see that there are millions of businesses that are either unsalable or will not be sold to an outside party. Solutions other than selling the business need to be applied to these millions of businesses. This book is one small step in a larger movement to address these issues.

Perhaps you are reading this book on the advice of an advisor who cares about you and your exit and has asked you to pay attention to some critical areas that can mean millions of dollars in preserved wealth for you. If this is the case, we are making progress, and you are tapped into the larger network of support that is crucial to set your exit in the right direction.

This book organizes complex concepts in an easy-to-understand manner in recognition of the fact that you are busy and there is a lot that you need to know. Case studies are provided throughout the book and almost every chapter has reference links to resources that provide further information on our companion Web site at www.exitingyourbusiness.com.

Enough has been said for now. Later you will thank yourself for the time that you invest in reading the pages that follow. Your business exit will cause many changes in your life; getting it right is critical as you move into your next phase.

Now let's get started on your business exit strategy.

ACKNOWLEDGMENTS

Many friends and associates contributed to the production of this book. My thanks to Rob Slee who had the foresight to write a textbook about the private capital markets and to give so much of his time working closely with me in developing an MBA course to teach this material and further refine my thinking in this growing exit strategy planning area. Thanks also to Mike Nall for introducing me to Rob many years ago—along with the countless other introductions that you have made over the years to assist in establishing the roots by which this book could be formed.

Thanks to Sheck Cho at Wiley for believing in this work and taking the initiative to bring it to the marketplace. And to my assistant Holly, who provided countless hours of interpreting my handwritten notes into legible form—without her assistance, this book would also not have any charts or exhibits.

Many professionals contributed to the technical content within each of these chapters. My thanks to David Neagle and everything that he has taught me about the mindset for success. Chapter 3 would not exist without his contributions to my understanding in this critical area. Also to the members of David's Mastermind group for the professional support and good energy they provided to this creative process. Along with David's strategic coaching, I owe a debt of gratitude to Liz Murphy—thank you once again for helping me see the bigger picture and for your tactical strategies that pushed this book out of my brain and onto the pages that follow.

To Chris Mellen—valuation advisor extraordinaire—your level of professionalism is unsurpassed and your counsel on the topic of valuations has been invaluable. To Monty Walker for your contributions to the tax and deal structuring section—thanks again. To Tony Perkins, thank you for your insights into legal agreements and how they assist with constructing exit strategies that truly meet an owner's goals. To Michael Pfeffer for adding thoughts to the private equits group recapitalizations section. To Ryan Boland for assisting with estate planning concepts. And to Phil DeDominicis for filling in the blanks and expanding the conversation surrounding ESOPs.

Also, thanks to Seth Mitchell who generously gave me his time earlier on when the book chapters were being sculpted. To Shariar Khaksari for his wisdom and guidance in creating this work. And to my friend Clark Ziegler who gave the early manuscript a read and told me it was good and to Tim Vac. for the initial cover design—you were all there when I needed you.

To all of my wealth management clients who allowed me to serve their best interests and who unselfishly released me from that responsibility: This book would not exist without the time that you allowed me to spend understanding the people behind each of these transactions. Particularly to Eric A., Tony B., and Ray B., —these fearless entrepreneurs taught me about trust in an advisor and belief in yourself. Thank you for your friendship and faith in my advice. I enjoyed going into battle with you to protect the wealth that you worked hard to achieve. Although I am no longer your wealth manager, we remain lifelong friends.

To my children, Catherine, Lizzie, Michael, and baby Nicholas. This book would not have been possible without your love and support—you were my inspiration to keep moving forward. And, most importantly, to my wife Chris, for all of the meals waiting on the counter and the laughter of you and the children coming from upstairs as I arrived home after dinner time, thank you—I love you.

ABOUT THE AUTHOR

John M. Leonetti, Esq., M.S. Finance, CFP®, CM&AA (Boston, MA) is the owner of Pinnacle Equity Solutions, an exit strategies firm. Pinnacle specializes in exit strategy training, design, and solutions for advisors and their privately held business owners. In addition, Mr. Leonetti has an extensive wealth management background, working directly with business owners in constructing and executing their exit strategy plans to protect their wealth. He has been a Financial Advisor with Smith Barney and Merrill Lynch Pierce, Fenner & Smith, as well an adjunct professor at Suffolk University, teaching Private Finance to MBA students as well as Certified Financial Planning (CFP®) courses to undergraduates. He has served as a Merger and Acquisitions Associate with a boutique firm in Boston and as a business owner in a family business in New York.

INTRODUCTION

Congratulations!

You made it.

Now let's do our best to protect it.

Your business has been built on your hard work and passion for what you do. The long hours, the battles with the finances, the incremental gains that you fought tooth and nail for are now more behind you than in front of you. For many readers of this book, many exciting challenges still await your careers. For others, a quick exit is what is most desired. In either case, you made it, and a warm congratulations is due to you for your accomplishment.

Now it is time to enter the equally challenging phase of keeping it. "It," of course, is the wealth that has accumulated in your illiquid business. That wealth is locked inside your business, much the same way that wealth is locked inside your home. Now, home may very well be where the heart is, but your business produces profits. If your business is where your heart is, then this book is a very good resource to assist you in viewing the business more as an investment and less as a job you love. The reason you want to think this way is because the majority of your wealth is likely tied up in your business, and without a plan to monetize or transfer that wealth, a great deal of your hard work may be lost.

Whether you want to exit over time or you are a get-me-out-right-away business owner who is burned out and dreads returning to work after enjoyable weekends and vacations, there is a way to begin planning your business exit today.

Business owners work a lifetime to accumulate their wealth, only to have it remain in illiquid form until an exit strategy is executed. All business owners will exit their businesses. This book is written to show you different options for exiting your business and to help you design the exit strategy that best fits your individual goals. The book also makes you aware of the obstacles

1

such as taxes, legal agreements, and professional advisory fees that you will encounter. As legendary investor Warren Buffett says, "You can have more success avoiding dragons than slaying them."

No matter where you are in your business life cycle, a written outline for your business exit strategy is a critical part of your planning. After all, your business is an investment, and every savvy investor knows when to exit a certain holding. The difference is that not every investment will have the emotional ties that come with owning and running a privately held business.

A process therefore is offered that, if followed, will bring order to this complex but critical planning area. This process will show you a range of options for your business exit and produce a result that is aligned with your overall planning goals. Insights are offered to virtually any owner of a privately held business who is looking to establish an exit strategy plan. This type of planning requires some effort and recognition that a change in your life is about to occur.

This book is a practical guide to the vast amount of knowledge that you will need. Turning your private business stock into cash (or passing it to heirs) requires a plan. Planning requires a process. It is precisely this process that this book offers.

This is not a book about selling your business. In fact, believing that an exit strategy is simply the sale of your business is a major trap to avoid. Owners of privately held businesses should consider many options for their business exit. This book not only discusses the major options available but also offers a framework for deciding which exit path is best for you. These options include private equity group recapitalizations, employee stock ownership plans (ESOPs), management buyouts, and gifting programs, in addition to the outright sale of a business. It is important to know that each of these options will give you a different amount of cash (or tax breaks) received in a variety of ways, in exchange for your business. Knowing these options and how each is likely to be valued will help you in assessing whether you will meet your goals with your exit. Again, this is not a sell-your-business book (although Chapter 5 covers this process in detail). Rather its aim is to provide information from which you can make an informed decision about an *eventual* exit from your business.

An exit strategy plan can be defined in this way:

> The written goals for the succession of a business's ownership and control, derived from a well-thought-out and properly timed plan that considers all factors, all interested parties, and the personal goals of the owners in a manner and a time period that accommodates the business, its shareholders, and potential successors and/or buyers.

Again, this does not say "sell your business."

GETTING IN IS EASIER THAN GETTING OUT

Building your business was not easy. It required a plan and a tenacious approach to competing in your marketplace. Exiting your business is equally challenging, and in many ways much more difficult.

An analogy will help put this in perspective.

On May 29, 1953, Edmund Hillary reached the summit of Mount Everest, the highest spot on earth.

But is Edmund Hillary famous because he was the first person to make it to the top of Mount Everest? Not necessarily. In fact, it is widely believed that others before him had made it to the pinnacle. However, Hillary became famous because he was the first westerner to navigate the descent back down the mountain without perishing. The others who went before him are still frozen up there.

Is climbing down a mountain harder than climbing up? Think about it. When you are ascending a mountain—or building a business—your weight is behind you, pushing onward and upward. By contrast, when descending from the mountain, your weight can work against you. You need to avoid missteps that send you tumbling down.

So, is exiting a business harder than building one? Very likely, yes. The next question is: Are you frozen in your business?

I'LL GET AROUND TO IT

One of the difficulties of business exits is the perception of it being overwhelming and complex. With so much information to be processed in a business exit, many owners procrastinate in doing anything. Often this results in a failure to plan an exit and, again, loss of hard-earned wealth in the illiquid business.

Begin your exit planning today.

Most business owners need to not only improve, but actually begin, designing their business exit strategy plans. Your preparation for the business exit will control the likelihood of you getting what you want. The more information you have and the more preparation you do, the better your odds of reaching your real goals and protecting your hard-earned wealth. Remember that your exit requires knowledge that spans many disciplines and is of varying levels of complexity. You need to know something about all of these different areas because you will be making decisions regarding all of them.

This author estimates that 85% of owner-operated business owners have one chance at a business exit. As with mountain climbing, the stakes are high. And mistakes can be permanent.

STRUCTURE OF THE BOOK

Part I of this book opens with some big picture ideas about how exit strategy plans are currently designed today and introduces a step-by-step process for improving your exit strategy planning. It discusses the way in which most owners view their business (i.e. more as a job than an investment) and it challenges the reader to ask whether or not their privately held business is generating a sufficient profit relative to the risk.

The current marketplace of advisors is examined, illustrating the gap that exists between transactional advisors (such as business brokers and M&A professionals) and relationship-based advisors (such as financial and insurance advisors, accountants and attorneys). These advisors are needed for your transaction so it is helpful to survey the landscape of advisors to understand why exit strategy planning is not currently as strong a focus as it should be for many advisors.

The book then measures the financial and mental readiness of an exiting owner in order to provide the key criteria in establishing an exit strategy plan. Your overall readiness for an exit will serve as the best starting point for your planning. The exit quadrant chart (Exhibit I.1) enables you to assess what stage of planning you are in from a personal perspective (i.e., what quadrant you fit into). Using the questions and worksheets provided, you will assess both your financial and your mental readiness to exit your business. Thereafter, you will determine which quadrant on the chart you best fit into and you will read about other business owners who fit into the same quadrant. Then you will be introduced to exit options that you can incorporate into your planning.

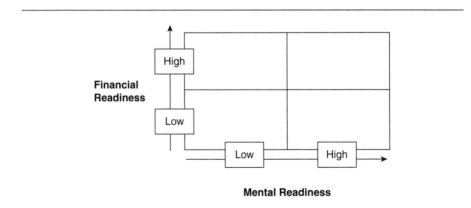

EXHIBIT I.1 EXIT QUADRANT CHART

This book provides a tool for developing a definite plan for the exit from your business and for the protection of your wealth by providing specific exit options no matter where you are in your personal and business life cycles.

Part I also introduces the reader to our hypothetical owner, Bill, who initially attempts to exit his business as if selling were his only option. Bill runs a successful business that he founded early in his working career. Bill is 56 years old and has grown tired of work. He is considering an exit from the business as a first step into retirement.

We examine this case study to illustrate the common traps that business owners fall into. Bill's story also highlights the planning that is missing from a well-conceived exit strategy.

Part II of the book explains the exit options that were introduced in Part I. Each chapter is dedicated to a certain type of exit option and each option is put into action with our exiting owner, Bill. Bill learns how knowing each of the different exit options would have changed his decisions and the outcome of his exit strategy.

Part III of the book presents technical aspects of an exit strategy that impact Bill's net, after-fee, and after-tax results. These technical areas, such as taxes and deal structuring, are essential to virtually any exit strategy.

For the majority of business owners the first major step toward to a successful business exit is to assemble the expertise of others through a team of experienced advisors. These attorneys, accountants, financial and insurance advisors, as well as transaction specialists—become critical to the success of a business exit. It is their past mistakes that will keep you out of trouble with your own business exit. Chapter 14 is devoted to forming and working with your advisory team. Although forming this team may be challenging, it is a critical step in a successful exit.

The book concludes with a chapter that brings all of these concepts together in a way that any owner can use to design their exit strategy plan.

So whether you want to exit over time or you are a get-me-out-right-away business owner, there is a way to begin planning your business exit today. After all, it is your lifetime of hard work that is being protected.

REVIEW

We have discussed:

- The necessity of an exit strategy to protect the wealth in your illiquid business.
- The challenges associated with developing an exit strategy.

We now turn our attention to preparing for your exit. It has been said that the first step in building a house—in our case an exit strategy plan—is not designing a blueprint, it's surveying the land. To that end, we begin our exit strategy planning with a survey of the marketplace of businesses, business owners, and advisors. This understanding will lay a solid foundation for you to develop an exit strategy plan that fits your goals.

I

PREPARING FOR YOUR EXIT

1

EXITING IS A PROCESS, NOT AN EVENT

Don't Limit Your Exit Strategy Planning with What You Don't Know

The general who wins the battle makes many calculations in his temple before the battle is fought. The general who loses makes but few calculations beforehand.

—*Sun Tzu*

You are what you are and where you are because of what has gone into your mind. You can change what you are and where you are by changing what goes into your mind.

—*Zig Ziglar*

Exit strategy planning is a complex endeavor. Currently millions of Baby Boomer business owners will be looking to exit their business and head into retirement. Statistically, the majority of their wealth will be tied up in their illiquid business. The problem is that business owners are in the business of building companies, not exiting them. In addition, the advisors who serve these owners are not well trained to develop comprehensive exit strategy plans that begin with the owners' motives.

An exit strategy is not the same as the sale of a business. Therefore, this is not a book about the viability of your business for sale or what you need to do in your business in order to improve its value so that a buyer will pay you more money. Rather, this book offers a process that begins with the personal readiness of the exiting owner—you—for an exit and how you can protect your wealth by understanding exit options in order to build and execute a customized exit strategy plan.

There are, in fact, a vast number of exit options for business owners who want to plan their exit and protect their wealth. Regardless of your choice of exit option, you, the owner, will want to liberate yourself from the business while simultaneously protecting your illiquid wealth. Because the process of exiting a business is so complex, most business owners (and their advisors) are ill-prepared to handle the exit effectively, potentially subjecting themselves to excessive taxes and advisory fees resulting in wealth depletion.

The good news is that this book was written to get you started on your planning today. This chapter introduces a step-by-step process for building an exit strategy plan. It also introduces exit strategy concepts as well as discusses the landscape of business owners, advisors, and the complexities involved with any exit strategy plan. This is a necessary perspective from which business owners can learn about why setting an exit strategy plan from their business can be so challenging. Accordingly, we say that your exit strategy planning should not be limited with what you do not know.

Let's begin with understanding how many business owners in the United States today are currently in need of this service.

BUSINESS OWNER MARKETPLACE

According to 2004 U.S. Census Bureau statistics, there are currently more than 22 million registered businesses in the United States today. Exhibit 1.1 ranks these businesses by the number of employees that each business hires.

WIDE BASE OF THE TRIANGLE

At the base of the triangle in Exhibit 1.1 are nonemployee firms—businesses that exist as sole practitioners or registered corporations without employees. This is far and away the highest volume of registered businesses in this country, numbering 17,646,062.

The next tier in the triangle represents businesses with between 1 and 19 employees. These are many of the businesses that we know well, the small businesses, usually run by the owner that vary in revenue and profitability metrics.

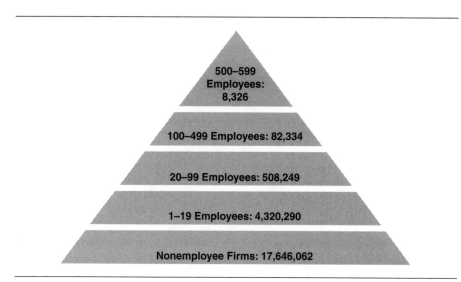

Exhibit 1.1 Number of U.S. Businesses Ranked by Employee Count

The tiers of this triangle continue upward to the pinnacle, where 500 to 999 employee businesses are highlighted. Many of these 8,326 companies are publicly traded with their common stock listed on an exchange that provides liquidity for the owners of those shares.

PUBLIC VERSUS PRIVATE

When a business grows large enough to attract capital from the public investing marketplace, it has the opportunity to go public through an initial public offering (IPO) process. The vast majority of owners of privately held businesses in the United States today, represented in Exhibit 1.1, will never have the opportunity to exit their business by selling equity to the general marketplace of publicly traded stock investors. What this means is that nearly 22 million business owners today need some form of exit strategy to protect the illiquid wealth that is in their businesses . . . and a lot of wealth it is.

TRILLIONS OF DOLLARS IN ILLIQUID WEALTH

Robert Avery of Cornell University has done extensive research into measuring the impact of retiring Baby Boomer business owners and what will happen to the illiquid wealth from those businesses. Avery states that "the majority of boomer wealth [in the United Stated today] is held in 12 million privately owned businesses, of which more than 70% are expected to change hands in the next 10 to 15 years."

He goes on to say that

> by 2050, virtually all closely held and family owned businesses will lose their primary owner to death or retirement. Approximately $10.4 trillion of net worth will be transferred by the year 2040, with $4.8 trillion in the next 20 years.[1]

With the huge number of businesses in existence today and the pending retirement of the founding Baby Boomer owners, the need for a comprehensive approach to exiting a business is clearly growing. As we will see, the more preparation that you apply to designing your exit, the higher the likelihood that you will achieve the goal of meeting your postretirement expenses (or alternatively, avoiding estate taxation) with a well-planned exit strategy.

SELLING VERSUS EXITING

An exit strategy is not necessarily the sale of your business. Owners should think of their exit strategy planning in broad terms, not just in terms of selling to someone else. Exhibit 1.2 compares the main differences between selling a business and developing an exit strategy plan. The concepts within this list will be referred to throughout the book as critical planning points.

As Exhibit 1.2 shows, the planning of an exit strategy is something that begins with the driving force behind the business—you, the business owner. It was your motives and goals that built the business, so it stands to reason that an exit strategy should be built around your personal objectives as you move into the next phase of your life. It is exactly this motive—i.e. what you want most from your business exit—that drives the step-by-step exit process detailed in this book.

EXHIBIT 1.2   COMPARING SELLING A BUSINESS WITH EXITING THAT BUSINESS

Sell the Business	Develop an Exit Strategy
Advisor motives rule	Owner motives rule
Advisors are "transactional"	Advisors are "relationship based"
Goal is "sale of business"	Goal is to achieve business owners' stated motives
Process includes "finding buyers"	Successors/buyers are found or "created"
Sales process at "mercy of market"	Transfer process is controllable
Outside party necessary for deal	"Internal" transfers considered with external ones
Company is "shopped"	Company examined for various transfer options
Negotiations center around "price"	Negotiations center around agreeable transfer
Large advisory fees and taxes	Taxes and fees can be controlled and reduced
Company sale is main consideration	Personal and corporate objectives drive process

EXIT PROCESS, STEP BY STEP

This book follows a process that begins with what an exiting owner wants most from their business exit. Exiting owners can establish the strategy that best meets their goals and protects their wealth once they follow the steps needed to determine the course that they should set with their planning. The steps in this process are shown in Exhibit 1.3.

The steps in this process are organized sequentially, chapter by chapter, in the design of this book. We start with how exit strategies are formed today. Then we move onto setting goals by determining your readiness for your exit. The exit quadrant chart and the exit options chart help you determine what type of exiting owner you most resemble and what exit options are ideal for you to incorporate in your planning today.

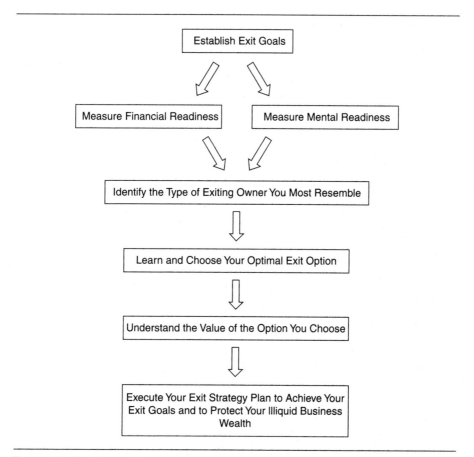

Exhibit 1.3 Exit Process Steps

Each exit option is explained and the valuation of each type of option helps illustrate the effectiveness of these different options in reaching an owner's goals. We answer the ultimate question, which is, "can you afford the exit that you most want?" Finally, the common obstacles that you will face including deal structuring, lifetime taxes, estate taxes, legal agreements, as well as the challenges of establishing an advisory team are examined. The book concludes with some closing thoughts on designing and executing your exit strategy plan.

This step-by-step process can assist any exiting owner with at least beginning to think about an exit strategy plan from the business. A careful study of this book's content will reveal a true guide for comparing and contrasting different exit options until you find the optimal solution for your exit strategy plan. Your optimal exit strategy plan is the one that allows you to meet your personal goals in the manner and time period that accommodates your objectives. Again, the process begins with your motives.

YOUR PERSONAL MOTIVES DRIVE THE EXIT PROCESS

It is your goals and motives that drive the exit strategy planning process. There is a methodology by which you can determine both how ready you are for your exit, and what type of exiting owner you most resemble.

If followed, these measurements will determine the path which your exit strategy plan will initially take. So, in order to analyze whether *you* are ready for an exit from your business, you will follow a process to answer these questions:

- Are you financially prepared for an exit from your business?
- Are you mentally prepared for an exit from your business?

Your financial and mental readiness will be ranked as either High or Low. Then, depending upon your readiness for an exit, you can check your alignment with four different types of exiting owners introduced in Chapter 4. Those four types of exiting owners include:

1. Get-me-out-right-away-for-the-most-money exiting owner
2. Well-off-but-choose-to-keep-working exiting owner
3. Stick-around-and-grow-the-business exiting owner
4. Rich-and-ready-to-go exiting owner

Together, the financial and mental readiness measurements marry you with one of the four types of exiting owner, as illustrated in Exhibit 1.4

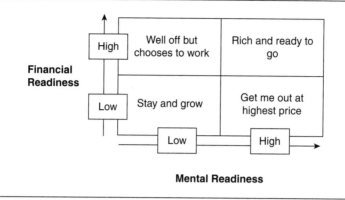

EXHIBIT 1.4 EXIT QUADRANT CHART

By the end of Chapter 4, you should have a very good idea of how ready you are for an exit and what type of exiting owner your most resemble. At that point in time, we use these measurements to identify the type of exit option that may be most appropriate for you to begin to analyze and develop your exit strategy plan.

RANGE OF EXIT OPTIONS

There are, in fact, many options for exiting a business. Some owners will simply close down the business. Others will liquidate and sell off their assets, if any remain. But others—many millions, in fact—will need a written plan to exit their business and protect their wealth.

Many of these business owners have a substantial amount of wealth tied up in their businesses. The five major transactions that owners can consider as the basis for their exit strategy plan are:

1. Sale of the business

2. Private equity group recapitalizations

3. Employee Stock Ownership Plans (ESOPs)

4. Management buyouts

5. Gifting programs

These five primary exit options are added to the exit quadrant chart to provide guidance to this complex planning area, as illustrated below with the exit options chart shown in Exhibit 1.5:

The options listed in each exit quadrant are alternatives for you to consider in your exit strategy planning. Each of these exit options is described in detail

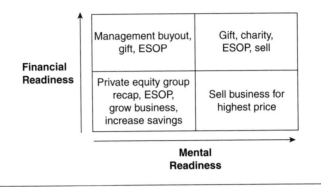

EXHIBIT 1.5   EXIT OPTIONS CHART

later in the book and applied against our hypothetical exiting owner, Bill. For now this concept is merely trying to show how this complex world of exit strategy planning can be made simple through the use of a few charts that help you determine how to get started.

After figuring out which options are the best to initially apply to your exit strategy planning, you need to understand that each of those options has a different value associated with it. And, given the demographics of Baby Boomer business owners who need to retire, we can assume that a great number of these owners are relying upon the proceeds from their exit strategy plan to fund their postexit lifestyle. Value, therefore, becomes a critical determinate of whether or not you can afford the exit option that you most desire. Let's take a quick look at concepts surrounding valuation of privately held businesses.

VALUATIONS VARY: RANGE OF VALUES CONCEPT

Privately held businesses do not have a single value. Rather, what you receive for your business will depend on who purchases it from you (or, alternatively, how you decide to gift it away). Starting in Chapter 4, and continuing thereafter, you will read about these value ranges and how to apply them to your customized exit strategy plan.

Sometimes the highest value is desired, as in the case of a sale to an outsider. Other times a lower value is optimal, as when you gift assets out of your estate—for estate tax planning purposes—to family members, employees, or charities. No matter what exit option seems optimal for your circumstances, you need to know the value measurement for each option to see if your personal goals will be met. After all, getting you an exit from your business that meets your goals (and protects your wealth) is the point of this book.

Value also is greatly impacted by the size, and hence the overall riskiness, of a business.

OWNER DEPENDENCY IS A MAJOR ISSUE

Exhibit 1.1 showed us that the majority of businesses in the United States today are small businesses. The wide base of the triangle completed this picture for us.

Small businesses can be more difficult to transfer than larger businesses because the owner, generally speaking, is integrally involved in the day-to-day affairs of the business. The riskiness (i.e., survival risk) of those businesses generally rises once the owner's presence is removed. When the risk increases, the price that someone else is willing to pay almost always goes down. As a result, many of these exiting owners need to understand the risk that an outsider perceives in their business. And, in the case of small and risky businesses, most buyers/successors will likely require the exiting owner to finance a portion of the transaction themselves (i.e., get paid over time to achieve a price that can sustain their lifestyle). Risk concepts are covered in this chapter, while deferred payments are addressed in Chapter 11.

In addition to the business depending upon the owner, the owner often times is equally dependent upon the business to sustain their lifestyle. These business owners are more dependent on the proceeds from the exit to satisfy their postexit financial expenses than an owner who has a high level of financial readiness for their exit (i.e., has substantial amounts of wealth outside of the business). This generalization stems from the fact that smaller business owners tend to live out of their businesses. And, for these owners, once the ability to draw income from, and expense personal items through the business is gone, that owner's lifestyle can be compromised. The natural conclusion is that getting a high price on a sale becomes very important to that exiting business owner.

Another way of saying this is that the owner's financial gap is large and needs to be satisfied with the highest price on the exit. We will examine this issue in Chapter 2 to see whether you have a gap in your financial planning. For now, it is important to realize that smaller business owners require greater attention to measuring their income replacement needs and that there is little integrated planning advice offered by transaction-based service providers at the small business level.

When faced with the dual prospect of receiving a lower price than desired, and potentially receiving payments in the future that may or may not come to pass, many owners of smaller businesses quickly conclude that it simply is not worth the risk to have a successor or a buyer pay them out over time. After all, if the business fails, the payments cease and the owner has to go back to work in a business that is now in need of repair. There may be a better way to structure your exit. Again, don't limit your exit strategy planning with what you do not know.

If you are such an owner and these concepts apply to your current situation and you have never seen it in these terms, then by reading these words your awareness is being raised and you are becoming better prepared to handle your exit. A proper amount of attention towards designing an exit strategy plan is what you need. If this does not apply to you, your exit may not be any easier, but it will not have these size challenges.

SIZE REQUIREMENTS FOR CERTAIN TRANSACTIONS

Not all businesses will qualify for the various options that are illustrated in this book because some exit options have minimum size requirements. For example, an S corporation that wants to install an employee stock option plan (ESOP) cannot do so with only a few people working in the business; you generally need 10 "unrelated" employees for the economics and requirements of an ESOP to work.[2] Another example of size requirements comes within the world of private equity group recapitalizations. In this case, companies with earnings of less than $1 million generally will not qualify for consideration of a recapitalization transaction. Other examples are given later in this chapter. For now, just be aware that size constraints limit your ability to take advantage of some options.

ECONOMY AND DEAL MARKETS MAY AFFECT YOUR EXIT STRATEGY

If you are considering a sale of your business to an outside party as your primary strategy to exit the business, it is helpful to remember that you can control your personal decisions as well as your business decisions, but you don't have control over the economy—and deal markets fluctuate with economies. And, as we will see, deal markets can contribute to the value of your business.

A helpful analogy is that of a sailor controlling the ship but not the winds and tides. Like economies, deal markets also run in cycles. There are periods of strength that offer a favorable environment to a selling business. There also are periods of recession, where buyers have the advantage.

Deal markets are impacted by a number of factors, including the overall economy, the availability of credit to finance transactions, and the supply-demand balance of buyers and sellers.

As an exiting owner considering a sale transaction, you will want to give some thought to your personal time frame so that you can "play" the transfer

	Deal Recession (Buyer's Market)		Prime Selling Time (Seller's Market)		Almost Recession (Neutral Market)	
1980		1983		1988		1990
1990		1993		1998		2000
2000		2003		2008		2010

EXHIBIT 1.6 10-YEAR TRANSFER CYCLE

Source: Reprinted with permission of Robert T. Slee, *Private Capital Markets: Valuation, Capitalization, and Transfer of Private Business Interests* (Hoboken, NJ: John Wiley & Sons, 2004, p. 444).

cycle. For example, you may be thinking that you will exit the business via sale to an outside buyer when you turn 65. If you use Exhibit 1.6 as a simple guideline, you may discover that the sale date that you are considering falls within a forecasted recessionary period.

If we assume that businesses that sell during this recessionary period of time generally command lower prices, we can begin to assess whether your desired selling date will provide you with the necessary proceeds to meet your financial goals. An exit strategy plan will consider this factor along with many, many others—such as whether or not a sale transaction is the best exit option for you. Again, only a small percentage of businesses will successfully sell to another party.

SALABLE VERSUS UNSALABLE BUSINESSES

According to a U.S. Chamber of Commerce Study only 20% of the businesses that are for sale will successfully transfer hands to another owner. The factors that make a business salable include good management teams, steady and defensible profits, customer and vendor diversification and loyalty, a solid reputation, predictable transferability, intellectual capital, and many others. Reasons why a business will not sell include:

- Owner is too involved in the business for it to transition successfully.

- Keeping family and key employees in the business is more important than selling to an outsider.

- Buyers in the industry cannot achieve financing.

- Poor economy is reversing the trend of profitability.

- Inappropriate or unreasonable price expectation of seller.

There are actually a wide number of reasons why a business will not (or cannot) sell. And there is an endless number of things that can be done to improve the salability of your business. However, if we apply the low percentage of businesses that will successfully exit via sale to an outside buyer (20% of businesses for sale) against the total numbers of businesses in the United States today, we see that there are millions of businesses that are either unsalable or will not be sold to an outside party. Solutions other than selling the business need to be applied to these millions of businesses.

So if millions of business owners are going to need help, what solutions are available? What is at stake if these businesses are not proactive in constructing exit strategy plans?

Before answering these questions, let's first take a look at the way in which many exiting owners view their privately held businesses. This will shed some light on why owners do not focus on exit strategy planning.

IS YOUR BUSINESS A JOB OR AN INVESTMENT?

When business owners begin to think about exiting their businesses, they need to consider whether they view the business as a job or as an investment. This distinction is critical in facilitating an exit because when the transaction is complete, business owners will be left with a financial reward. This financial reward can be structured in many different ways. There may be a lump-sum amount of cash for 100% of the value of the business delivered to the owner at the closing of a sale transaction. Often, however, a portion of the value will be received at a date after the closing transaction. If a business is transferring to employees or to family members, there may be no lump sum at the closing but merely a stream of income transferring to the business owners over time.

If business owners can picture this sum of money in their minds, then they can see that their business is truly an investment. Instead, most see the business as a job. Often they see themselves as the boss, king or queen of the castle, so to speak. It is dangerous for business owners to be complacent about having a job, particularly when it comes to exit strategy planning. When business owners begin to view their businesses as investments and not jobs, they begin making better financial decisions.

Because this investment represents the majority of an owner's wealth, that owner needs to know how the value of that business will be delivered to them according to the exit option that is chosen. Business owner exits depend on a visualization of trading shares for cash (except in the case of gifting). Often this includes the owner departing from the business.

How much cash would you be willing to accept for operational and financial control of your business today? Sadly, the answer to this question is often twice the true value of the company. Business owners have this inflated value in their minds because they measure what they want by what is needed to sustain their personal lifestyle. The amount is not based on what an outside investor would pay for that business. The limited view that an owner holds of the riskiness of their business (because they see it as a job and not as an investment) prevents proper and objective financial decision making.

Now, from the perspective of a buyer of a business, no matter who that buyer may be, this money machine needs to generate a return on investment. The return that is required is related to the risk that is being assumed in owning that privately held business. The risk is compared to that of owning other assets into which money can be invested.

The risks of illiquid privately held businesses are higher than the risks of liquid (i.e., publicly traded) companies for the simple reason that a trading market exists for the stock holdings. For example, shares of equities in the stock markets in the United States, going back 50 years, have provided investors with returns averaging approximately 12% per year. These returns need to be compared to the potential returns of a privately held business relative to the risks that are being assumed.

Too many exiting owners do not appreciate the amount of risk that truly exists in their businesses. Therefore, they create unrealistic expectations for their exit price and, in fact, fail to do much planning at all for their exit. Let's further examine these concepts surrounding risk to put the concept in better perspective.

RISK VERSUS RETURN

Your Company's Risk Factors

Very generally speaking, buyers or successors to your business will pay you a multiple of your company's cash flow, depending on the risk that they perceive to be in your business. The higher a perceived risk, the lower the price someone will pay.

Risk factors also come into play when considering internal transfers, such as transfers to employees, family, or co-owners. Ultimately, a business is valued based on the predictability and quality of the future cash flows to the new owner. As we will see, small business owners can compromise those future projections in many ways, creating a lower value for the business enterprise and a depletion of their total wealth.

When owning a privately held business, risks come in many forms. For the most part, buyers of privately held businesses expect annualized returns in the 20% to 40% range (this issue is addressed in Chapter 5). As we will see, it is important that you are able to see your exit strategy transaction through the eyes of your buyer/successor. Understanding the true risks in your business is a large part of this process.

The business has provided a personal return on investment for you and your family for a long period of time. However, is that return suitable to the objective level of risk that your business possesses as will be seen by buyers/successors?

Hidden Risks

Business owners—particularly those who have built a business from the ground up—generally do not appreciate the riskiness of their enterprises. For you, pledging personal assets and working exhausting hours is simply what needed to be done in order to survive. If this sounds familiar, then you likely do not appreciate the risk that exists in your business or you have not gone through the exercise of trying to see it from a buyer/successor's perspective.

To put this in focus, let us start by taking a look at what liquid investments can return for you.

Investments in publicly traded stocks and bonds historically have provided a certain level of returns that many investors use for long-term financial planning. As stated early, US equities have provided high single-digit and low double-digit returns for many years. These are historical liquid returns that an investor can use in making assumptions of appreciation, over time, from a portfolio of diversified investments. Your business returns have likely been significantly higher than the promise of returns from liquid investments—but you have had a higher level of risk.

As an investor moves from bonds (lower risk) to stocks (more risk) to small stock returns (greater risk)—historical rates of return increase. The old saying "You get what you pay for" applies to investments. You can expect a return that is matched by the level of risk that you choose from your portfolio. The process of choosing a level of risk is known as asset allocation—a way of purchasing different types of assets with separate risk/return criteria.

Most privately held business owners have unknowingly chosen the largest allocation of their wealth to be in their privately held business, an inherently risky asset class. Many exiting owners are now interested in protecting that wealth through diversification of their total base of assets both liquid and illiquid.

A PRACTICAL QUESTION TO ASK YOURSELF IS:

- If I had the opportunity, would I reinvest all of the money that someone would pay me for my business today back into my company?

Most likely the answer to this question is no. You will want a diversified portfolio of investments that provides income to meet your post exit expenses with a relatively low level of risk. For those business owners stepping into retirement, this is the financial goal that they are trying to achieve to meet their long-term personal goals. Having an understanding of the risk/return measurements between liquid investments and illiquid business assets is critical to determining whether you can afford to retire with peace of mind.

You may be thinking that the return figures for liquid assets seem rather low relative to the returns that you have achieved with your business over time. This may be true, but again, you need to also account for the risks that you incurred in the business during your ownership.

An interesting dynamic is that rarely do business owners fully appreciate the riskiness of their companies until a buyer or successor begins to ask questions, such as "What will *my* return on investment be once I take over this company?" A business owner who is not prepared with some discussion points on this topic will be missing a big piece of the exit strategies puzzle.

Accordingly, we provide a formula to help you determine your return on investment (ROI) for owning your business.

Return on Investment in Your Company		
Your private business's return on investment can be measured.		
ROI Calculation:		
Potential Sales Price:		$ 8,000,000
Less:	Fees & Taxes:	$ 2,000,000
		$ 6,000,000
Excess Draw/yr. net of tax	$ 100,000 ×15 years	+$ 1,500,000
		Total Return
		$ 7,500,000
Initial Investment	Investment Time	Annualized Return
$ 200,000	15 years	27%

In this example, the business owner projects that her exit via a sale of the business will yield a gross selling price of $8 million. At the closing, there will be two major expenses for advisory fees and taxes (covered in detail in Chapter 11 and throughout this book). With a net amount of $6 million, this owner adds back the additional compensation that was drawn from the business for each of the 15 years that she owned it—resulting in a $1.5 million "add-back."

This owner's total return on the investment in her business is $7.5 million. She then takes the $200,000 initial capital that was contributed in the beginning of the business and comes to the conclusion that the annualized return on investment for owning this privately held business is: 27%.

This business owner achieved a return in excess of the returns that could have been achieved by investing in liquid stocks. The primary questions then becomes whether those profits will continue in the future and will a buyer be willing to assume the risks of owning your privately held business in order to achieve returns that are consistent with his or her return criteria. Remember that investors in your business have liquid alternatives with investments in publicly traded stocks. And, again, public equities are generally less risky; size and liquidity are two of the main reasons for this reduced level of risk for publicly traded investments. Also noteworthy is that investment in publicly traded securities provides a return on an investment without having to work in that investment. Hence the term *passive income*.

Once you grasp this concept, a few observations can be made:

1. You realize that the wealth that is trapped in your illiquid, privately held business is actually shrinking as your business fails to grow, and/or

2. You become empowered to make detailed, cogent arguments to buyers/ successors as to why owning your business is a better investment than publicly traded securities or other investment alternatives.

In the absence of this analysis, buyers/successors will be reluctant to purchase your business because of the lack of risk/return reward that they are seeking. This book reiterates many times that it is your responsibility to explain the benefits of your business to a buyer or successor. If you miss this step and place the burden of making this assessment on potential buyers/successors, they will be doing so with imperfect information and will likely lower their offering price to compensate for the risks that they cannot see or do not understand. Understanding the high levels of risk in your privately held businesses helps to protect your wealth for external transfers as well as being a very important concept for transfers to insiders. Either way, we are addressing your total wealth and how it can be best protected.

Said another way, the wealth that is concentrated in your illiquid business could be invested in other types of assets that are providing a return that is equal to their level of risk. The overall point of protecting your wealth through exit strategy planning is to provide protection against giving back what you have already accumulated. Your goals and motives are likely changing as you begin to seriously consider an exit strategy from your business. It is natural that you desire more security. And, from a financial planning perspective, the need for security is satisfied through one simple word: diversification.

DIVERSIFICATION AND THE FIVE BUCKETS OF WEALTH

Being diversified is the equivalent of the old saying that you shouldn't have all of your eggs in one basket. Most business owners have all of their eggs in the basket called their privately held business. The risks that you took to build and grow the business were worth it at the time. However, now you will want to protect the wealth that you have built by diversifying your holdings.

There are five primary buckets, or pools of wealth in which to invest. These categories of wealth are:

1. Cash
2. Bonds
3. Equities (publicly traded securities)
4. Real estate
5. Privately held business

A diversified wealth portfolio for a business owner will include allocations to each of these asset classes. Of all the asset classes just listed, the most distinguishing characteristic of privately held businesses is the difficulty you face when entering or exiting this asset class. Actively traded markets exist for the purchase and sale of most stocks and bonds. Real estate, though not as liquid, generally serves as adequate collateral for a financing source to allow for favorable lending terms—hence the dynamic mortgage and commercial lending markets in this country.

For the privately held business, however, each exit needs to be constructed on its own merit. In Chapter 4 we discuss concepts of valuation of privately held businesses that incorporate the riskiness of owning businesses and the manner in which such risk is measured when businesses change hands. For now, recognize that a business exit is a difficult task. And, since a majority of your wealth is likely tied up in that business, you should ask yourself this question:

What percentage of my total net worth is tied up in my privately held business?

Again, helping you, the business owner, convert your illiquid assets to liquidity and achieve greater diversification for your wealth is a major objective of this book.

But, the more immediate question for your consideration is *who* is supposed to be helping you with this type of complex decision making process. We now examine the marketplace that currently provides this type of guidance and the possible reasons why you have struggled to find someone willing to do this type of planning for you.

MARKETPLACE FOR EXIT STRATEGY ADVICE

Let us now turn our attention to today's marketplace of advisors who provide business owners with business exit strategy planning and advice. This discussion reveals a few alarming statistics regarding exit strategy planning that will help you understand why what you may not know can hurt you.

With millions of Baby Boomer business owners seeking an exit strategy from their business, the demand for advice in this area is very high. However, the supply of trained advisors who can assist with this type of planning is disproportionately low.

If we accept that business exits are difficult, we can extrapolate that help from advisors is necessary. At a minimum, you will need an attorney to draft documents for the transfer of shares of stock or assets. Ideally, you are guiding a team of qualified advisors through an exit plan that you designed to meet your personal goals. Between these two options lies the universe of possibilities that helps to define the current marketplace of advisors to business owners. Unfortunately, the vast majority of advisors do not currently have the background or support to offer exit strategy planning tools and advice. Consequently, the demand for this advice currently outweighs the supply.

For example, we know that 8.4 million businesses (8.4 million is 70% of 12 million businesses cited) in the United States will be changing hands in the next 10 to 15 years.[3] Therefore, we can make some projections about the capacity of advisory services required to fulfill this need that will illustrate this supply and demand point.

An exit strategy is a complex planning engagement. Let's say that 50 to 100 hours of work is a good estimate of the time needed to formulate and execute an exit strategy plan. By multiplying the number of businesses that will transition by the estimated 50 to 100 hours of advisory work, we conclude that 420 million to 840 million hours of advisory work will be required in the next 10 to 15 years.

Many types of advisors are available to assist business owners with their exit strategy planning. There are an estimated 700,000 such advisors in the United States today: legal advisors, financial advisors, insurance advisors, accountants, business consultants, business brokers, and mergers and acquisitions professionals.

With a lack of focus in the area of exit strategy planning and the great demand for this advice, Baby Boomer business owners can draw a few conclusions.

1. Most business owners will be alone in designing their exit strategy plans.

2. You should seek out advisors who have a working knowledge of the complexities of exit strategy planning.

You need to be proactive in finding these advisors (Chapter 14) because, as mentioned in the introduction, exit strategy planning is more difficult and delicate than growing a business. This is not the time to be learning on the job; the protection of your lifetime of work and effort that is trapped in your illiquid business depends on the successful execution of your exit strategy plan.

Who is currently providing this service? Who can help the millions of business owners who require assistance?

Let's survey the landscape of service providers currently available to assist with this type of planning to further illustrate the important point of working with a strong advisory team.

Objective Advice Is Hard to Come By: Who Can Help with the Exit Strategy Plan?

A business owner requires a team of advisors in order to complete an exit successfully. Going it alone is not an option. Therefore, it is important to have a solid perspective on the types of advisors who can be of assistance with an exit strategy from a privately held business.

The world of advisory services can be broken down into two primary types of service providers:

1. Transactional service providers, who get paid for completing a single service

2. Relationship-based service providers, who get paid on an ongoing basis for being in steady service to the business owner

Neither advisory service provider is optimally suited to deliver a complete set of exit strategies advice and service to you. Current relationship-based advisors are not trained on exit strategy planning, and transactional advisors have financial incentives that prevent them from being totally objective. We can understand this first critical point by examining the motives of these types of advisors.

TRANSACTIONAL VERSUS RELATIONSHIP-BASED ADVISORS

Relationship-based advisors generally aim to provide the proper level of service—whether it is legal, accounting, or financial advisory—in order to keep you as a satisfied client, year in and year out. In doing so, their advice is often limited to what they know and how they get paid. For their businesses to remain profitable, relationship-based advisors need to stay focused. Only a few of these advisors have learned enough about exit strategies to be able to incorporate it into their practices.

On the other hand, transaction-based service providers have an extensive base of knowledge around business sale transactions. The motives of a transaction-based advisor are, generally speaking, to complete a specific transaction for which they get paid, no more, no less. If a deal gets done, they get paid; if not, no reward. Since this is the case, what incentive does that advisor have to provide a complete set of exit options to a business owner?

In fact, offering comprehensive exit planning advice and tools works against transaction-based advisors' profitability (unless they separately charge a fee for this type of planning, which very few currently do). Transaction-based advisors effectively create their own competition when they provide comprehensive and objective exit strategy advice. After all, if a transaction is not going to happen (i.e., an ESOP or a gifting program is chosen), how will they get paid? The exception here, again, is the transaction-based advisor who has accepted the challenge of offering *completely objective advice* to a business owner while still charging for that advice.

This dichotomy in the way advisors are compensated is the first reason why no one has explained the options for exiting your business to you. To examine this further, let's look at who *sells* businesses in the Unites States today so that we may better understand the motives of these players. This is an important insight because speaking with a transaction-based service provider is the first step for too many business owners who are beginning to consider an exit from their business.

LANDSCAPE OF TRANSACTIONAL ADVISORS

If you have fallen into the trap of perceiving selling your business as your only exit option, it is logical that you would go to the people who actually sell businesses for a living. Once you meet with these transactional advisors, you also will tend to use your current business skills to negotiate the agreement while believing—or hoping—that it will be an easy process. After all, you may think, this person gets paid only if he brings me the deal that I am willing to accept.

EXHIBIT 1.7   TRANSACTIONAL SERVICE PROVIDER OFFERINGS BY DEAL SIZE

Business Brokers	Mergers and Acquisitions Professionals	Investment Bankers	Mid–Large Firms
Small business	$5 mm–$25 mm	$25 mm–$100 mm	$100 mm+
Up to $2mm –$5 mm in enterprise value			

In my experience, this is an optimistic and rather incomplete understanding of how a business exit strategy should proceed.

Exhibit 1.7 illustrates the types of transactional advisors that represent owners of privately held businesses in their sale transactions and the representative size transaction that each type of advisor will engage.

Business brokers primarily handle smaller businesses of less than a few million dollars in total value. These transactional advisors typically handle a large number of engagements, with buyers ranging from individuals to strategic, industry buyers. For the most part, a business broker "listing" is one that can be purchased by an individual buyer—someone who is interested in a "lifestyle business." Often such a buyer is a corporate refugee—someone who has retired or was pushed into an early retirement package by a former employer and wants to stay engaged in a business endeavor.

Mergers and acquisitions (M&A) professionals handle larger transactions than business brokers. The M&A professional follows a process for bringing a business to market. This process includes packaging the company in a marketing document and distributing the information to prescreened, qualified buyers who can pay the highest value for the business. Ideally, the M&A professional gets many buyers to compete among each other for the purchase of the business, thereby driving the price higher and benefiting the exiting owner.

Investment bankers generally engage in a number of corporate finance–related projects including capital raising, acquisitions for their client's businesses, or the outright sale of a business to an industry buyer or private equity group. These investment bankers likely are licensed professionals and have a minimum transaction size in the range of $25 million. These are experienced, sophisticated, and well-paid advisors who have teams of people assisting with their transactions. Generally, the head of such a group originally was part of a mid- to large firm and has now chosen the simpler life of running a smaller firm that caters to a few business owners on a selective basis. These transactional providers often have minimum fees ranging from $500,000 to $1 million.

Mid–large firms work with companies that are close to going public, or are already publicly traded and are in need of additional financing. These firms will have dedicated research teams covering certain industries and sectors, keeping a close eye on developments in their respective fields for their clients. Often the mid–large firms have investment banking departments, research departments, and retail wealth management services, so as to provide an entire suite of corporate and personal financial services to a large firm (+$100 million) and its executives and employees.

The statistics offered earlier indicate that most business owners will be working with business brokers and M&A professionals. There is a large difference between the manner in which a business broker delivers their services and how an M&A professional works with an exiting owner. Therefore, if your business is valued at more than a few million dollars (roughly speaking, your company earns about $500,000 per year in profits), you should be considering the higher-touch services of an M&A service provider over a business broker.

However, as we will continue to emphasize, the first step in establishing an exit strategy from your business is not to take a meeting with one of these service providers. Rather, it is to learn about options for exiting your business according to your personal goals and then to seek advisors who can execute on the exit plan that you have created. Before we move into the specifics of this type of planning, let us take a closer look at the motives of the transactional advisors; doing so will help to reinforce the overall point that exiting a business is a process, not an event.

TRANSACTIONAL ADVISOR MOTIVES

To most business owners, the motives of transactional advisors appear to be rather straightforward—to get you the highest price for the business, thereby earning the high fee that they are charging. After all, you may think, if your business has an estimated value of $8 million and an M&A intermediary is able to find a buyer willing to pay $10 million, it seems logical that he or she would be entitled to a $500,000 fee. These transactional advisors derive their fees based on a schedule called a *double Lehman* formula (see Exhibit 1.8).

The value propositions seems rather straightforward. In fact, you may think you would be rather indifferent—maybe even glad—to pay the fee for such an outcome. After all, just as with running your business, you are paying for results, right?

Well, in theory, this outcome is possible. So, the dance begins. The contract is agreed upon and the process of selling the business commences. What was

```
10% of the first $ 1,000,000 = $ 100,000
8% of the next $ 1,000,000 = $ 80,000
6% of the next $ 1,000,000 = $ 60,000
4% of the next $ 1,000,000 = $ 40,000
2% of the next $ 1,000,000 = $ 20,000
Plus 2% of each additional $1,000,000
```

EXHIBIT 1.8   DOUBLE LEHMAN FORMULA

left out of this process so far? Years of experience in working with transactional service providers indicates that there is quite a bit more to the story that many exiting owners do not initially realize.

To begin with: Did you consider that your transactional service provider gets paid *only* if a deal closes?

Did you consider that because of this fact, the transactional service provider may in fact, be more motivated to close *any* deal than to get you the deal that you think you want?

Did you look at the contract and realize that the transactional service provider also has a large interest to protect? In fact, these types of advisors know from experience that they could wind up doing a tremendous amount of work, only to have you reject what would appear to be a perfectly suitable sale transaction (i.e., you don't like the buyer that they bring you). Many transactional advisors are also motivated to protect themselves against an unscrupulous exiting owner going back to the buyer that the advisor found and, at a later date, striking his own deal with them, eliminating the requirement that the transactional advisor's fee be paid. Transactional advisors protect themselves from this scenario with what is called a tail provision, meaning that you will have to pay their commission for a period of time after which you terminate the agreement, usually 18 to 24 months.

You may initially agree that this tail provision properly protects both parties. However, what if the transactional service provider does not work hard to find you a buyer or produces poor results? The reality of the transactional marketplace is that if a deal does not appear to have strong appeal to buyers right away, service providers will limit the amount of time they spend on your transaction so that they can focus on transactions that are more attractive and are more likely to close.

You need to carefully choose your transactional service provider, one with a solid record of closing deals that they engage. Because in this situation described above you are most likely still liable for paying a fee even if you want to make a change and go to another M&A provider.

Does this type of process and result happen often? Unfortunately, the answer is yes. Too many owners of privately held businesses believe that selling the business is the only way to exit. They do not understand the (hidden) motives of the players, and, more important, they do not understand their options for exiting the business. As a result, they seek the counsel of transactional advisors and engage their services with less than perfect information.

Can you avoid this scenario with some good exit strategy planning information?

We believe that you can. This book provides a guide to avoiding these traps. First, however, let us consider yet another scenario.

Here you, the business owner, believe that selling the business is the only option for an exit. This time, however, the well-intentioned transactional advisor determines that your business is not currently marketable, so they cannot currently work with you (remember the statistic of only 20% of businesses for sale actually being successfully sold). They do, however, leave you with a few ideas of changes that you can make over the next few years to get your business in a better position to be sold.

In this case, you end up with no advisor, no exit strategy plan, and only some general information on how to spend the next few years making changes that lead to the sale of your business. What other options have you considered along the way to protect your wealth? What other resources are available to you? Remember that this situation applies to the majority of exiting owners in the United States today.

If you, as an exiting owner, have already done your homework and surveyed all of your exit options to determine that selling the business is your optimal exit strategy, then the transactional service providers' advice is well founded, and you probably should make those changes to your business. If, however, you have not received any advice on the options that are available to you, you have fallen into the classic trap of thinking that exiting is the same as selling, and you are continuing to make decisions based on incomplete information that may or may not be in your best interest.

We can summarize the points above in this way. Most transaction–based advisors are not financially motivated to deliver options that will allow you to customize your exit while meeting your personal goals—unless your personal goal is to sell control of your business and try to get the highest price in the market.

Why do we pay so much attention to the motives of advisors?

Because this book was written to show exiting owners a better way to establish an exit strategy plan. This plan will be aligned with an owner's primary motive for his or her exit and the exit strategy will be led by their goals, not those of their advisors.

RECENT CHANGES IN THE MARKETPLACE

While we are on the topic of advisors and their motives, it is helpful to share a bit of information regarding the current status of transactional and relationship-based advisors. You now know that exit strategy planning should be a part of your total business planning at every stage of your business. Further, not only is exit strategy planning new to you, it is also relatively new to the marketplace.

A helpful analogy is to think back to the mid-1980s and how stocks were sold to the investing public. Transactional stockbrokers would call clients, pitch an idea, and receive a commission for the sale transaction. Over time, however, clients began to ask important questions, such as: If you are making a commission for any stock idea that you sell me, I have to ask if these calls are more in my best interest, or are they more in yours?

Technology, legislation, and market changes have forced that industry to mature. Yesterday's stockbrokers are today's wealth managers. These service providers are now seeking higher and higher professional designations so that they can offer more complex and comprehensive services on a relationship-driven, fee basis rather than for commissions on stock trades.

The transactional community for business sales is at the early stages of a similar evolution. At the time of this writing, the Securities and Exchange Commission (SEC) is well along in its efforts to bring mandatory licensure standards into this transactional community. This initiative is being made to bring order to this highly fragmented and loosely regulated marketplace of advisors. Such legislation would be a benefit to most exiting business owners.[4]

There are also a growing number of business owners seeking exit strategies specialists to assist them with a customized exit from their business. These advisors understand business exits and can offer business owners an objective, comprehensive, and expansive array of exit strategy options to consider and apply to their personal and business situations.

Owners are also turning to their trusted advisors and asking them for greater assistance with this type of planning. These owners want to work with someone that they know and trust to determine whether or not selling the business is the most appropriate exit strategy to help them reach their overall planning goals.

CUE THE RELATIONSHIP-BASED ADVISOR

Relationship-based advisors include financial advisors, insurance advisors, accountants, and attorneys. These are advisors who have an interest in starting and maintaining a relationship with you, the business owner, over many years.

Along the way, these advisors earn (relatively) smaller fees than transactional or M&A advisors, but they provide ongoing services to you every year. The goal of these advisors is to keep you happy by providing good representation, good service, and attempting to add value to your business and personal situation where they can.

The trouble with any of these relationship-based advisors, however, is that selling businesses (or exit strategy planning) is not their specialty. More important, these types of advisors are generally more affable and accommodating than the hard-hitting, tough-negotiating transactional advisors who know how to lock horns with buyers and get them to pay what is being asked.

But remember what we said about traps that business owners fall into. Selling is not your only option for a business exit. And the advice that your trusted advisor carries may be the first step in a long and well-thought-out process for exiting your business.

Recently, the relationship-based advisors have been taking the lead in offering exit strategy planning services to the business owners they serve. This is a welcome development in the exit strategy industry; these cutting edge advisors are beginning to realize that the transactional advisor does not have the same level of commitment and concern for the client as the relationship-based advisor. Barriers between these two worlds are slowly being broken; these two types of advisors are just now learning how to work together to benefit the business owners by protecting the wealth in the privately held businesses (see Exhibit 1.9). This is a trend that has every indication of increasing to the business owners' ultimate benefit. The end result should be coordinated advisory services that focus on your motives and not on the advisors'.

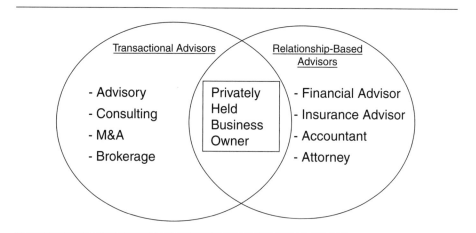

EXHIBIT 1.9 RELATIONSHIP VERSUS TRANSACTION-BASED ADVISORS

YOUR MOTIVES

While having a softer touch may not qualify a relationship-based advisor to negotiate your highest selling price with a buyer, it likely does qualify that advisor to do something far more meaningful to the exit strategy process: to discover your motives and personal objectives in exiting the business and to deliver objective information and solutions to assist you in meeting those goals.

Designing a business exit strategy includes planning for an exit and not (necessarily) selling your business. It therefore stands to reason that you should plan an initial meeting about your business exit with someone who asks questions not only about your business and what you are trying to achieve, but also about your personal situation and what type of results you would like to see from this business exit so that your overall goals in life can be met.

A relationship-based exit strategy process focuses on the total and holistic goals of you, the owner. It begins with a conversation about your goals and your readiness to leave the business. It then leads to a sharing of information on the pros and cons of different types of exit strategies and which exit option(s) will work best in helping you achieve all of your goals, within the time frame of your choosing. Think of this process as an advanced form of financial, retirement, insurance, estate, and business planning, all wrapped into one business exit strategy plan.

How can you begin to think about an exit strategy that is broader in scope than the sale of your business?

PRIMARY MOTIVES OF EXITING OWNERS

Let's survey a few situations that begin with an exiting owner's motives and build toward customized solutions for the transfer of their business and protection of their wealth.

What if your motive is to stay with the company—keep your job—but you are interested in some personal diversification and taking some chips off the table?

Maybe an ESOP could be installed to accomplish the goal of personal diversification, allowing you to create a buyer for the shares of your stock and to pull some money out of the company without having to bring in an outside buyer or financing. In fact, under the right circumstances, your sale of stock to the ESOP may qualify for a tax-deferral under Internal Revenue Code Section 1042. Additionally, you keep your job and continue running the company and may even increase your cash flow in the business through annual, non-cash, deductible employee contributions. ESOPs are discussed in Chapter 7 and illustrated in a case study as being powerful planning tools for exit strategy planning.

For now, note that selling your business precludes you from the benefits of establishing an ESOP. After all, you no longer own the business.

Further note that ESOPs have a tremendous amount of flexibility, allowing for leveraged transactions or prefunded transactions. We describe each structure to show how easily the ESOP is incorporated into other exit strategy planning techniques.

Perhaps you have an interest in keeping your job but transferring your business risks to another party. This modified form of exit strategy planning is possible through a private equity group recapitalization (recap). Recapitalization transactions are discussed in Chapter 6. Here a group of financial professionals invest in your business, purchasing a controlling stake in your company; a recap generally includes the purchase of 80% of your company stock. In addition to being paid for your stock ownership, you also receive a multiyear employment agreement to continue running operational—day-to-day control—of the business. Theoretically, the recap also contributes additional capital to the business in order to assist you in executing a growth plan for the business. Under this scenario, the recap is designed to project another exit strategy from its investment in your business, typically, five to seven years in the future. At this point in time, you, as the owner, get a "second bite at the apple" (explained in further detail in Chapter 6) as your 20% continued interest in the company is sold along with your investor's 80% interest.

Whether a recapitalization will work for your exit is largely determined by your mental readiness to exit the business. If you want some diversification and some additional financing but choose to continue working, you can take on such a partnership with a private equity group that will monetize your currently illiquid asset while also providing for future growth potential.

Or perhaps your management team is extremely capable and is, in effect, currently running your business. You may have thought about a management buyout (Chapter 9) but you have not pursued it because you did not want to negotiate with your own employees for the succession of your business.

Sadly, as mentioned earlier, statistics indicate that many businesses are not salable. Therefore, an internal transaction, such as a management buyout, may be the best alternative for an exit from the business. Too many business owners take no action when considering a management buyout. They believe that the employees both do not have the money to execute a buyout and that they will not be willing to take the risks that the owner originally took when starting and growing the business. These two facts may independently be true, but this should not prevent an exiting owner from considering a management buyout as a viable option—particularly when such an exit can result in the best value that the owner can extract from the business.

Or perhaps your motive is to pass some wealth to your heirs (Chapter 10 covers gifting strategies) but you do not know where to begin because the stock in your company is illiquid. Would it help to know that certain discounts are permitted by the Internal Revenue Service that allow you to transfer large amounts of illiquid (nonmarketable, noncontrolling) business wealth during your lifetime? In fact, if your primary motive is to avoid paying estate taxes (which currently hover at the federally mandated 45% rate for all assets that exceed the applicable exclusion amount for an individual), an exit strategy can be engineered to accommodate these estate planning objectives.

Once again, selling your business precludes you from this opportunity (assuming that you have not made the transfers prior to the sale transaction).

Or perhaps you are charitably inclined and would like to pass a portion of your illiquid wealth to a nonprofit organization of your choosing (also covered in Chapter 10). There are tax advantages to making this type of transfer as well, even allowing you to take a stream of income in return and utilize potentially valuable tax deduction in the year that you make the transfer.

The outright sale of a business may not preclude this charitable gifting— after all, you could always give away the cash that you receive in the sale transaction—but losing control of the company stock would reduce the positive tax effect that could occur if the transfer were to happen prior to a sale.

Maybe you really enjoy what you are doing with your business and simply are interested in reducing your current tax burdens and saving for a future retirement date. This form of exit strategy planning is very forward thinking and allows a business owner to begin to save today with the awareness that more options will be available at a future date and time if her financial readiness ranks high at the time of exit.

These are a few of the primary motives that business owners have that do not include selling the business to a third party. In each case, a carefully constructed exit strategy plan can be the first step in determining which options are feasible and whether the wealth that is trapped in the illiquid business can be monetized and protected while the business transfers to the intended succeeding party.

So we see that exiting owners have many motives other than simply selling the business to an outside party. An exit strategy plan will guide an owner towards executing the exit option that is most aligned with her primary motive.

The tools in Chapters 2 and 3 will allow you get started with analyzing your exit strategy needs and options. First you will measure your financial and mental readiness to exit the business. Then you will learn which options, other than selling, will assist you in customizing your exit strategy and in reaching your exit goals. Finally, you will measure how each exit option is affected by fees and taxes so that you can determine if the net amount that you receive at the conclusion of your exit strategy plan will be sufficient to meet your personal and financial goals. A successful exit strategy includes the realization of the business owner's personal goals and motives.

What if your first step in exit strategy planning was not down the path of selling but rather down the path of learning? What if the first step that you took towards developing a business exit strategy plan was to learn about the options for exiting and how they could be applied to your personal situation?

Are we claiming that transactional service providers will not play a role in your exit strategy? Not at all. However, your choice of advisors depends mostly on what you are trying to achieve. Know that first and then bring in the right team.

The purpose and intention of this book is to help you, the successful business owner, construct a customized exit strategy plan that protects the wealth that is trapped in your illiquid business. A well-conceived exit strategy plan can provide you with the information necessary to establish a plan to protect your wealth and transfer ownership of the business to the desired successor.

GETTING STARTED

As stated earlier, many business owners will be on their own with developing a business exit strategy plan. That is why this book is written in a step-by-step manner toward helping you define and achieve your goals. We start this process by asking two simple questions:

1. Are you financially prepared for your business exit?
2. Are you mentally prepared to leave your business?

The answers to these questions will start you down the proper path to begin your exit strategy planning. This book develops a structure for analyzing different types of exit alternatives to determine which one will work best of you.

If you are ready to learn about whether you are financially and mentally prepared for a business exit and how to determine your exit goals, turn to Chapter 2.

NOTES

1. Robert Avery, "The Ten Trillion Dollar Question: A Philanthropic Gameplan," Cornell University (February 2006).

2. Menke & Associates provided evidence that of the 2500 ESOPs that they have installed over the past 34 years, only rarely will businesses smaller than this size be able to effectively install an ESOP.

3. Robert Avery, "The Ten Trillion Dollar Question: A Philanthropic Gameplan," Cornell University (February 2006).

4. For more information and updates, visit www.exitingyourbusiness.com.

2

SETTING YOUR EXIT GOALS

If you go to work on your goals, your goals will go to work on you. If you go to work on your plan, your plan will go to work on you. Whatever good things we build end up building us.

—*Jim Rohn*

Before you can really start setting financial goals, you need to determine where you stand financially.

—*David Bach*

If you are reading this book, there is a good chance that you are looking for a way to remove yourself from your business while still maintaining certain aspects of control, financial security, family legacy, continued income, or perhaps simply the thrill of continued success that can come about only by overcoming obstacles in creative and profitable ways within your business.

The first step in your exit strategy planning process is to determine which of these motives is most important to you. Do not make the mistake of waiting until a future date to design your exit. Once your cash machine is up and running, you should have a firm idea as to how you can convert it into liquid proceeds or a legacy.

You must figure out exactly what you want and get there!

What do you really want?

Have you taken time to consider what it is you really want from your business exit strategy? Or does the business of running your business prevent you from doing so?

Set aside time to reflect on why you started your business and what you would ultimately like to get from it. Your life's work is wrapped in your business. How you exit it is an essential piece of your overall life and wealth puzzle.

WRITE IT DOWN

Have you written down what you want to achieve with your business exit?

If you stopped reading now and spent the next few hours detailing your goals in writing, this book will have accomplished part of its primary goal: to get you prepared for your business exit.

Think about it: You probably formed a business plan when you started and/or grew the business. It made sense then. Doesn't it make sense to develop a plan for your exit?

Get it done. Start writing your exit strategy plan right now—today! It is a work in process; it will change as you read this book and as the business evolves. The important part is to get started now by writing down your ideas.

Reducing your exit strategy to writing, and starting with what you want, provides an anchor to a process that can be rather challenging. As you journal your thoughts, remember to begin with the end in mind.

QUESTIONS TO ASK YOURSELF TO GET STARTED

- What amount of investable assets would I be comfortable with in my account?
- At the closing, will I know the tax impact to the check that I am being handed?
- Am I familiar with the legal agreements that I will need to sign as I exit my business?
- Can I see the opportunity to own this business from the buyer's/successor's perspective and, if so, what are the most important considerations for the business's success in someone else's hands?
- What am I going to do with my time when I am no longer needed in the business?

These questions engage your mind in the exit strategy process. None of these questions will be asked of you in your daily business operations. You need to be proactive in detailing your own goals.

We have seen already that a business exit strategy consists of many options. If you are able to write down and/or clearly express what it is that you are trying to achieve with the business exit, then you can begin to survey the array of exit alternatives to see which one is the best fit for you.

Without a complete understanding of what it is that you would like to achieve with your exit, the default pattern is usually to get the most money and to fall into the classic trap of considering only the single option of selling the business.

This book highly recommends that you find a trusted advisor with whom you can share your exit strategy thoughts. The key to choosing this advisor is to focus on the person's knowledge of exit strategy planning and transactions, just as you chose a financial advisor because of his or her knowledge of investments or legal advisors because of their knowledge of the law and their ability to communicate it to you in a manner in which you could analyze, interpret, and apply the information to your personal situation.

Two heads are better than one in this creative process. It is not uncommon for this initial confidant to be a spouse or another business partner. However, these trusted advisors likely do not have the technical background of a professional advisor. They may help you to discover what you would most like to achieve with your exit, but an experienced, professional advisor will help you form your exit strategy plan and keep you on track to meet you goals. Filling this role in your advisory team is critical, as we will later see. The best plan is to be pro-active and begin the search early; it may take awhile.

Always remember that when your exit is complete—whether it takes six months or six years—you alone will need to determine if your goals have been met. This book gives you many of the tools necessary to formulate your exit strategy, but without knowing the end result that you would like to achieve, you cannot take definite action in any one direction. Use the guide shown in Exhibit 2.1 to help you organize your exit thoughts.

Take action—today.

Put your written exit strategy plan in a manila folder and place it in your desk drawer. You will review and update it on a regular basis. For additional guidance, go to www.exitingyourbusiness.com to download a form for writing down your exit goals and to find additional exit tools.

ADJUSTMENTS TO YOUR BUSINESS

You know that things will change after you are gone. Consider those changes now and begin to adjust the way your business is run to accommodate a successful execution of your exit strategy plan.

I want to achieve _____ with my exit strategy.

Examples
- ☐ Get most money.
- ☐ Time and money freedom.
- ☐ Continue running the business but diversify my estate.
- ☐ Leave a legacy—maintain family harmony.
- ☐ Pay as little taxes as possible.
- ☐ Keep control as long as possible, diversify along the way.
- ☐ Pass on to employees.

The reason that this is most important to me is because

_____.

I would like to achieve this by _____, _____ .

                          Month / Day   *Year*

I am going to achieve this by:

- _____ reading this book.
- _____ writing out my goals.
- _____ studying whether my goals are achievable.
- _____ analyzing my options for liquidity.
- _____ making changes in my routine to accommodate this plan.

I will know that I have reached my goal when these outcomes manifest:

The business is owned / run by _____ (insider/outsider).

I have $ _____ in after-fee and after-tax money in my investment account.

After the exit I will engage my mind in these activities:

_____   _____   _____

EXHIBIT 2.1 SUMMARY SHEET OF PERSONAL GOALS

After writing down your exit goals, every alteration that you make to your business should be directed toward achieving the end result of having the business continue in a profitable manner without your participation. For example, if your goal is to achieve the highest value and retire by selling to an outside party, then you will need to begin to consider how involved you are with the day-to-day operations of the business. If your absence will compromise its value, then your retirement goal may be difficult to achieve according to the way your business is run today. Your planning should include a time period in which these changes will occur. Remember that organizational changes can take many years to implement and, depending upon your mental readiness for your exit (Chapter 3) you may be short on time for implementing this plan under your optimal time line. This is a major reason why it is critical to begin with a written plan today.

Using another example, if your goal is to simply achieve some diversification while still maintaining control of the business, begin to examine your borrowing capacity and banking relationship in order to consider funding a leveraged employee stock option plan (ESOP) transaction. By finding a lender who will provide capital to an ESOP transaction, you can sell a portion of your stock today while still running the company. In this case, you can begin to meet your exit goals not through operational changes today but rather through changes to your business partnerships and adjustments to the ownership structure of the company.

Examples of preparations that you can make today are endless. Your written goals will guide the adjustments that you need to make to your business and will determine the amount of time required to meet those goals. Throughout this book we are going to focus on executing the written goals that represent your true motive for your business exit. The fact that this process takes time and that you will have to make adjustments to your business reinforces the fact that exiting a business is a process, not an event.

IS THERE A FINANCIAL GAP THAT YOU NEED TO ADDRESS?

As mentioned, there are really two types of exiting business owners: those who are depending on the proceeds of their business exit to meet their long-term financial goals and those who are not relying on that income to meet their financial goals. If you are one of the fortunate few who are *not* depending on the proceeds from your exit, you can afford to get creative with your planning. Perhaps charitable donations or family and employee gifts are a part of the design.

If this is the case, then you can rank yourself as very high on the financial readiness scale. But are you mentally ready to check out of the business? Have you given full consideration to what your life will look like without work and your business consuming the majority of your thoughts? Our discussion on this topic continues in Chapter 3. For now, if you are financially prepared for a business exit—meaning that even a failed exit would not disrupt your ability to meet your financial goals—then you can proceed to Chapter 3 to score your mental readiness to leave the business.

On Exhibit 2.2, plot a point on the chart (bottom = low; top = high) to indicate your financial readiness to leave the business.

If, however, you are like most business owners today, you *are* depending on the proceeds from your exit to satisfy your lifestyle. In this case, the contents of this book can really make a difference to your exit strategy as you consider,

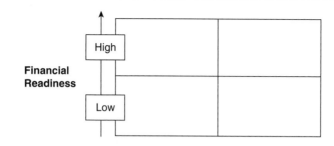

EXHIBIT 2.2 EXIT QUADRANT CHART: FINANCIAL READINESS

for example, whether you can afford to conduct an internal transfer or whether the taxes you will pay in the transaction will kill your deal (see Part III).

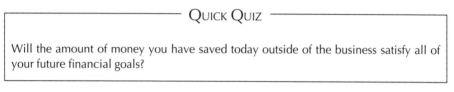

QUICK QUIZ

Will the amount of money you have saved today outside of the business satisfy all of your future financial goals?

If the answer is no:

Do you have any idea as to what you need in after-tax, after-fees, risk, and inflation adjusted net proceeds from your business exit in order to meet your financial goals?

Measure this financial gap. Work with your financial advisor on this step. If your current advisor does not understand these concepts, get a new one. This is a critical point to exit strategy planning. Think forward and recognize that you will have to decide how and when certain proceeds will be paid to you in exchange for the shares (or assets) of your business. If you do not know the minimum amount of investable assets that you need to satisfy your financial goals, any offer will create a great deal of confusion in your mind. As we will see in Chapter 3, confusion leads to frustration, which leads to inaction, which leads to failed transactions.

Knowing the amount of net proceeds that you require in exchange for your business is a critical planning point. In order to examine this further, let us take a look at how your lifestyle is currently tied to your business.

DO YOU LIVE OUT OF YOUR BUSINESS?

For you to have confidence in your exit strategy, you need to understand the concept of passive income from investments and whether you have enough of an asset base to generate a sufficient stream of income to meet your postexit financial expenses.

You cannot turn over the reins of your business without a firm understanding of these concepts because financial situations change after a business exit. Dinners, cars, and travel are no longer deductible expenses. Health benefits may be lost. Discretionary bonuses are gone. Your entire personal financial picture may be overhauled as you lose the opportunity to enjoy certain personal expenses that were previously run through the business.

ADDING BACK PERSONAL EXPENSES

The financial objective of private business owners is to increase their personal net worth, not necessarily to increase the value of the business. If this is true for you, then you will need to follow the steps in these few paragraphs to determine if you can afford to exit your business at this time.

Take a look at your lifestyle. Do you find yourself running certain personal expenses through the profit and loss (P&L) statement? The answer is probably yes, at least to some degree. Now, before the transfer is upon you, is the time to take stock of the business and personal decisions you have made over the past several decades.

If you do live out of the business, you should know the answers to these questions before your exit:

- Which bank and/or investment account will pay the living expenses after the business exit?
- Do I understand how the income that I require will be generated within that account?

Your primary personal goal likely had been to maximize personal wealth through business income and perks. Usually this goal includes minimizing your tax bill. The objective in a successful exit is to demonstrate to your buyer/successor the true profitability of the company without your owner perks and additional compensation depressing the company's true profitability. The process of adding back these expenses to reflect the business's true profitability needs to be understood by you, the exiting owner, because buyers/successors will need an explanation as to how and why this business will benefit *their* investment return expectations. Again, it is your responsibility to explain this to a buyer or successor, not theirs to discover.

BEING LIQUID: INCOME REPLACEMENT AFTER THE EXIT

One seemingly illogical truth about exiting a business is that your money could be working smarter for you than you are currently working to earn that money. Seems like an easy decision, right? You trade one asset—the business—for another asset—liquidity.

Chapter 3 addresses the emotional reasons why a business owner does not routinely make this trade. Chapter 8 further illustrates the lost opportunities that owners experience when they get emotionally stuck in their businesses. For now, however, let's take a look at how income will come to you from passive investments.

Your postexit financial reality may be dramatically different from your current owner lifestyle. For example:

Our business owner drives a company car. Sometimes he uses it for business travel . . . but not always. The company makes lease payments of $500 per month. The business owner is accustomed to running that lease payment (and insurance payments, and fuel payments, and maintenance costs) through the business. He has come to rely on the business as his piggy bank to pay for everyday personal expenses.

Consider what happens to this owner's financial situation when he exits the business.

In order to replace the auto allowance "income" from the business, a business owner—only spending interest income (not dipping into principal)—will need more than $150,000 in investable assets, earning 6% per year, to make the same payment.

To calculate the interest income required for the replacement auto allowance expense:

Divide the annual payment—here, the annual auto expense paid for by the business—by 1 minus the business owner's tax rate (here we assume a 35% tax rate):

$$\$6,000.00/0.65 = 9,231.00$$

Then divide the interest income required by the rate of return achievable:

$$\$9,231.00/0.06 = 153,850.00$$

To conclude, we see that $153,850.00 of liquid/investable assets earning 6% a year is required to produce enough after-tax income to satisfy the car payment after the exit from the business. It is important to note here that this calculation does not account for growth in any investment or changes in tax laws; nor does it account for rising inflationary pressures in car lease payments or the use of the principal sum of money to assist with making the car payments. It also assumes that 100% of the car payment was attributed to business expenses. Your actual results will vary. A conversation with your accountant is helpful for this step of planning.

This is one example of running expenses through a business. Perform this calculation for all expenses your business covers. Then you can see the amount of liquid proceeds (or continued income stream) that you'll need to continue in your current lifestyle including salary replacement. Is there a financial gap between your current asset base and what you need to maintain your lifestyle?

☐ _____ Yes

☐ _____ No

If yes, can you fill in the blank in the next question?

I need $ _____ in investable assets to replace the income from my business after the exit.

In later chapters we will be learning about different values for private businesses. A key step in the exit strategy process is to figure out whether you can afford the exit that meets your primary motive. If you can afford it today (i.e., you have scored high for financial readiness), then you will not have to make adjustments to your business due to a need for more liquid wealth.

However, if the exit strategy that you desire does not produce a value that will meet your personal financial goals (i.e., your financial readiness is low), then you can: (1) grow the business to meet your goals; (2) execute a partial exit today in order to diversify yourself while still maintaining control of the business; or (3) reduce your postexit living expenses. These calculations go into your written exit strategy plan.

MEASURING THE GAP

Here we are analyzing the personal financial planning component of exiting your business. This critical planning area requires that you are comfortable with how you will maintain your financial lifestyle after your business exit. If you have a high financial readiness to exit your business, you will be able to explore many options for your exit. This is a fortunate position to be in because you have choices that you can execute today. The choice of which one will work best for you is then determined, in large part, by how mentally ready you are to leave.

If you have a low financial readiness today, you should still begin to establish an exit strategy. You can begin either to plan for an exit at a later date or execute a partial exit strategy that will allow you to take some chips off the table. There are, however, a few more practical points to touch on prior to moving into Chapter 3.

GROWING YOUR BUSINESS WITH YOUR EXIT IN MIND

As we will see, owners with a large financial gap in their exit strategy planning and a reluctance to leave the business often must face the fact that they need to continue growing their business to accommodate their desired future exit.

If the dollar figure that you entered in the previous exercise far exceeds the most optimistic estimated value for your business, you may need to set a multiyear exit strategy. In this case, you are envisioning continuing to run the business until a future time when it will be worth a much higher value. In fact, this type of exit analysis is the essence of ownership in any investment and a very healthy—arguably necessary—way to always look at ownership in your private business. Remember, ownership in your privately held business is an investment, even if you view it primarily as a job.

For more information on growing your business for a future exit, visit www.exitingyourbusiness.com for resources to assist with management consulting and business building exercises.

SPECIAL NOTE ON FAMILY TRANSFERS

Perhaps financial issues are not most important to you. Rather, what you want is to transfer your business to a family member. These three questions will assist you in considering, and detailing in writing, your plan to transfer your business to family members:

1. Will this family transfer affect your financial security?
2. Is this family member capable of running the business?
3. How will the grooming process impact your goals? In other words, for how long will you have to stick around?

Family transfers are a study unto themselves. Much research has been completed on the ways in which family harmony can be maintained while the business survives the succession of ownership. For purposes of this book, we will not focus on family dynamics but rather provide the technical tools for assessing the existing majority owner's financial and mental readiness for an exit, independent of family influences on that decision. Then, as the book proceeds into the options quadrant (Chapter 4) and the alternatives for exiting and succeeding the business (Chapters 5 to 10), your imagination will begin to flow.

This book's companion Web site lists resources for addressing family dynamics within a business. Visit www.exitingyourbusiness.com for more information.

EMPLOYEE TRANSFERS

Chapter 9 goes into quite a bit of detail regarding transfer of a business to a management team. There are unique challenges to this type of transfer, and the likelihood of success for this exit option can be highly dependent on the business, the industry, and the circumstances and personalities of the players involved.

If your primary motive is to transfer your business to employees or a key management group, you must answer three important questions before proceeding:

1. Will your employees risk their personal assets to buy you out?
2. Do you understand the inherent risks involved with negotiating the transfer of your business to your management team?
3. Do your managers need to become entrepreneurs? Can they make that shift?

The first question goes to the heart of why your employees work for you. Sometime, perhaps long ago, you decided to take control of your destiny by owning your own business. The sacrifices that you made are hard for your employees to appreciate. Now that the business is up and running and produces profits, the risk in the business appears very low, at least compared to what it used to be. To your employees, however, the risks of ownership will likely appear to be very high compared to the risks they currently take as employees.

Further, you need to consider how failed negotiations with your management team may impact your business relationships with them and, by extension, your personal net worth. Consider for a moment that it may be very difficult for an employee to return to a role in your organization after failing to come to terms with you on the succession of the business. This employee's mind-set has likely turned to an interest in owning the business. Be cautious of the damage that this can cause, particularly when you consider that the employee in question is likely your top person. One solution to avoiding this type of negative outcome with your key people is to have a neutral third party handle these initial talks. At a minimum, you will remove yourself from some of the emotional exchanges that accompany this type of internal transfer.

Finally, it takes a special group of employees to convert from a mentality of working for you and drawing a steady paycheck to stepping up to becoming a partner in a business. Again, Chapter 9 discusses management buyouts and addresses these issues in more detail.

IN CLOSING

Your goal-setting process is unique to you. It is the most important part of your exit. After all, you built the business, so why not exit it according to your motives and goals? This book will continue to show you a process to assist you in identifying your readiness for an exit and then helping you understand the options, values, and obstacles standing in the way of reaching your goals. This chapter has laid a foundation for you to determine your financial readiness for an exit. You should rank your financial readiness and use the next worksheet for additional support.

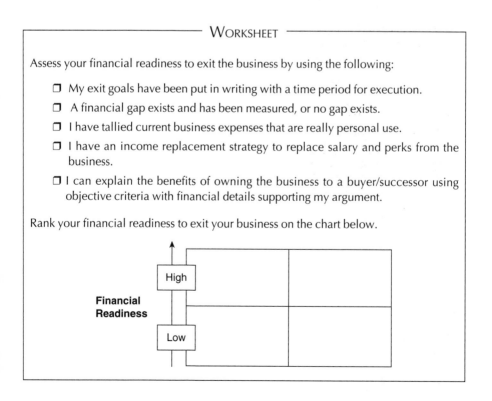

WORKSHEET

Assess your financial readiness to exit the business by using the following:

❑ My exit goals have been put in writing with a time period for execution.

❑ A financial gap exists and has been measured, or no gap exists.

❑ I have tallied current business expenses that are really personal use.

❑ I have an income replacement strategy to replace salary and perks from the business.

❑ I can explain the benefits of owning the business to a buyer/successor using objective criteria with financial details supporting my argument.

Rank your financial readiness to exit your business on the chart below.

Financial Readiness

High

Low

REVIEW

So far we have discussed:

- Your exit goals, writing down what you want most.
- Determining your financial readiness for the exit.
- Measuring the amount of net proceeds required to satisfy your estimated financial expenses after the exit, including items that were previously run through the business.
- Your income replacement formula for the proceeds from the exit.
- The risk and return measurement for illiquid versus liquid investments.
- Growing your business with your exit in mind.
- Special notes on family and employee transfers.

The next point that needs to be plotted on the exit quadrant chart is your mental readiness. In other words, are you really ready to exit the business you built?

3

ARE YOU READY TO LEAVE?

The Mental Game of Business Exits

Your past was essential for you to become who you are and prepare you for what you are going to do now and in the future. However, you need to let go of anything that might be affecting new decisions you will be required to make.

—*David Neagle*

An amazing thing, the human brain. Capable of understanding incredibly complex and intricate concepts. Yet at times unable to recognize the obvious and simple.

—*Jay Abraham*

The responsibilities of a business owner can at times be overwhelming. Usually thoughts of running your business are the most pressing and dominant in your mind. The price that you—knowingly or unknowingly—pay for the privilege of managing a successful business is that your personal needs often are overlooked or subordinated to the interests of the business. In order to execute an exit strategy plan successfully, exiting owners need to be aware of their personal mental readiness for their business exit.

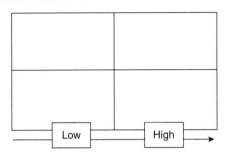

Mental Readiness

Exhibit 3.1   Exit Quadrant Chart: Mental Readiness

Now that you have assessed your financial readiness to exit your business, the next step is to assess your mental readiness. Are you really ready to leave the business? In this chapter you will plot a point on the chart (left = low; right = high) to indicate your mental readiness to exit the business (see Exhibit 3.1).

Questions that you should ask yourself about your mental readiness to exit the business include:

- How involved am I in the day-to-day running of the business?
- Do I have a plan as to how I will spend my time away from the business?
- Are my thoughts and habits of running my business so routine that I will not know what to do after the exit?
- Do I view my business as growing and providing a good return on my invested capital, or am I more interested in the lifestyle that the business provides?
- Will I be able to think clearly throughout the exit process so that the decisions I make are based on objective criteria instead of the subjective way in which I feel about the exit?

The majority of business owners reading this book will not have solid answers to these questions. Therefore, being mentally prepared for your exit may be the largest challenge that you face. Again, we emphasize that having a low mental readiness to exit does not mean that you should put off planning for your exit—in fact, just the opposite is true. Accordingly, we offer a few critical points to exiting owners in this chapter and then illustrate the concepts through a case study introducing our exiting business owner, Bill.

If you are not involved in the day-to-day running of your business and you treat the business as an investment and not a job, then you can jump ahead to

Chapter 4. You can also congratulate yourself, once again, because you are one of the rare few.

YOU ARE YOUR BUSINESS

You are your business. And your business is you.

There is no simpler way to describe the multifaceted owner-operator of a business than to discuss that person and the business together. This fact holds true with rare exception. Your business is the outward manifestation of your beliefs, personality, skills, and creativity. You are your business and your business is you.

So how can you exit yourself?

Is what you want for your business consistent with what you want for yourself?

Have you asked yourself what it is that you—not your business—truly want?

This is where we begin our examination of an owners' mental readiness to exit their business.

On the outside, you are a successful businessperson. That is because on the inside, your mind is conditioned to certain success habits from running your business. Thoughts of exits, instead of growth, are new. At first, these new exit thoughts are unrecognizable to your conditioned, successful mind.

THE CONDITIONED MIND

Know that your conditioned mind is insidious. Its programming is not easily altered by new thoughts. Initially, most exit thoughts are new and hence rejected by the conditioned mind, which is more accustomed to processing growth thoughts. When new thoughts enter the mind that go against the ordinary processing of more routine thoughts, resistance occurs. This internal resistance lurks in the darkness of your subconscious mind, silently corroding your exit plans. Resistance creates doubt in the conditioned mind. Doubt creates confusion. And confusion kills successful exits.

Have you ever heard someone say that retirement is the same as death? Well, for them, that may literally be true. That owner is expressing the feelings that his subconscious mind is sending to his body: Change is going to be difficult, if not impossible.

Life is a series of choices. And habitual conditioning of the mind automates certain thought processes. Your awareness of this internal struggle between how your mind is conditioned towards running your business and the new exit strategy thoughts that you are trying to embrace will aid you in dealing with the resistance that naturally arises as you begin to formulate an exit strategy plan.

IT'S YOU AGAINST YOU

In the game of business exits, you are often battling yourself first and foremost. A privately held business represents the primary investment vehicle that manufactures wealth for stakeholders involved with the enterprise. In addition, it provides a job for the business owner. When building the business, the business owner created certain habits and certain ways of doing things that developed into successful financial outcomes, which encouraged more of the same. In the process of growing a business, the business owner experienced ideas that worked and ideas that did not. All successful business owners develop routines for generating results that foster confidence and success. A key insight is to realize that the mind and body are actually connected and that success in business is connected to the owner's physical makeup.

Inside the mind, the business owner creates ideas to drive his or her business. The years of building a business produce two very dramatic consequences to the body and mind. The first are what the eyes can see and feel and touch and witness, which are the habits of that business owner. These habits will win the business owner labels such as hardworking, diligent, persistent, early riser, detail oriented, control oriented, intelligent, experienced, personable, and so forth. These are criteria that are identified as common denominators among successful owner/operator business owners.

In addition to the outer characteristics are the harder-to-see inner characteristics, which likely include a physical addiction to the business. This level of understanding is not something that can be easily seen with the eyes but exists in the brain and in the body.

For all human beings, experiences create certain emotions. When an experience occurs, the brain registers it through charges in its neural network. This is true, as science has proven, for all human beings. What, then, is the significance of this physiological connection to business owners and exit strategies?

ARE YOU ADDICTED TO YOUR BUSINESS?

If we take this chemical reaction and understand it, we can extrapolate the notion that your body may have a physical addiction to your business. Simply put, addictions occur when the brain habitually delivers certain peptides into the cells of the body. When the body does not receive the expected dose of peptides, the body physically craves what it has grown accustomed to. We, as emotionally driven human beings, will actually *create situations* that feed the body the experiences that it is looking for. Many times this happens without our awareness that we are creating situations to feed our body and this is the process that is actually driving our behavior.

To draw a simple analogy, when the body no longer has food, it registers a signal that it is hungry. In response, we go get something to eat. This analogy helps in understanding that behavior and habits create certain dependencies that a body craves. The body of a business owner has a dependency on certain experiences that the business provides, and it is these cravings that subconsciously drive the decisions within the business. This is why many business owners believe that exiting their business is when they will die. Simply put, after the exit, their bodies will not be fed the necessary doses of chemicals required from the business addiction. Their bodies will experience a certain amount of withdrawal from the business. And it is precisely how much withdrawal exiting owners are ready to experience that determines how mentally prepared they are for their business exit.

Because many business owners are not aware of this issue, they may say "I know that I need to do something about transferring my business," but fail to move forward. Subconscious resistance is preventing them from protecting the wealth that they have accumulated in their businesses over many years.

Understanding that you may be addicted to your business is important to recognizing why you procrastinate on your exit strategy planning. Furthermore, this resistance will only increase when your actual exit is taking place and radical changes to your future are being proposed. Knowing that a resistance to change is what is occurring in your subconscious mind is an important step toward preparing yourself mentally for the exit from your business. In addition, the objective financial criteria that you wrote down in Chapter 2 will provide you with criteria that will support your decision making as this resistance begins to occur.

Without this level of understanding, your mind and body will automatically resist your exit strategy. As the case study of our exiting owner, Bill, illustrates, this resistance creates doubt in the mind of the exiting owner. That doubt creates hesitation and confusion. And confusion kills. It is what will send you tumbling down the mountain.

CLEAR THINKING

Think clearly. Recognize that you are making a major life change, and keep a vigilant eye on resistance that leads to doubt and confusion. Stop this doubt dead in its tracks. Again, Chapter 2 had you set financial goals to get you focused on achieving an objective target as a means of blocking out thoughts of doubt. Your written goals are your guide to your exit and your shield against any doubt and confusion that may creep in. By understanding whether you are mentally ready to exit the business, you are completing the initial tasks of developing your exit strategy plan.

PLOTTING THE POINT

As you copy your separate answers from Exhibits 2.2, your *financial readiness*, and Exhibit 3.1, *your mental readiness*, onto the exit quadrant chart (Exhibit 3.2) your answers will give you a framework for focusing on the components of an exit strategy that are most important to you right now.

As you enter your information for the first time, consider the optimal exit that you have envisioned. Then, as you read through the case study, reflect on the decisions that Bill is making in attempting to exit his business to see if you would have acted the same way. This is a very helpful exercise before moving into Chapter 4, where we begin to examine types of exiting owners and the different options for exiting a business to determine which one is optimal for your current situation.

CASE STUDY: BILL BROWN'S FAILED EXIT—LESSONS APPLIED AND LEARNED

Our story begins with Bill Brown—our Baby Boomer business owner. We take what starts as a rather straightforward proposition, that his exit strategy planning is leading with a sale of his business to a competitor as his primary

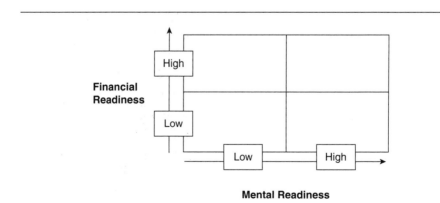

Exhibit 3.2 Exit Quadrant Chart

exit strategy. We see right away that Bill falls into the classic traps that we described in Chapter 1:

1. He believes the selling is his only option for an exit.
2. He believes that his success as a business owner qualifies him to design and execute his own exit strategy.
3. He believes that the process is going to be easy.

Let's have a look at Bill's story to illustrate mental preparedness for a sale and to see where his thinking could have been improved in order to execute the exit strategy that would have been best suited to his personal goals.

I'LL SELL YOU MY BUSINESS, IF . . .

Bill Brown started his career at a major beer distributor at age 22. He has always loved great beer, but for years he did not see domestic brewers producing the kind of quality beer he and his friends liked to drink. So he started making beer in the basement of his house in 1991. He was 40 years old at the time. Soon after, he started his own brewery. This was about the time craft breweries cropped up all over the country so competition quickly grew fierce. He poured all his cash into growing the business, worked 100+ hours a week, and did not sleep much.

By the late 1990s, the craft beer industry had matured and many small breweries had gone out of business. Hard work paid off for Bill, and his company has thrived. Now his company generates annual sales of $12 million with earnings of $2 million. Bill is 56 years old and is the sole owner with no obvious heirs to take over the business. He's starting to feel burned out. (Clue: Does beginning to feel burned out mean that you should think about selling? Keep reading.) Sure, he is a wealthy man, but all of that wealth is tied up in his company. Bill enjoys nice vacations at the company's expense and drives a high-end company car. In addition, he receives a bonus at the end of every year. If he could pull out a significant percentage of the company's value, Bill could retire early. The problem is that he does not know how or when he wants to exit the business. He simply has not made time to think about it.

Bill won't trust just anyone with a business he has nurtured and grown from infancy. He regularly receives buyout offers from big industry players with deep pockets, but he doesn't want to see his hard work turned into a commodity. He would rather work until he is 75 than see the business suffer under the wrong ownership. (Clue: Getting the highest price suddenly does not seem like Bill's underlying motive. He actually cares about who takes over the business.)

Time passes, and Bill starts to feel overwhelmed. He sees his grandchildren growing up and wants to be more involved in their lives. One day he calls up an industry buddy, Jim, who owns and runs one of the bigger concerns in the industry. Thinking he knows Jim rather well and will get a fair shake, Bill says that he would consider selling to Jim. Bill has not detailed or written down his personal goals or studied his mental readiness, but selling the business sounds like a good idea. And besides, what are his other options? This seems like the only way to liquidate his ownership.

At first, everything goes smoothly. Competitor Jim seems more than willing to grant Bill the respect he deserves for building the business from scratch—he thinks highly of Bill and assures him a consulting role in the business for as long as he wants to stay on. The two talk generally over dinner. It sounds like a dream come true; Bill can hand over the reins to Jim, whom he trusts, and cash out and step away from the headaches of running the business.

Bill is ready to get the ball rolling so he calls his accountant. Said accountant suggests an experienced merger and acquisitions advisor to relieve Bill of the direct negotiations with Jim and to assist with the transaction. Bill thinks, Who needs to pay hard-earned profits to a bunch of bankers? He's known Jim for years. And, after all, Bill is a successful businessman, certainly capable of negotiating a deal. Surely two intelligent, like-minded businessmen can come to a fair agreement.

Bill and Jim set a date to sit down and hammer out the details. During the two weeks leading up to the meeting, Jim sends over a list of things he'll need to see at the scheduled meeting. Bill starts to sweat. Here is where resistance, doubt, and confusion come storming in. Jim wants to see the books? What if Bill isn't ready to lay open his livelihood? What about confidentiality? Even if Jim honors the confidentiality of the information that Bill shares, Bill knows that he is still turning over trade secrets and other important business information in the process. What if this deal doesn't go through? What damage could it do to Bill's business? And what if the employees discover that Bill is in talks with Jim? After all, Bill's salespeople have been fighting it out with Jim's company for competitive positioning in the market for many years. Will the employees be concerned about their job security? What if the industry finds out? Will Bill be able to operate autonomously if suppliers, distributors, and customers believe that he is about to sell out to Jim? Is Bill really mentally ready to exit the business?

What will Bill retire into? He begins to wonder what he will do with his time . . . (more *doubt*). How will he fill his days? Without the business to keep him occupied, how will he engage his mind? And will he have enough post-tax, postfee money from his net proceeds to replace the income and perks that he currently pulls from the business every year? These financial and emotional components have not been reduced to writing so that Bill can analyze this sale transaction objectively. Furthermore, Bill realizes that at age 56 he may still be able to increase the value of his business. Perhaps he is selling too early in the life cycle of the business and not getting enough value for the company.

The day of the meeting arrives. Bill walks into a barrage of unanswerable questions about his personal expenses, Jim's projected return on investment, and a variety of other details that Bill has not considered. Bill simply has a price in his mind of what the business is worth and a rough idea of what the tax hit is going to be. After all, Bill thinks, Jim wants to buy the business from him; why should he answer his questions? Isn't having the answers to all of these questions Jim's problem, just as running the business has been Bill's problem all these years? (Clue: Remember that buyers/successors are not interested in your game—they are interested in theirs, and the money that *they* can make with your business. If you can help them to understand the potential for a return on their investment, your exit process will go a lot smoother.)

Without the information needed to make a return on investment assessment, Jim is not willing to meet Bill's price. In fact, there is a heated discussion about what Bill perceives to be excessive questioning, particularly for a first meeting. Bill accuses Jim of seeking to attain industry information at Bill's expense. The meeting does not end well; both sides have entrenched themselves into positional bargaining, unable to communicate or find common interest other than what Bill was demanding for a price. End result—*no deal*.

Bill has done nothing but go in circles. Now he is back to the start, minus a friend and having wasted a whole lot of time.

ANALYSIS AND INSIGHTS

What went wrong here?

Well, a lot of things. Bill's main problem was his *mind-set* and his lack of preparation. He was too focused on what he did not have (liquidity and time) and not on what both parties were trying to achieve. He knew two things heading into his meeting: He wanted to leave behind the headaches of running the business, and he needed enough money on which to retire. Bill had not been a very good saver and as a result felt pressure to achieve the highest price possible. Had Bill followed the rather straightforward steps illustrated in this and the previous chapters, he would have had a plot on the exit quadrant chart as illustrated in Exhibit 3.3 below:

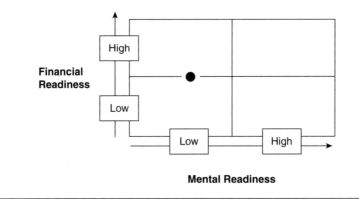

EXHIBIT 3.3   BILL'S PLACEMENT ON THE EXIT QUADRANT CHART

With a relatively low mental readiness for an exit and an average financial readiness for his exit, Bill should have considered many other exit options besides selling to Jim. In fact, as we will see, the sale option would have been rather far down the list of options to consider given Bill's positioning on the exit quadrant chart—more on this later.

In fact, Bill saw an opportunity and jumped and ran with it, in much the same way he has approached business all his life. Bill was using his existing tools and skills of business to handle his exit strategy. Although first mover's advantage is a key to competitive business, the qualities of foresight and patience are more useful when it comes to business exits. Bill also erroneously believed that the business transfer would be easy and that selling to Jim was his only option.

By skipping ahead before fully examining his readiness and options, Bill entered a situation that was going to fail.

Consider what Bill could have done differently that would have radically changed the outcome of his meeting with his potential buyer, Jim. Before the meeting, Bill should have prepared a written exit strategy plan that armed him with these eight items:

1. The minimum amount of postfee, posttax money that he would need to net from his transaction with Jim in order to accept any deal.

2. A plan of action that results from an awareness that this process is not going to be easy, but rather, fairly difficult. This plan would include written and objective goals that he is looking to achieve with the business exit.

3. A detailed list of retirement items that Bill has been looking forward to engaging in, including more time with the grandchildren at the top of the list.

4. An awareness that Bill's mental wiring is geared towards running, not exiting, a business and an expectation that some resistance is going to occur when Bill attempts to let go of the business if Jim agrees to Bill's asking price.

5. A further assessment of his mental readiness to leave the business, including:

    a. Investing a good deal of thought into the personal satisfactions and standing in his community that Bill receives from owning and running his business.

    b. Time spent visualizing his life without the business and has resolved how he will occupy his mind without the challenges of running his business every day.

6. A prepared consulting agreement that Bill is ready to honor.

    a. Bill is not completely ready to retire and wants to continue to receive income for his involvement in the business. He puts this stream of income into his retirement projections.

    b. Bill's time will not be completely devoted to the company and includes a work schedule that accommodates his personal wants.

7. A signed confidentiality agreement with Jim that Bill stands ready to enforce should any information leaks occur.

8. Documentation that illustrates the benefits of Jim owning Bill's business, including:

    a. Justification as to why Jim should pay the amount that Bill asks, including details on his financial statements that add back the additional expenses that Bill has been compensating himself over the years.

    b. A lucid explanation as to why his company is worth what he is asking and an illustration that shows the benefit of these earning streams to Jim's business once the acquisition is complete.

    c. A professional valuation report (which Bill does not share with Jim) that determines the market value of the business, i.e. the low-end of Bill's asking price and the rationale behind the determination of value that Bill will use in his negotiations with Jim.

All of these items are helpful to the meeting with Jim, but Bill is also armed with some eight additional pieces of information in his written exit strategy plan.

BACKUP PLANNING

1. Bill's projected net after fees and tax proceeds from a sale of part of the company to an employee stock ownership plan (ESOP), where he retains his position at the company while achieving diversification and liquidity.

   a. Sensing that the ESOP value would be lower than what he could get from a full sale to Jim (see the ESOP discussion in Chapter 7), Bill decides to pursue the agreement with Jim because his financial preparedness to exit the business scored average.

   b. Bill holds on to the ESOP option as a backup plan in the event that the deal with Jim does not work out.

2. A second backup plan includes offering his management team an opportunity to buy him out over time.

   a. Bill has prepared projections on how a management buyout could be structured. The collateral asset base of his company is debt-free, so he believes that those assets could be pledged as a loan for the existing management team to structure an internal buyout that could get him quite a bit of up-front money. This would also allow his capable management team to pay him the balance, with interest, over a five-year period. (See Chapter 9 for a discussion of management buyouts.)

   b. Bill has not discussed the possibility of selling to his management team with any of the members of that team. However, he knows that a management buyout is another viable backup option for his exit if the meeting with Jim does not produce the results that he is looking for.

3. A detailed understanding of the taxes that Bill will be paying at the close of the sale and the advisory team (and the approximate cost of their fees) that will be required in order to complete the due diligence that Jim or any other prospective buyer/successor will require.

4. Bill's income replacement strategy for reinvestment of the proceeds that he will get from the deal with Jim (i.e., a projected portfolio of investments including stocks, bonds, and other investments that will provide him a sufficient amount of passive income to meet his retirement needs).

5. A review of the legal agreements that he will be required to sign, including a purchase and sale agreement, an enforceable confidentiality agreement, and a noncompete agreement, as Bill recognizes that Jim will want to protect the interest that he is purchasing in Bill's company.

   Bill recognizes that he does not want to see these legal documents for the first time at the closing of the business sale.

6. A review of the impact of this transaction on Bill's estate planning.

   Given that Bill's total estate far exceeds the applicable exclusion amount allowed by the federal and state estate tax laws, he needs to know the amount of his wealth that is exposed to estate taxes so as to reduce his risk of paying out his hard-earned wealth (45 cents on the dollar—2008, Federal level estate taxation) to the government in the form of estate taxes. (See Chapter 12 for a discussion of estate tax planning.)

7. A backup plan for receiving health insurance coverage in the event that Bill is not able to achieve employee status with Jim's company and avail himself of Jim's corporate plan and benefits.

8. A strategy for business growth that Bill can execute if none of his exit options materialize. This new plan is designed to prevent Bill from mentally checking out of the business while giving consideration to the variety of exit options.

WRITTEN EXIT STRATEGY PLAN

Bill puts all of his thoughts and alternatives into a written exit strategy plan that details the structure of each alternative as well as its net financial effect to him. His written exit strategy plan has changed the course of the meeting with Jim. Bill is confident in knowing that he has examined all of the options that are available to him for the exit and transfer of his business. He walks into the meeting with his competitor fully prepared to execute the largest financial transaction of his life or go back to work competing with Jim. Bill has done the work; he has examined his options for exit and is ready to execute his optimal exit strategy.

Bill's exit strategy plan began with his personal goals for the business exit, including his financial and mental readiness for his business exit. Armed with this knowledge, Bill moved ahead in constructing options for exits other than the sale of his business to this competitor. By knowing his personal and mental readiness as well as his options, Bill was able to deliver a cogent argument for why the sale to his competitor should be executed at the price that he suggested in practice, buyer makes first offer. More important, Bill was able to *think clearly* through the execution of this exit strategy and negotiate from a position of strength with his competitor. Bill used this written plan as his guide as the resistance and doubt crept in.

REVIEW

Up to this point, we have considered:

- The importance of planning the exit
- Financial readiness for your exit
- Mental readiness for your exit
- Introduction to the exit quadrant chart
- Case study of Bill the business owner who:
  - Originally falls into the common traps that were identified.
  - Then makes the common mistakes that many exiting owners make.
- How Bill's situation could be improved with a well-thought-out, written exit strategy plan that considers all of his exit options and measures their net impact on him from a business and personal perspective.

As we take a look at Bill's situation, we need to ask about the process he used to determine which exit options were the right ones to consider, and how and where he could get such organized information. You will need a process to develop your business exit strategy plan, and it begins with the exit quadrant chart and the four types of exiting owners discussed in the next chapter.

If you are ready to learn how Bill discovered and analyzed the many options that were available to him for his exit and how he followed a simple process to get started, turn to Chapter 4. There you will learn about four different types of exiting business owners and how you can use Chapters 2 and 3 and the exit quadrant chart to begin your exit strategy planning.

WORKSHEET

Assess your mental readiness to exit the business by using this worksheet:

- ❏ Love job.
- ❏ Involved in it day to day.
- ❏ Firm idea of how to fill time when not running the business.
- ❏ Perceive exit as a healthy, natural step.

4

WHAT TYPE OF EXITING OWNER ARE YOU?

One of the marks of excellent people is that they never compare
themselves with others. They only compare themselves
with themselves and with their past accomplishments
and future potential.

—*Brian Tracy*

This chapter is not about comparing your success with that of
other exiting business owners. Rather it is a framework from
which you can learn about four types of exiting owners and
use them to begin to find solutions that work for your exit
strategy planning and wealth protection.

Here we build on the work that you did in Chapters 2 and 3 to lead you to a
point where you can assess the optimal way to begin building your exit strategy plan.

Four types of exiting owners are discussed in this chapter:

1. Get-me-out-right-away-at-the-highest-price exiting owner

2. Well-off-but-choose-to-work exiting owner

3. Stay-and-grow-the-business exiting owner

4. Rich-and-ready-to-go exiting owner (can use any option)

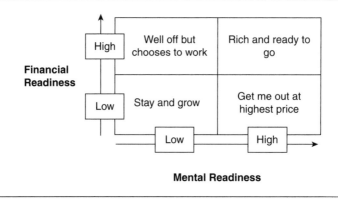

Mental Readiness

Exhibit 4.1   Exit Quadrant Chart

IDENTIFY YOUR READINESS, LEARN YOUR EXIT OPTIONS

Each of the listed business owners represents a certain level of financial and mental readiness that primarily defines their attitudes toward an exit. The exit quadrant chart (Exhibit 4.1) organizes these types of exiting owners within an easy-to-use framework.

The framework of this chart is then filled with exit options, as illustrated in Exhibit 4.2. The options that fit within each quadrant are those that are best aligned with the financial and mental readiness of that exiting owner. Hence, this is the optimal place from which to begin your exit strategy planning. (These options are described in Parts II and III.)

Our exit quadrant chart now offers exit options that can be considered based on the exiting owner's financial and mental readiness for exit. Exit options listed in the chart are most applicable to the readiness of each of those exiting owners. Your ability to relate to any one of these types of exiting owners will guide you toward options that you can consider for your exit and will set you on a course for building an exit strategy plan suited to your personal goals.

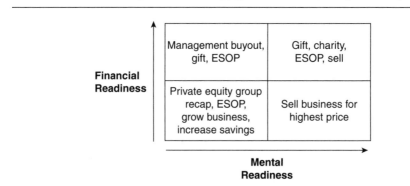

Exhibit 4.2   Exit Options Chart

There is a wide array of exit options to choose from. Having all of these options available is both a blessing and a curse. On the positive side, forward-thinking exiting owners can create any exit strategy plan that satisfies their primary, personal motive—the Chapter 2 concept that stated what you would like most to accomplish with your business exit.

This book is about using the process of determining your personal readiness for an exit in order to follow a system for starting to build your exit strategy plan. Once you have put the necessary thought into your exit and have constructed a blueprint of what you want your plan to look like, you will want to consult with legal, tax, deal structuring, and financial advisors to execute the plan and determine if your goals can be met. (Part III)

Again, this is not a book about the viability of your business for sale or what you need to do to improve the value of your business. Rather, this book offers a process that begins with your personal readiness for an exit and how you can protect your wealth by understanding exit options in order to build and execute a customized exit strategy plan.

UNDERSTANDING VALUATION

It is critical to understand that your privately held business has many different values and we examine those different values at the end of this chapter. Unlike the stock of a publicly traded corporation, which has ready buyers and sellers, to exit from your business, you will have to create a market for the shares of your business. And, how and when you get paid for your shares will determine whether or not your postexit expenses will be met. Part II, starting with Chapter 5, discusses various external and internal methods for transferring your shares and illustrates how those options are applied through case studies involving our exiting owner, Bill. Again, the exit option you choose will be determined by your personal desires and readiness for the exit. However, each exit option has different values that you will need to know to meet your goals. Exhibit 4.3 is an illustration of how these value ranges can be understood.

The fair market value standard and the market value standards are explained in detail later in this chapter. For now we simply note the important point that the value of your business is a range concept. This means that you cannot know the exact value of your business without first knowing who is going to own it after you have exited. It is important to realize that the exit option you choose will be the largest determinant of what value you receive. And whether your goals will be met most likely depends on the value that you receive.

The exit strategy planning process therefore continues to follows the steps shown in Exhibit 4.4.

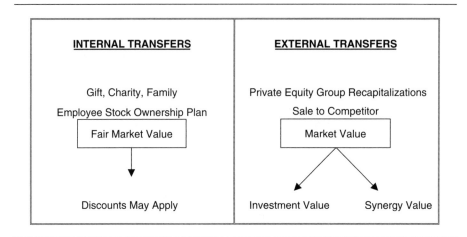

EXHIBIT 4.3 INTERNAL VERSUS EXTERNAL TRANSACTION VALUATIONS

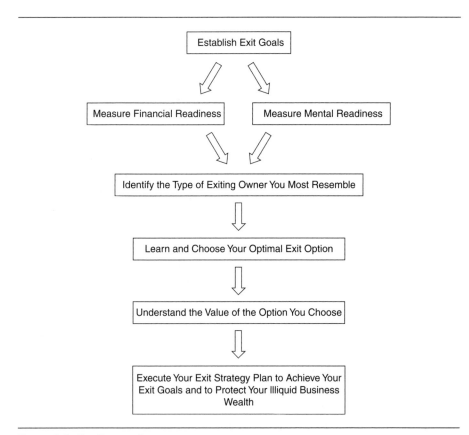

EXHIBIT 4.4 EXIT PROCESS STEPS

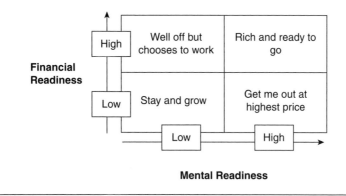

EXHIBIT 4.5   Exit Quadrant Chart: Four Quadrants

FOUR TYPES OF EXITING OWNERS: WHICH QUADRANT ARE YOU IN?

Let's take a look at the descriptions of the four types of exiting owners who fall within the exit quadrant chart. By understanding the mind-set and readiness of each type of exiting owner, you will be able to choose the type whom you most resemble and then identify the exit options most suitable for you to begin to build your exit strategy plan.

We are now going to give initial direction to your exit strategy planning by plotting both your financial and mental readiness within the four quadrants listed in Exhibit 4.5.

A general profile of the exiting owners that fit into each quadrant is provided so that you can position yourself within this world. Then we give exit alternatives as a starting point in constructing your exit strategy plan. For example, a stay-and-grow exiting owner—who has low financial and low mental readiness—may begin building an exit strategy plan by studying recapitalizations with private equity groups. Or this exiting owner may be more inclined to install an employee stock ownership plan (ESOP) to increase the cash flow of the business while also planning for a future sale of stock to the ESOP trust.

We will also return to our exiting owner, Bill, to see how the use of these different exit options helped him to optimize the value of his exit and to meet his personal goals with his new and much-improved exit strategy plan.

EXITING OWNER 1: RICH AND READY TO GO

Rich-and-ready-to-go exiting owners have a high financial and mental readiness for an exit from the business (Exhibit 4.6). Virtually any exit options are

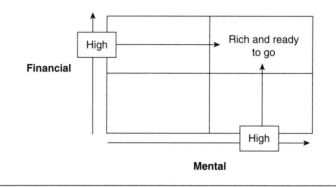

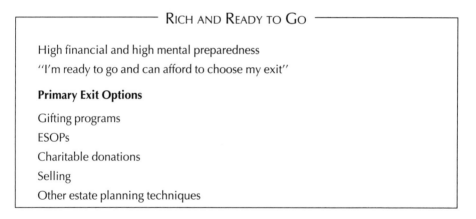

Exhibit 4.6 Rich and Ready to Go

available to them, as most of their wealth is not concentrated in the business. Many factors will contribute to which exit option they choose, but they have a good deal of flexibility in choosing an option and in executing their exit strategy plan.

RICH AND READY TO GO

High financial and high mental preparedness

"I'm ready to go and can afford to choose my exit"

Primary Exit Options

Gifting programs

ESOPs

Charitable donations

Selling

Other estate planning techniques

Here, business owners are just cruising along in their business with plenty of investment assets and/or personal wealth in the form of real estate or other assets outside of the business. Work has turned into a hobby for them, a sort of game to keep the mind occupied. For some reason, these businesspeople are now motivated to exit the business right away. They have no emotional attachments to the business, and a failed exit would be meaningless to their lifestyle because they do not rely on the income from the business to support themselves.

In fact, these fortunate business owners often have large estate tax issues that occupy their minds.

Options for owners in this quadrant include:

- **Gifting programs** permitting the transfer of shares of the business to family, friends, and employees, thereby reducing the owner's estate tax exposure.

- **ESOPs** as a tax-efficient way to get some liquidity and transfer shares, over time, to employees.

- **Charitable gifting strategies** to take advantage of tax-deductions today, manage low-cost basis positions, and generate current income.

- **Selling the business** if no known successor or family members are present.

MATCH YOUR CURRENT PERSONAL SITUATION WITH

"Rich and Ready to Go"

❑ Personal involvement is not critical to day-to-day running of the business.

❑ Personal savings or outside income is sufficient to sustain lifestyle.

❑ Work is viewed as more of a hobby than a chore.

❑ Limited emotional attachments to the business.

❑ Estate tax issues are present and need to be incorporated with the exit.

❑ Owners were not interested in exiting until now.

If you match these criteria, you are a rich-and-ready-to-go exiting owner, and you can begin to learn about the exit or transfer strategy that is going to fulfill your primary, personal motive.

EXITING OWNER 2: WELL OFF BUT CHOOSES TO WORK

These hardworking exiting owners (Exhibit 4.7) are simply that, hardworking. In fact, they are so hardworking that if they don't have a business to report to every day, they are not sure what they would do with their time. The business keeps their minds engaged, and their mental readiness for an exit is low. They

---

WELL OFF BUT CHOOSES TO WORK

High financial, low mental preparedness

"I can afford to leave but I'd rather keep my job; what else would I do?"

Primary Exit Options

ESOP

Management buyout

Gift

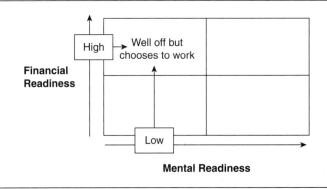

EXHIBIT 4.7 WELL OFF BUT CHOOSES TO WORK

have been good savers but are likely addicted to their business (concepts discussed in Chapter 3).

This type of exiting owner is quite common. These business owners have been rather diligent at saving for the future and have an eye towards retirement but are not mentally ready to exit the business. These owners enjoy working but are looking ahead to when they would like work to be optional. There may be some pressure from home to spend more time with the family. In addition, there may be health issues causing them to begin to consider their own mortality. Or the idea of simply taking some chips off the table has a very nice ring to it after years of concentrated, illiquid wealth trapped in the business.

These exiting owners are often involved in day-to-day operations due to various factors. First and foremost, their work is what they truly enjoy doing—sometimes to the detriment of being able to let go of certain responsibilities within the business. They have tried to delegate tasks to others but experienced frustration when the quality of execution dropped. As a result, their approach to the business is that if something has to be done right, they have to do it themselves. These exiting owners are not eager to leave. However, they realize that they cannot continue to run the business forever. And by insisting on being the hub in the wheel, they have at times caused the business to miss out on certain growth opportunities. These owners generally work a lot of hours but constantly remind themselves that they're not working as much as they used to. They have thought about selling the business but are not mentally prepared to stop working.

These exiting owners can look to these exit options:

- **ESOP plans,** where they can increase cash flow in their business with certain tax deductions while achieving personal diversification from the business today.

- **Management buyouts,** where key employees are offered an opportunity to buy out the owners over time.
- **Gifting programs** to transfer shares to key employees or family members.

MATCH YOUR CURRENT PERSONAL SITUATION WITH

Well Off but Chooses to Work

❏ Likely critical to day-to-day running of the business.

❏ Personal savings or outside income are close to sustaining the owner's lifestyle.

❏ Work is viewed as something enjoyable.

❏ May or may not be emotionally attached to business.

❏ Estate tax issues are likely.

❏ Considering a controlled and phased exit from the business.

If you match these criteria, you are a well-off-but-chooses-to-work exiting owner. You can begin to learn about the exit or transfer strategy that is going to fulfill your primary, personal motive including your desire to keep working.

EXITING OWNER 3: STAY AND GROW

These exiting owners are not ready to leave the business, either financially or mentally (Exhibit 4.8). Most of their wealth is tied to their business, and the business pays for most of their lifestyle. Without the business, these owners would be without a means to engage their mind and without a source of income to pay personal bills. Many business owners fall into this category and forgo doing any exit strategy planning but rather focus on business-building strategies and planning. This is a mistake, as all owners will exit their

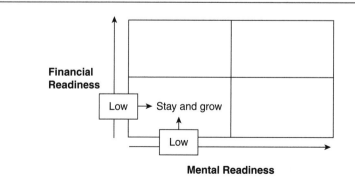

EXHIBIT 4.8 STAY-AND-GROW EXITING OWNER

businesses, and having an exit strategy plan will increase the focus on what is happening with their business-building plans. These owners have most of their wealth trapped in the business. Although that wealth may still be growing, an exit strategy plan for realizing that wealth is essential.

Stay and Grow

Low financial and mental preparedness
"I'm not ready to stop working and I have not been a great saver."

Primary Exit Options

Private equity group recapitalizations
Leveraged ESOP
Grow business
Increase savings

There are several options available to these exiting owners depending on age, the size of the business, and their relative skill sets. It seems clear that these owners need to continue with their businesses for some time, both financially and emotionally. And fortunately, it is what they prefer to be doing. Their mental readiness to exit is low, so even if they sold for top dollar, they would still want to work for a number of years. In fact, this type of owner may not technically qualify as an exiting owner by standard terms. However, as this book has illustrated, all owners are exiting owners if they are truly treating their business as an investment. A number of options exist for owners who need to bolster/diversify their personal financial situation but would like to continue working.

- **Private equity group recapitalizations** can be considered if the annual profits of the business are at least $1 million and the business lends itself to a decent growth path. Or the company (and its exiting owner) can serve as a platform company in an industry that is primed for consolidation.

  Here the exiting owner sells a majority (controlling) stake in the business to a private equity group while retaining a small percentage of equity in the company. The owner is retained under a multiyear employment agreement to assist with the growth objectives of the business plan formulated by the equity group.

- **Leveraged ESOPs** allow the owner to sell some of shares to the ESOP potentially in a tax-deferred transaction and achieve some personal diversification.

In a leveraged ESOP, the company obtains a bank loan whose proceeds are put into an ESOP trust. The ESOP trust purchases shares of the company from the exiting owner.

- **Grow business/increase retirement plan savings** is always an option for owners who have been slow to provide for their personal finances because they always reinvested profits back into the business or for owners who enjoy their position in their market and want to align the business to a future exit at a much higher value. Often this is the case of an owner who has a value gap (discussed in Chapter 2) and is not yet ready to exit the business.

MATCH YOUR CURRENT PERSONAL SITUATION WITH

Stay and Grow

❏ Younger business owner who wants to continue working.

❏ Interested in focusing the growth of the business on a future exit.

❏ Enjoys work but would like to diversify personal wealth.

❏ Some emotional ties to working but not necessarily to the business.

❏ More of an entrepreneur than a business owner.

❏ Would like to save for the future in a tax-efficient manner.

EXITING OWNER 4: GET ME OUT (AT THE HIGHEST PRICE)

These owners want out of the business yesterday (Exhibit 4.9). The problem is that the majority of their wealth is locked inside the business, and that is how their lifestyles are currently maintained. As we will see in Chapter 5, these owners have few options for an exit other than an outright sale to a synergistic buyer (i.e., selling at the highest price).

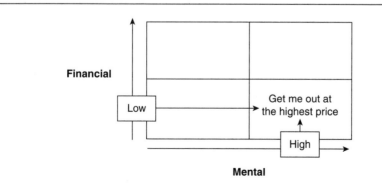

EXHIBIT 4.9 GET-ME-OUT-AT-THE-HIGHEST-PRICE EXITING OWNER

┌─────────────────── Get Me Out at the Highest Price ───────────────────┐

Low financial, high mental preparedness
"Get me out yesterday to whoever can pay me the most money."

Primary Exit Option
Sell business for highest price

└──┘

One of the foundational concepts behind this book is that most business owners have a number of options for exiting their business. In fact, however, for business owners who fit this category, the options are actually quite limited. These owners have not prepared themselves financially for their business exit and are highly motivated to stop working and to leave the business. Selling the business appears to be the best—and likely the only—option available. When the business sells, these highly motivated owners will leave the business and hope to get as much money at the closing as possible.

These exiting owners will need to enter a process for selling the business— described in detail in Chapter 5—that ideally will include many buyers who can enjoy synergies from acquiring this target company and who are competing with each other to buy it. These types of exiting owners will pay their taxes and advisory fees, close the value gap, and proceed into retirement, living off the income generated from their liquid investment portfolio.

OUR OWNER BILL

We will return to our exiting owner, Bill, who thought in the last chapter that he was a get-me-out-at-the-highest-price exiting owner. Bill thought this because he incorrectly believed that selling the business was his only exit option. Once he tried to negotiate his own transaction, however, he found that he did not know what he was going to do with his time. He was not mentally ready for a complete business exit.

If Bill had read about these four types of exiting owners, he could have determined his financial and mental readiness and surveyed the exit quadrant Chart to see what type of exiting owner he most resembled. Thereafter, he could refer to the exit options chart to determine what options were available other than the sale of his business to a competitor. Ultimately, Bill could have—and will in Parts II and III—designed an exit strategy plan that suited his personal needs and in a manner and time period that was most accommodative to him.

This book is written for the exiting owner who, like Bill, needs to develop an exit strategy plan to protect the wealth that is in an illiquid business. To that end, we present an overall review of what we have covered so far. Then we enter into an important discussion about business value. In Parts II and III we detail the exit options available for building a customized exit strategy plan.

OVERALL REVIEW

In Chapter 1 we saw that a great many business owners are heading into retirement and looking for solutions for the illiquid wealth that is trapped in their businesses. The health of the business and the strength of the economy are important to an exit, but not nearly as important as the personal readiness of an owner to leave (or transfer) the business. Exiting owners who can see their business more as an investment and less as a job will understand that an exit strategy is necessary for protecting their wealth. Many options exist for a business exit, and a team of advisors will be required to assist with the execution of your exit strategy plan.

In Chapter 2 we stressed the importance of writing down what you want most from your business exit strategy. We used a few tools to measure the return on investment of the business as well as to assess your income replacement strategy. We also noted that your exit strategy plan will need to change as more information is made available to you.

In Chapter 3 you were asked to consider how mentally ready you were to leave the business. Many business owners really enjoy the positions that they hold in their companies. Furthermore, after years and years of experiencing success in their businesses, they can become addicted to their businesses. Realizing what is happening on a subconscious level is critical to understanding resistance to your business exit strategy planning. Overcoming that resistance is one key to a successful exit.

WHAT TYPE OF EXITING OWNER ARE YOU?

You should now be able to identify with one of the four types of exiting owners introduced in this chapter. Now that you know what type of exiting owner you most closely resemble, review what you wrote down in Chapter 2 describing what you want from your business exit. You should have a clearer view of what is possible for designing your exit strategy plan given the structure of options described in this chapter so far. Whether you are a stay-and-grow-at-the-highest-price exiting owner or a get-me-out right away owner, you should now have an understanding of how to begin your exit strategy planning.

EXIT OPTIONS CHART

You have now plotted points on the exit quadrant chart, taking an accurate measurement of both your financial and mental readiness for a business exit. If you feel that you are close to plotting a point that is *on* one of the lines, that is fine. For now, we are simply trying to have you position yourself within the range of choices available to most exiting business owners, enabling you to think about the alternatives available to you.

We examine the exit options in Parts II and III, highlighting the pros and cons of each to help you determine whether that option will assist you in reaching the exit goals that you wrote down in Chapter 2.

Where do you fall in the quadrant chart?

EXIT OPTIONS AVAILABLE

A few observations can be made about where you place yourself on the exit options chart (Exhibit 4.10).

HIGH MENTAL READINESS

If you are mentally ready to leave the business behind—high mental preparedness to exit—you will need to measure your financial ability to execute the transaction of your choosing. For some exiting owners, this will be obvious. All of their net worth is in the business, and they want to get it out. However, for other exiting owners—owners on the line—the measurement becomes a crucial part of the exit strategy plan. You need to be able to answer the question: "Can I afford an exit other than the sale of the business at the highest price?"

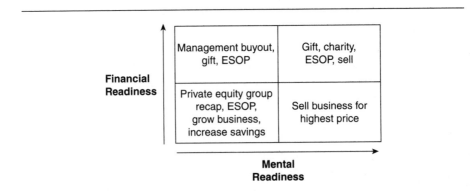

EXHIBIT 4.10 EXIT OPTIONS CHARTS

If your planning reveals that you can afford an alternate transaction, survey the upper-right-hand quadrant of the chart. If your financial planning reveals that you cannot afford another exit, i.e., you are a get-me-out-at-the-highest-price exiting owner—bearing in mind that you are really ready to get out— you may be ready to meet with a transaction-based advisor to begin the process of selling your business.

LOW MENTAL READINESS

If you are interested in keeping your job, you really need to decide what the near-term prospects for your business appear to be. Will you be growing the business and making further personal guarantees to the bank over the next few years, or will you be aggressively grooming a successor so that you can begin to step back from the business? Or perhaps you can sell control to a private equity group that can help finance the growth while you achieve personal liquidity. In any event, learning about your options for exiting over a longer period of time will serve you well.

In many respects this book was written for you, owners who sense that they do not want to sell but have an interest in learning about options for exiting the business.

ESOPs ARE FLEXIBLE EXIT STRATEGY PLANNING TOOLS

You will note that the ESOP option is present in three out of four of the exit option quadrants. Therefore, if you are not in a position to sell the business today (low financial, high mental readiness), you should be familiar with what an ESOP is. At a minimum it will help you to understand how a flexible and creative exit planning tool can be used to potentially customize a strategy for you that you control. It may turn out to be much more than that for your exit plans.

MOVING AHEAD

You have measured your financial and mental readiness to exit the business. You have found a place on the exit quadrant chart where you believe that you fit. And you have been introduced to the four types of exiting owners to reinforce your assessment. Each quadrant of the options chart contains a list of exit options available to owners who fit the respective description.

A complete exit strategy plan will examine all of these options to determine which is the best fit for helping you achieve your overall goals.

Easy enough so far?

One final point before we explain the options available so that you can apply them to yourself.

VALUATION

We need to focus our attention briefly on the topic of business valuation. This is a topic that should be near and dear to your heart because it directly impacts the amount of cash (or the value of a gift) you may receive (or transfer away) with your business exit.

As we have mentioned, business owners often believe that selling a business is the only exit available. In fact, many other options exist. However, in order to examine the outcome of each the options on your personal goals, you need to know something about the range of values that exists for privately held businesses.

BUSINESS VALUATION AND THE RANGE OF VALUES CONCEPT

You may ask whether a high value and getting the most money aren't of paramount importance in an exit strategy.

Well, not exactly. Receiving a net amount of money that will secure your financial goals is really the most important objective of an exit strategy.

Does this mean that you are leaving money on the table if you do not sell for the highest price?

Well, again, not exactly. Selling your business to a competitor probably generates the highest value that you can receive at the closing. However, consider for a moment that the sale of your business likely subjects you to a loss of more than 25% of the business proceeds to taxes and advisory fees (more on this in Part III). In addition, you lose your source of income, your company perks, perhaps some health benefits, and your standing as a business owner.

You may very well end up ahead of the game, in terms of net proceeds, by examining all of your options and executing a multiyear, controlled exit where you keep your job, your income, your standing, and your benefits.

How is valuation relevant to each exit option, and what tools can you use to figure out the net result that will be achieved from each exit?

Let's learn about different types of valuations so that we can later apply the concepts against exit options available.

EVERY PRIVATE BUSINESS HAS A RANGE OF VALUES. . .

. . . it depends on the type of transfer the seller chooses.

All business owners want to know the value of their business. You, as an exiting owner, need to understand that the value of your company is a range concept; there is no single value for the shares of your privately held business.

Rob Slee, author of Private Capital Markets, helps us understand this otherwise confusing concept by defining this range of different values as "value worlds." Slee states:

> Because each value world is likely to yield a different value indication for a business interest, private business valuation is a range concept. Thus, a private business interest has *at least* as many correct values at any given point in time as the number of value worlds.[1]

We are primarily interested in two of the value worlds that Slee describes: the worlds of fair market value and market value. (We discuss both in this chapter.) Within the world of market value, we will look at both investment value and synergy value to understand how our choice of who succeeds you in your business directly impacts the value that is placed on it. (This will become clearer once these concepts are applied to the case studies in Chapters 5 through 10.)

THE VALUE OF YOUR BUSINESS DEPENDS UPON WHOM YOU CHOOSE TO TRANSFER IT TO

Your business value at the time of your exit is directly tied to the type of exit you choose. And the type of exit you choose is tied to your financial and mental readiness to exit the business. The easiest way to understand this range of values concept is to use the options chart to determine whether an internal transfer—gifting programs, family transfers, ESOPs, or charitable transfers—will satisfy your goals, or whether an external transfer—private equity group recapitalization or a sale to a competitor—is required for you to meet your exit strategy planning goals.

Another way of understanding this range of values concept is to see that valuations vary primarily according to which type of transfer, internal or external, you choose (Exhibit 4.11).

INTERNAL TRANSFERS: FAIR MARKET VALUE STANDARD OF VALUATION

FAIR MARKET VALUE DEFINED

In the world of valuations, there exists a standard called fair market value. This standard of measuring a company's worth is used by the tax courts and the Internal Revenue Service (IRS) when evaluating a stated value for a business. According to Slee, "The Fair Market Value world hypothetically embodies the value of a business interest. In terms of standards and processes, fair market value is the most structured value world."[2]

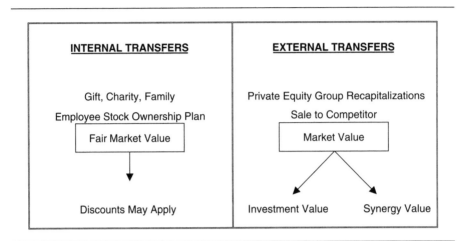

EXHIBIT 4.11   INTERNAL VERSUS EXTERNAL TRANSACTION VALUATIONS

IRS Revenue Ruling 59-60 defines fair market value as:

> The price at which the property would change hands between a willing buyer and a willing seller when the former is not under any compulsion to buy and the latter is not under any compulsion to sell, both parties having reasonable knowledge of relevant facts . . . the hypothetical buyer and seller are assumed to be able and as well as willing, to trade and to be well informed about the property and concerning the market for such property.

Slee explains further that

> The world of Fair Market Value is the most cohesive and fully developed of the value worlds. There are highly specific purposes for these appraisals, and each entails a specific process and set of standards. Fair Market Value appraisals are used to establish value in estate and gift tax valuation, Tax Court cases, and the creation and updates for ESOPs.[3]

WHY FAIR MARKET VALUE MUST BE USED WITH GIFTING AND ESOPs

In the absence of such a standard, many business owners would be able to claim that their business was worth very little, thereby structuring internal transfers to family members that minimize or avoid both gift and estate taxes. However, owners who want to gift shares of their business must use the mandated fair market value process to place a value on those shares. This mandated value also applies to sales of stock under an ESOP or under a charitable transfer.

Note: Fair market value appraisals are conducted by professional appraisers who are trained in valuation methodologies. It is adherence to the process for developing a fair market value appraisal that is defensible in tax court if the value is challenged at a later date in tax court.

Valuing shares under fair market value uses a process that is cohesive and fully developed. Use of this generally accepted process allows for proper passing of assets to children, ESOPs, or charities with an idea as to how the IRS will later view the transaction. The IRS is well aware that wealthy business owners are looking for ways to transfer their wealth to family members while minimizing estate and gift taxes. In the case of ESOP plans, the fair market value standard applies due to the fact that an ESOP is a *qualified* retirement plan that falls within the purview of the Employee Retirement Income Security Act (ERISA) laws (discussed in Chapter 7). Specific guidelines are established and the fair market value standard is mandated to impose consistency to the valuation of certain types of transaction so that interested parties, such as employees or the IRS, know that certain rules were followed—and a level of self-interested subjectivity was minimized—in the process of determining the value.

FAIR MARKET VALUES ARE GENERALLY LOWER THAN MARKET VALUES

As a general rule, fair market value appraisals will produce lower valuations than open market transactions, such as selling the business. Thus, fair market values are more in line with what a financial investor who brings no synergies to the table would pay for the business. The question, however, for exit strategy planning purposes is whether the fair market value is sufficient to achieve the business owner's financial goals and optimal exit. If so, that owner can begin to consider some very creative ways in which to exit the business.

If there is a large value gap, as measured from Chapter 2, owners may need to sell the business in an external transfer in order to get the highest price to be comfortable in meeting their postexit lifestyles.

Even though the fair market value standard may be lower than what owners could otherwise achieve in the open market, internal transfers allow greater levels of flexibility, which may be important to exiting owners. Flexibility quickly translates into more control for exiting owners. As we have already seen, this control comes at the price of a lower value. (See Exhibit 4.12.)

MAJORITY SALE VERSUS MINORITY SALE OF STOCK
AND DISCOUNTING THE VALUE

Many business owners will consider the idea of a partial exit strategy. Often owners want to take a step back and gain some time and money freedom

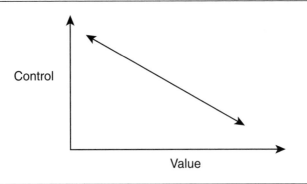

EXHIBIT 4.12   INVERSE RELATIONSHIP BETWEEN VALUE AND CONTROL

(diversification), but they still want to have a hand in the operations of the business. What are the options?

Business owners can sell or transfer either a controlling—majority—or a noncontrolling—minority—interest in the company. Often business owners will structure a minority transfer of stock in the company in order to reward valuable employees (sometimes including family members) or to reduce estate tax exposure.

In short, selling anything less than a majority stake in the business requires *discounts* to be applied to the value of those shares. Two of the prevalent discounts include the:

1. Discount for lack of marketability
2. Discount for lack of control

Discounts
When fair market value is used for an internal transfer and less than a majority (or control) stake in the company is sold or given away, discounts are applied to the value of the shares. This minority block of shares may be discounted for having a *lack of control*. This term means that the owner of this minority amount of stock does not have any authority regarding the strategic and/or financial decision making in the company. The shares may also be further discounted for a *lack of marketability*, recognizing that shares of a privately held business do not have a ready market for their transfer.

Discounts Can Work for You in Achieving Your Goals
It is often advantageous to apply discounts to shares of stock when implementing an estate tax strategy. The lower value allows for larger amounts of assets to leave the owner's estate, which is a primary consideration in a gifting

strategy. Selling or transferring minority blocks of stock is likely a part of a larger estate plan designed to minimize future estate taxes. Here discounts work to the benefit of exiting owners because they can transfer a greater amount of wealth out of their estate by utilizing applicable and allowed discounts. We visit this concept again in Chapter 10.

Discounts Can Also Work against You Achieving Your Goals
However, if owners are conducting a sale of stock to an ESOP, these discounts can work against them. In this case, the fair market value standard is still being used, but the owners want to exchange their shares for cash, not give them away. When the value of shares is reduced, owners cannot get the highest amount of money for the sale of those shares. Usually the more cash exiting owners receive, the greater the diversification and the closer the financial goals are to being achieved.

CONCLUDING THOUGHTS ON FAIR MARKET VALUE AND INTERNAL TRANSFERS

With few exceptions, the fair market value standard will generate a lower value than an open market transaction. When conducting a gifting program or a sale of stock to an ESOP, the fair market value standard must be used. Now let's examine the features of an open market sale of the business to better see how value intersects with motives and the exiting owner's choice of exit option.

EXTERNAL TRANSFERS: VALUE OF TRANSFERRING TO FINANCIAL BUYERS AND COMPETITORS

INVESTMENT VALUE VERSUS SYNERGY VALUE

We now look at your business valuation from the perspective of market value, which involves two different types of buyers who use two different types of valuations: financial and synergistic buyers. We start with the financial buyer and investment value.

The investment value of a business is the open market value that a financial buyer is willing to pay; the term *investment value* is suggestive of what is actually happening.[4] This is a value that does not include synergies.

The synergy or synergistic value, however, is an open market value that a synergistic (or industry) buyer will be willing to pay for the purchase of the business. In this case, the synergistic buyer is able to marry her existing business with the acquired business and generate additional revenues and/or profits through the combination. Synergy value is the highest value that an exiting owner can achieve.

Unlike fair market value, which operate according to a defined process applied by valuation experts to determine a hypothetical value of the business, investment and synergy values are generated by actual market players and the amounts that they are willing to pay to own the business.

MARKET VALUE VERSUS FAIR MARKET VALUE: VALUE VERSUS CONTROL
Investment value and synergy value are prices that the market will pay for your business. As a general rule, market values are higher than fair market values. However, a market value—or an open market transaction—generally includes selling control of the business, resulting in your loss of financial and strategic control. (However, as we will see with private equity group recapitalizations in Chapter 6, you may retain operational control under a multiyear employment agreement.)

In short, investment and synergy values in external transactions offer exiting owners less flexibility in making future business decisions. Also, exiting owners lose a good deal of control over the timing and tax structuring of the transaction.

Fair market value, however, mostly produces a lower value for shares, particularly when discounts are applied. But owners have more control over the transaction, and the types of transfers can be very flexible. In other words, owners can control how many shares are transferred, when they are transferred, and how and when payment will come for those shares. And, as mentioned earlier, these owners can keep their job, benefits, and income. (See Exhibit 4.12.)

KEEPING CONTROL
Control is an important consideration when building your exit strategy plan. Since most business owners got into business to control their destinies and their income and lifestyles, then, naturally, the amount of control that business owners lose or retain becomes an important consideration in the exit strategy process. Again, Chapter 3 surveyed an owners' mental readiness to exit the business. If maintaining control of the business is important to the exiting owners, they need to survey the exit options chart to see what options are available under the low mental readiness sections.

PUTTING IT TOGETHER
Now, having briefly mentioned different values for the business, it is important to see how the concepts fit together. If your goals from Chapter 2 are to transfer to family or to an ESOP, then fair market value will be your valuation measurement and you need to figure out how this (almost certainly) lower value will meet your financial readiness to exit.

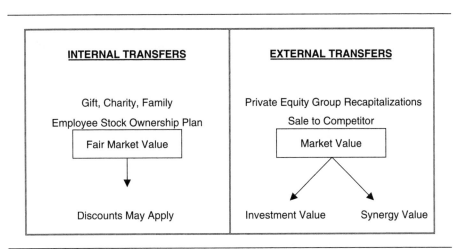

Exhibit 4.13   Internal versus External Transaction Valuations

If you need to get the highest price for your business because of your financial situation, you need to focus on investment and synergy values involving what an outside party would pay you for your business.

Many of these concepts are repeated and applied to the individual exit options detailed in Chapters 5 through 10. The concepts introduced here will become clearer in subsequent chapters as they are brought together in case study format.

Exhibit 4.13 summarizes internal versus external transfers.

REVIEW

The book's Introduction provided an overview of the importance of business exit strategy planning as well as the current marketplace for executing exit strategies.

Chapter 1 detailed the size of the marketplace, types of advisors, their motives, options for exits, and distinguished the sale of a business from the development of a business exit strategy plan.

Chapter 2 outlined the important steps is establishing exit goals, including an assessment of your financial readiness to exit your business. It discussed analyzing the business in objective terms, including an assessment of the business's return on investment.

Chapter 3 further challenged you to begin to assess your mental readiness for a business exit. The chapter suggested that you may, in fact, be addicted to your business. If so, you should keep a vigilant eye out for behavior that prevents you from protecting the wealth that has accumulated in your illiquid business. The chapter also introduced Bill, our Baby Boomer business owner, who is interested in exiting his business but made many mistakes in his initial exit attempt, including not preparing a written exit strategy plan.

Chapter 4 has put the exit quadrant chart and the exit options chart introduced in Chapter 1 to work by having you plot your financial and mental readiness in order to assist you in considering different exit alternatives. You were introduced to four types of exiting owners to compare yourself to so that you can see how different options could apply to your situation. The chapter also introduced the important concept of business valuation, explaining that internal transfers to family, employees, or charities would be measured using the fair market valuation standard (with or without discounts), while external transfers to financial buyers or competitors would produce a higher value (investment or synergy value) but would also require relinquishing control of the company.

As we have seen, there is an inverse relationship between value and control. Your goals for the business exit will determine how much of a business value you need to achieve. Personal goals for a business exit strategy plan range from the parents who are financially well enough off to give the business (or a portion thereof) to their children, to owners with no successors who need top dollar from an industry (or synergistic) buyer in order to declare the exit a success.

In Chapters 5 through 10, we explore the different types of exit options. Also, we reintroduce our exiting owner, Bill, as we detail each exit option and list its pros and cons and apply each exit to Bill's situation.

If you are ready to learn the details of the different exit options and see how they are applied to Bill, turn to Part II, Knowing Your Options.

NOTES

1. Robert T. Slee, *Private Capital Markets: Valuation, Capitalization, and Transfer of Private Business Interests* (Hoboken, NJ: John Wiley & Sons, 2004), p. 34.

2. Ibid., p. 88.

3. Ibid.

4. The business valuation community refers to this value as "the value to a particular investor based on individual investment requirements and expectations."

II

KNOWING YOUR OPTIONS

We now turn our attention to learning about the different types of exit options that are available to establish an exit strategy plan.

Exit options discussed in this part include:

- Sale of the business
- Private equity group recapitalizations
- Employee Stock Ownership Plans (ESOPs)
- Management buyouts
- Gifting programs (including charitable gifting)

5

SELLING THE BUSINESS

The point to remember about selling things is that, as well as
creating atmosphere and excitement around your products,
you've got to know what you're selling.

—Stuart Wilde

We begin our survey of exit options with the highest-value
exit, the sale of a business. It is human nature to want to know
the most money that you can potentially get for your business.
So, let's examine the get-me-out-at-the-highest-price exiting
owner who ranks low on financial preparedness but high on
mental preparation for exit. (See Exhibit 5.1.)

SELLING IS NOT THE ONLY EXIT OPTION,
BUT IT MAY BE FOR YOU

If you scored low on the financial readiness but high on the mental readiness,
you are likely a get-me-out-yesterday type of exiting business owner who has
most of your wealth tied up in your illiquid business. Or you may simply be an
entrepreneur who wants the highest value for your investment.

For exiting owners who are mentally ready to leave but cannot afford a
failed business exit (i.e., low financial readiness), a sale is likely the optimal
exit option.[1] If we can assume that your business is salable, then you need to
understand the basic components of a sale transaction in order to better prepare yourself for what lies ahead. The value that you are going to receive for

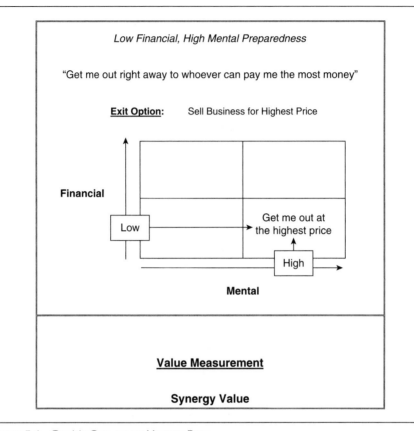

Exhibit 5.1   Get-Me-Out-at-the-Highest-Price

the sale of your business is simply whatever the market will bear—or, quite simply, whatever a buyer is willing to pay you. (Note: If you sense that your business is not salable, visit our Web site at www.exitingyourbusiness.com for a list of items that buyers look for when purchasing businesses.)

If your business is salable, then these concepts should sound simple enough. Look back at the work you did in assessing your financial readiness for an exit in Chapter 2. You need to know whether you will be able to accept an offer that an outside buyer puts in front of you. In other words, do you know your get-out-price for exiting your business today? This price should somewhat resemble what a buyer would be willing to pay for your business while also being the minimum amount that will fill the value gap that exists in your planning. Before we discuss value, let's first examine the process that is used to create a market for the sale of a business.

Question: What are you selling when you sell a business?

Answer: Future cash flows and the predictability of those cash flows without you there.

At the end of the day, after all of the talk in a deal, buyers are interested in your cash flows and their ability to achieve a return on investment that meets their investing criteria. For the exiting owner who has reviewed the exit options and is ready to sell the business to an outsider, we offer some very useful guidance toward understanding the process of selling a business as well as maximizing the sales price.

PROCESS OF SELLING A BUSINESS

The sale of a business requires a process through which interested buyers can be located. Two methods of selling a business exist. The first is a negotiated transaction. In this type of business sale, owners identify a limited number of buyers for the business; usually it is a short list of competitors and other players in the business. This is a rather straightforward transaction, where exiting owners feel confident that there are only a handful of buyers for the business, and they do not want to advertise to everyone and anyone that the business is for sale.

The second type of sale process includes an auction. Here exiting owners are interested in contacting as many potential buyers as possible, to see which one(s) will attribute the highest value toward the purchase of the business. In this case, owners usually hire a transactional advisor/intermediary to develop lists of potential buyers and to send those prospective buyers invitations to learn more about the opportunity to purchase the business. In the ideal scenario, many interested buyers are brought into the process and made to compete with each other for the purchase of the business. This will drive the price higher and give exiting owners leverage when negotiating pricing, terms, and deal structuring (see Chapter 11).

MARKETING THE BUSINESS

An intermediary is generally hired to handle the marketing and sale of privately held businesses. This transactional service provider follows a process that includes the initial potential steps shown in Exhibit 5.2.

In short, the company is described in a one-page confidential flyer that is distributed to the initial buyer list. Exiting owners may have potential buyers that they do not want contacted for various reasons; they are removed from the initial buyer list. Transactional advisors assist with forming the list of potential

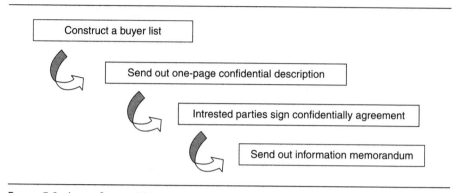

EXHIBIT 5.2 INITIAL STEPS IN MARKETING A BUSINESS FOR SALE

buyers and include names of parties, such as private equity groups, that would likely be interested in purchasing the business. Interested potential buyers contact the transactional advisor and request an information memorandum, which includes a full description of the business, its ownership, basic to intricate details from the financial statements, as well as the value drivers for profitability.

In order to receive this information memorandum, potential buyers must sign a confidentiality agreement stating that they will use the information about the company only for the purposes of considering a purchase and that they will not share this information with anyone else. This initial marketing and sales process also includes phone calls by your transactional advisor to all interested buyers to answer any questions that they may have. If the auction process is conducted properly, multiple offers are generated for the business, and exiting owners choose the one that will help them to meet their goals.

Choosing a buyer for your business is usually not as simple as taking the highest offer. As discussed in Chapter 3, many business owners feel a certain way about their business—as our hypothetical owner Bill did about his brewery. The assessment of what type of buyer you want to sell to is an important consideration. As the selling owner, you sign one letter of intent (LOI discussed in Chapter 13) from the buyer that you have chosen. The auction process ends with the selection of this buyer, and the selling process moves into a discovery, or due diligence, phase. At this point in the transaction, buyers need to have all of their questions answered about how the company is run as well as make assessments of their ability to transition the business to new ownership once you are gone.

NOTES ON PRESALE DUE DILIGENCE: GETTING THE HOUSE IN ORDER

Buyers/successors must have access to great amounts of information in order to complete a transaction. One of the primary issues surrounding privately held businesses is the lack of transparency, or information sharing that takes place. By contrast, publicly traded, liquid companies, are mandated to disclose information to shareholders on a regular basis. Since your buyer will now own your business, they need to understand all of the details of how it runs and what makes it profitable.

The buyer will typically have long lists of items that they want to review prior to closing. This includes all customer and vendor contracts that the company has entered into, attestations that the corporation is in good standing, procedures manuals for the operations, employment files, asset lists, inventory lists, accountings of tangible and intangible property, etc. . . . The lists can be quite exhaustive. Assembling all of this information is an onerous task for an exiting owner. Again, as stated in Chapter 1, smaller transactions generally also will have a harder time accumulating this information because it is primarily the principal owner who has negotiated and handled all of these agreements. Therefore, it is he or she alone who can locate and explain them to the buyer. Note: Larger Businesses have CFO's and other advisors who make this process easier on the exiting owner.

Exiting owners should organize their documents and begin a cleanup of all the outstanding items within the corporation prior to a sale: small claims by and against the corporation, grievances of every kind, environmental issues (if resolvable), employee-related matters, and the like. Also do not underestimate the importance of the business having a clean physical appearance. First impressions count. Many experienced buyers of businesses place a lot of emphasis on how clean the office and/or facility is when they come for an initial visit.

Due diligence items need to be disclosed as a matter of course; exiting owners are well advised to be proactive about addressing these issues up front. Depending on the number and severity of the various claims, exiting owners will need a certain amount of time to address these items. This is often referred to as getting a business ready for sale. It is a good idea to begin keeping all salient corporate contracts and agreements in electronic data form. Technology can assist in organizing these agreements and contracts. For a small expense, the corporation can also conduct an internal legal due diligence exercise so that you, the exiting owner, can proactively address any skeletons in the closet as part of the overall execution of your exit strategy. Getting your house in order tells buyers/successors that you are transferring a well-organized business. (For a sample due diligence request list, go to www.exitingyourbusiness.com.)

Again, many exiting owners believe that the sale of their business will be easy, similar to the way in which they may have once sold a home. Recognize the unfortunate reality that many deals go into due diligence—after the LOI— never to come out of it. Forewarned is forearmed. Due diligence items will be addressed in the main closing document, the purchase and sale agreement, which we will discuss in Chapter 13.

After the due diligence phase, if no surprises arise, legal agreements (discussed in Chapter 13) will be presented for the transfer of the business from you to the buyer. Your advisory team (discussed in Chapter 14) will work with you to understand the tax implications (discussed in Chapter 11) of the transaction so that you can see if your financial goals will be met with your net-of-tax, net-of-fee proceeds from the transaction.

The entire process of creating a market, negotiating the sale, and executing the agreements takes anywhere from 9 to 24 months. We repeat again that exiting a business, particularly via a sale transaction, is never an easy process. So many factors are involved with the sales process that entire books have been devoted to this topic alone. Here we offer only the highlights of the transaction and indicate the inherent difficulties involved in completing a sale. In addition, a major contributing factor to a successful business sale is the timing of the transaction.

THE ECONOMY MATTERS

Strong economies produce active buyers and ready access to capital. Unfortunately, you cannot control the economy. Using our earlier sailing analogy the winds and the tides that need to be considered in your exit via a sale of your business are the economic conditions present at the time that you are in the process of selling your business.

Accordingly, we offer again the 10-year transfer cycle for your consideration (see Exhibit 5.3).

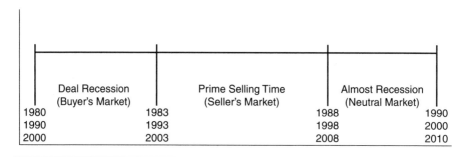

	Deal Recession (Buyer's Market)		Prime Selling Time (Seller's Market)		Almost Recession (Neutral Market)	
1980		1983		1988		1990
1990		1993		1998		2000
2000		2003		2008		2010

Exhibit 5.3 10-Year Transfer Cycle

Source: Robert T. Slee, *Private Capital Markets: Valuation, Capitalization, and Transfer of Private Business Interests* (Hoboken, NJ: John Wiley Sons, 2004, p. 444).

Remember, your personal timing (i.e., your financial and mental readiness) is the key determinant in your sale decision. However, as a general rule, the value of your business will fluctuate with the economic cycle. When you are working towards protecting your wealth, you need to recognize that your personal timing may not coincide with the optimal environment for the sale of your business.

During slow economic times, buyers are reluctant to forge ahead with new acquisitions. In addition, bank financing is not as readily available. Slowing economic times bring anticipations of loan defaults. And, without financing, many transactions via sales to third parties simply cannot get done.

If you are going to consider an exit via a sale transaction, you should consider the 10-year transfer cycle (Exhibit 5.3). Your intention of running the business for a few more years may result in the closing of a window of market opportunity and the compromising of your ability to receive the synergy value that you require to meet your financial goals. If this is the case, and the value of your enterprise declines with a slowing economy, you may be stuck with the business for some time going forward.

An exit strategy that includes an outside party is, in effect, a shifting of the risk from you, as owner, to your buyer. Your decision to sell the business to someone else is concurrently a decision to forgo sharing in future profits of the business. For owners who will exit their business once in their lifetime, this can be an overwhelming change, creating doubt, confusion, and resistance in the mind. Ideally, exiting owners who have chosen to sell understand the process that is involved and are resolved in their minds that a sale transaction is the optimal exit strategy to execute. These exiting owners know their synergy value (defined later in this chapter) and are able to accept it once it arrives. They also know that this sale price will satisfy their personal financial goals, allowing them to meet postsale expenses and lifestyle. At the closing, you should be confident that this sale transaction has met your financial goals (assessed in Chapter 2).

Selling a business can be a trying endeavor. The best sales transactions occur when the owner's readiness, the business's readiness, and a strong economy and deal market are aligned for the sale. In addition, a great deal of planning must accompany the transaction to assist the exiting owner in reducing its complexity.

Now let's see how you can achieve the highest value for the sale of your business. We turn our attention to a discussion of valuation of a business and how to understand and achieve the highest value available, synergy value.

HOW TO ACHIEVE MAXIMUM VALUE FROM THE SALE OF YOUR BUSINESS

We said earlier that what you are selling in a sale transaction is your future cash flows. The value that you receive for your business very simply put, will be a multiple of its cash flows. To succeed in any exit strategy, it is important to see the transaction through the eyes of your buyer. For myopic business owners who have always been primarily focused on their business operations and profitability, this can be a difficult mind-set shift. Let's review a calculation of those cash flows to begin to understand how a buyer will value your business:

$$\text{Cash flow} \times \text{Risk factor for your company} = \text{Selling price}$$

As stated in Chapter 1, buyers of privately held businesses have a return expectation that generally exceeds those available in liquid investment alternatives. The return requirements are higher because the riskiness of a privately held business is also higher than other liquid alternatives. The multiple that buyers will pay for your cash flows is dependent upon how risky those buyers perceive those cash flows to be. To translate these concepts into an offering price for your business, divide the buyers' return expectations (which you can estimate in the selling process by looking at comparable sales of other businesses in your industry) into 100 to determine the multiple of cash flows that they can afford to pay. Let us look at the example:

$$\frac{100}{35\%} = 2.9 \text{ times multiple of cash flows}$$

$$\frac{100}{17\%} = 5.8 \text{ times multiple of cash flows}$$

According to the return expectations that range from 17% to 35% annualized returns, the multiples of cash flows that a buyer will be willing to pay for your business falls into a general range of 2.9 to 5.8 times cash flow of your business.

In the case of our exiting owner, Bill, the business's cash flow was $2 million. Therefore, for a business such as Bill's, the amount that buyers will pay will range from $5.8 million to $11.6 million.

This is a very large range, and Bill's personal financial goals are highly dependent on the price that he receives within this range. Buyers will determine the amount of risk that they perceive in owning a business and adjust their purchase price accordingly. Different buyers will perceive different amounts of risk in acquiring your business. Therefore, it is your job (or that of your transactional advisor) to make cogent arguments for a lower level of risk while also understanding your buyers' reasons for assessing a higher level of risk and, hence, a lower offering price for your business. An understanding of how buyers arrive at a value for your business is critical to any exit strategy (even for gifting, the topic of Chapter 10, which assigns a fair market value to your business). Once you grasp these concepts, you are empowered to negotiate with buyers using their language and to present detailed examples of how an investment in your company will provide them with a solid return.

Let us return to our exiting owner, Bill, to apply these pricing concepts. As we saw earlier, Bill is interested in a negotiated sale transaction to his competitor, Jim. Bill has corrected his prior mistakes by making two very important discoveries in his exit strategy planning:

1. He measured his financial readiness to exit the business, taking into account his personal lifestyle and the bonuses and other additional income that he takes from the business each year. He spoke with his financial advisor about the required amount of investable, liquid assets that he would need to sustain his postexit lifestyle and determined that he had a medium financial readiness for his exit. Consequently, Bill has determined that he needs to fill the financial gap by selling his business for the highest price. Bill also met with a valuation specialist to assist in determining the minimum asking price for his business.

2. Bill gave great thought to, and wrote down in detail, how he would spend his time after his business exit. He knows that his feelings of being burned out are likely to increase over time, and he has been feeling badly about not having time for his family. After all, he thinks, what is his business success worth if he cannot enjoy it? Bill now ranks himself high on mental readiness to exit his business. He has resolved in his mind that if Jim, his competitor, can meet his asking price for the business, he will accept the offer and move into his next stage of life.

Having made these assessments, Bill plots himself on the exit quadrant chart, as illustrated in Exhibit 5.4.

Bill gives thought to the other exit alternatives in the chart but concludes that those other options will serve as backup plans only.

VALUATION

Since Bill will be selling to a buyer in his industry, he will be looking to achieve the highest value for the sale of his business—synergy value. Bill recognizes that he and his competitor have many duplicate functions that

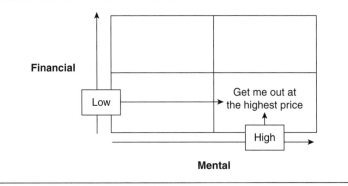

EXHIBIT 5.4   GET-ME-OUT-AT-THE-HIGHEST-PRICE EXITING OWNER

Jim could eliminate, such as accounting, finance, and some administrative functions, which will increase the business's value to Jim. In addition, by purchasing Bill's business, Jim will eliminate a competitor and gain access to new accounts.

These combined benefits to Jim represent synergies in the sale transaction. Bill knows that Jim will be reluctant to discuss and to share these synergies. Bill, however, will argue for, and expect to get, an improvement in his selling price to Jim because of the synergies that Jim will receive in the purchase of Bill's business.

Bill estimates his new synergized value and uses that sum as the basis of a separate set of projections that he and his financial advisor are preparing for his retirement.

GETTING THE HIGHEST PRICE

We know that Bill's brewery business has $2 million in annual cash flow. When Bill meets with Jim, Bill asks the right questions to discover Jim's annualized return expectation for the business, which is 20%. Therefore, Jim values Bill's business at approximately $10 million, as detailed next.

First, Bill determines the trading multiple, using Jim's return expectations:

$$\frac{100}{20\%} = 5 \text{ times multiple of cash flows}$$

The 20% figure in the denominator represents Jim's annualized expected return from the purchase of Bill's business. The 5 times figure represents the multiple, or the number of times the company's cash flow that Jim should offer for Bill's business

Next Bill determines the price that Jim can offer:

Bill's Annual Cash Flow × Trading Multiple = Buyer's Offering Price

$$\$2,000,000 \times 5 = \$10,000,000$$

IMPROVING JIM'S OFFER

Bill will attempt to increase the sales price that Jim offers him by arguing that Jim will benefit from a higher cash flow because of synergies in the combined businesses. Bill can further argue for a higher price by understanding Jim's motives for buying the business and speaking in terms of future benefits that Jim will get by owning the company.

Bill estimates Jim's annualized cost savings, postacquisition, at $500,000. So he will argue that Jim is going to gain an annualized increased benefit to earnings of $500,000 after the purchase. Therefore, Bill needs to argue or negotiate the point that Jim should share some of the $ 2.5 million in synergized cash flows with him as a part of the selling price. Bill expects Jim to share 15% to 30% of those synergies, resulting in an additional $375,000 to $750,000 price improvement from the initial offer Jim was expected to make. That is quite a healthy increase for doing a bit of homework and making a solid argument. Let's review to see how these numbers calculate:

Synergized Cash Flows
Bill's Brewery Cash Flows:

$$\$2,000,000 \times 5 = \$10,000,000$$

Cash Flows Benefits to Buyer After Purchase:

$$\$2,500,000 \times 5 = \$12,500,000$$

LESSONS LEARNED: WHAT DID BILL DO RIGHT THIS TIME?

Bill has come a long way in his thinking. Recall from Chapter 3 that he originally went into the meeting with Jim focused only on what he, Bill, wanted out of the deal. This time, however, Bill frames his arguments in terms of the benefits that Jim, his buyer, will receive by owning Bill's business. And, by extension, he helps Jim to see the reduced risk level as well as the opportunity that would be lost if Jim was not able to buy Bill's business (i.e., if another competitor wound up purchasing it instead).

When Bill was introduced to us in Chapter 3, he had not gone through any exercises to prepare himself to handle his exit. He worked from instinct, as he had worked to build his business. Bill did not understand the component parts of a valuation or the concept of explaining the reasons that owning the business would benefit Jim in the short and long run. He thought that his exit would be easy if he could simply call Jim and strike a deal with him. Bill thought that his skills as a successful businessman would prevail in the negotiations, but he was not armed with the knowledge of synergized cash flow projections, return on investment details, and a competitive process that would force Jim to make a substantial offer or lose the opportunity to purchase the business. In addition, Bill had not objectively assessed his financial and mental preparedness for an exit. He was focused only on what he was looking to get out of the transaction, relying more on hope than strategy. Moving ahead with a plan that was based only on what he wanted limited his ability to actually get it and created many problems, some of which could have resulted in permanent damage to Bill's company.

By understanding the type of transaction that he is undertaking and how to determine value, Bill can now bargain from a position of strength.

FURTHER NOTES ON EXTERNAL TRANSACTIONS TO INDUSTRY BUYERS

Not all sellers will be able to accurately determine the risk factors that a particular buyer sees in your business. As stated earlier, an easy way for you to find out what a buyer's return expectations will be, for your industry is to research the selling multiples of businesses comparable to yours. Actual market transactions are very helpful in determining the likely risk factors that buyers will perceive in your business. By double-checking your estimates of risk with actual market transactions, you are strengthening your argument for your buyer to pay what you ask. Both transactional service providers and valuation professionals assist with this process. For more information on finding comparable transactions for your business and industry, visit the Web site www.exitingyourbusiness. com for databases that offer comparative multiples.

RESTATING EARNINGS TO REFLECT THE TRUE PROFITABILITY OF THE COMPANY

The Introduction stated that most owners of privately held businesses are more concerned with increasing their personal net worth than with raising the value of their businesses. Accordingly, most business owners will look to reduce the earnings that they show in their business in order to pay less taxes. This is not a great secret—almost all business owners conduct their affairs in this manner to some extent.

The point here is that these suppressed figures on your financial statements can work against you in a sale transaction because they represent a lower earnings potential (i.e., they show a reduced annualized cash flow). Buyers will not explain to you that the cash flows will be higher once you are gone. They will simply base their purchase multiple on the cash flows that you show them, offering you a lower amount for your business.

In order to normalize your income statement, you will want to add back any excessive perks or salary that you take from the business and explain these add-backs to your buyer. Think of it this way: If your selling multiple is five times your earnings, then for each $1,000 of add-backs that you show, buyers are going to add $5,000 to the price they offer.

You need to list and explain these owner add-backs so that buyers will understand them—another area that Bill failed to address in our earlier scenario.

TAXES AND FEES

Remember that it is not what you get that is relevant to a sale transaction but rather what you keep after you pay your fees and taxes.

Selling a business causes you, the seller, to realize the gain on the sale of your business in the year that it is sold. Accordingly, a tax is due. We discuss taxation of deals in more depth in Chapter 11. For now, remember that it is not what you get but what you keep that matters most when selling your business.

If you work with transactional advisors to initiate and manage your sale process, you will also want to consider their fees. Begin your process of interviewing transactional service providers to see which one can be of the greatest assistance to your exit. These transaction-based service providers play a vital role in achieving your exit goals in a sale transaction. Review the details in the introduction to make certain that you are equipped with the right questions to ask these service providers during your interview process.

Because an advisor's fees can be a meaningful part of the costs of your transaction, we present the double Lehman chart again for your reference (Exhibit 5.5).

Transaction advisors are the market makers and the lifeblood of external transactions, such as sales of businesses to outside parties. For this service, they are justly rewarded. Since this is a book about protecting an exiting

10% of the first $ 1,000,000 = $ 100,000
8% of the next $ 1,000,000 = $ 80,000
6% of the next $ 1,000,000 = $ 60,000
4% of the next $ 1,000,000 = $ 40,000
2% of the next $ 1,000,000 = $ 20,000
Plus 2% of each additional $1,000,000

EXHIBIT 5.5   DOUBLE LEHMAN FORMULA

owner's wealth, the focus is on any and every circumstance that could reduce the net amount of assets that you would keep from a transaction. The transactional advisor and his or her fee is a necessary part of the sale process. Our advice is to understand the issues and to choose your advisor prudently.

Exhibit 5.6 illustrates a general step-by-step process by which the amount of money that you get from a sale transaction is reduced by fees and taxes to leave you with what you keep in this transaction (more on these concepts in Part III).

Note: The second to last step in determining what you keep versus what you get includes assessing whether or not your corporate form of organization is a flow-through entity. If you are going to conduct a sale transaction, then you must know that your financial projections could be altered greatly if you are not aware of the differences between asset sales and stock sales and how your corporate formation will be impacted. (See Chapter 11.) The deal structuring aspect becomes particularly relevant when the buyer is offering to purchase your assets, not the stock in your company.

As will be explained in Chapter 11, a majority of transactions in the under $10 million value range are asset, not stock, sales. If you are a C corporation and an asset purchase is being offered, make certain to discuss the tax consequences with your tax advisor. Many deals have fallen apart over this very issue, resulting in loss of time and money. For a detailed explanation of this issue, visit www.exitingyourbusiness.com.

REVIEW

We have offered insights for business owners who have concluded that selling their business is the exit strategy that will best assist them in reaching their personal goals. These insights have been discussed to better understand sale transactions:

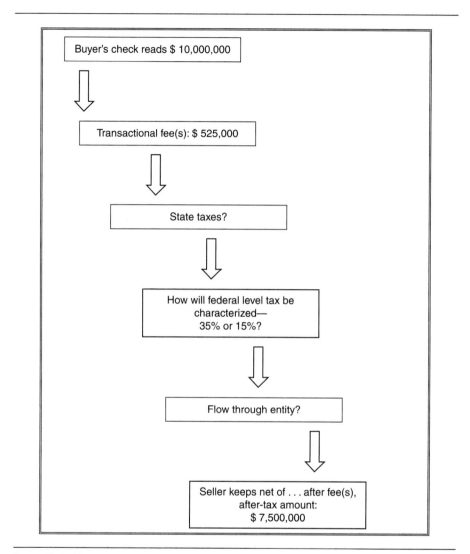

EXHIBIT 5.6 WHAT YOU KEEP VERSUS WHAT YOU GET IN YOUR SALE TRANSACTION

- You are selling financial and strategic control of the business.
- The highest price is available under synergy value.
- You should understand how your buyer will value your business.
- There is a process for creating a market for the sale of your business:

- ○   Negotiated transactions

- ○   Auction process

- We illustrated the lessons that Bill learned once he applied these concepts to his exit strategy.

- Deal markets run in cycles, just like economies, so be aware of the timing of your sale decision and how it can impact value.

- We noted that owners should add back the personal excess expenses that a buyer will not incur after purchasing the business.

- We mentioned taxes and fees that you will pay before arriving at the net amount that you receive to meet your personal goals.

Remember, selling your business is not your only option. In fact, now that we have covered the details, pros, and cons of selling your business, we can examine the universe of other options that are available to you, the exiting business owner. In fact, a great number of owners are not mentally ready for their business exit but would like to know how to protect the illiquid wealth that is in their businesses today.

Our attention is now turned another outside transaction, the recapitalization transaction with a private equity group. In this transaction an exiting owner still sells financial and strategic control of their business, but they maintain operational control. In other words, they keep their jobs, but diversify themselves personally. In addition to keeping their jobs, they also receive salary, benefits, and a small percentage of the equity in the company, making them a partner in the future success of the business.

What if Bill's plans for the future growth of his brewery included a major expansion into a new and profitable market? Bill is not ready to sell the business completely because he believes that he is close to achieving a large increase in the profitability within the business through an expansion into new areas. However, this potential expansion requires investment capital.

How will Bill finance this expansion while still keeping a vigilant eye on his not-so-distant projected retirement date? If he sells the business outright to a competitor, he loses the upside potential, along with control.

The private equity group recapitalization is the second major exit strategy option that we examine for an owner who is not mentally ready to leave the business.

NOTE

1. However, for many of the reasons stated in Chapter 1—business size, type of business, the challenge of finding a third-party buyer—an external sale may not be feasible. Some business owners are simply so inextricably tied to their businesses that a sale to someone else is likely a worse result than hanging on and staying involved with the business.

6

PRIVATE EQUITY GROUP
RECAPITALIZATIONS

The political tradition of ancient thought, filtered in Italy by
Machiavelli, says one thing clearly: every prince needs allies,
and the bigger the responsibility, the more allies he needs.

—*Silvio Berlusconi*

If you can run the company a bit more collaboratively, you get a
better result, because you have more bandwidth and checking
and balancing going on.

—*Larry Page*

If you scored low on financial readiness and low on mental
readiness you may need to continue growing your company
and saving more money, or you may need to consider bringing in a financial partner.

If you fit the profile of the exiting owner in Exhibit 6.1, you are not ready to
leave your business. You can continue growing your business and set a date in
the future for an exit. If you want to get the highest price, then you need to
grow your business by focusing on reducing company risk (as a buyer would
perceive it) and increasing company cash flow (i.e., generating more profits).
This combination will drive your value as you build your company to demonstrated defensible profits, low risks, and a transferability that would not

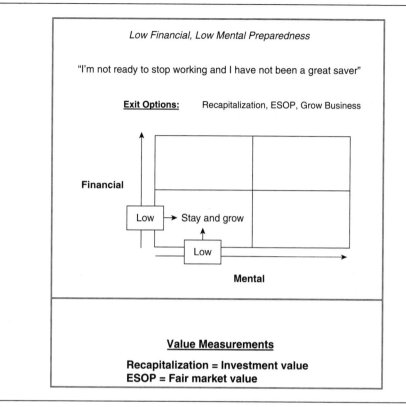

Low Financial, Low Mental Preparedness

"I'm not ready to stop working and I have not been a great saver"

Exit Options: Recapitalization, ESOP, Grow Business

Financial

Low → Stay and grow

Low

Mental

Value Measurements
Recapitalization = Investment value
ESOP = Fair market value

Exhibit 6.1 Stay-and-Grow Exiting Owner

require your involvement to continue generating those profits. If you want some liquidity today, financing for the business and partners who have experience achieving these results, a private equity group recapitalization may be just the thing to begin considering in your exit strategy planning.

Private equity is simply that: private, not public, money that is invested in privately held businesses. These private equity investors are formed as groups, hence the term *private equity groups*. The purpose of such groups is to aggregate the investment dollars of individuals and institutions and to invest those monies into private businesses that can provide returns superior to those available from other investment choices.

EXPLOSION OF PRIVATE EQUITY

Recently *private equity* has become a commonly used term in the world of corporate and private finance. As business around the world continues to evolve and adapt to a global environment, private equity has become a large contributor to the privately held business marketplace.

John Chapman from *The American* magazine describes private equity and its role in U.S. privately held businesses in this way:

> Prior to the advent of the modern private equity sector, there was an unmet need for long-term patient capital that could be deployed to co-opt growth opportunities or to compel change in companies or industries. Existing financial institutions did not have the risk appetite, requisite knowledge, or capital availability to undertake long-term equity investing. Additionally, the United States has long had a complex regulatory regime for financial institutions that effectively divorced "banking" from "commerce." Prior to 1980, regulations limiting pension fund investments also limited the formation of a modern private equity sector.
>
> But after 1980, the combination of pension reform, financial deregulation, and shrewd entrepreneurship led to private equity's rapid expansion, with firms now managing over $2 trillion in leveraged capital (up from about $5 billion in 1980). The boom in private equity has in turn played a critical role in the growth of U.S. productivity and corporate profits over the last quarter century, which has spurred the creation of jobs and material wealth.[1]

You may be thinking that's great, but what does it have to do with my exit strategy planning?

Well, these private equity groups offer the ability for you, the exiting owner, to both monetize the majority of your illiquid business asset and also keep your job and grow your company. The trick is to pick the right partner.

CAPITAL FLOWS TOWARDS OPPORTUNITY

To understand private equity group investment structures, we must first recognize that investment capital flows to where it is best maximized. In recent years, the world of private equity has grown tremendously as more and more investors are clamoring to participate in the superior returns traditionally available through the ownership of privately held businesses. One may ask, "Why would private investors who hold this capital invest in privately held business to find riches?" The answer is that private equity has the ability to exploit inefficiencies in the marketplace of private business ownership, thereby generating greater returns for those investors. Recently more and more investors are interested in chasing these types of returns.

In fact, historical returns for private equity investments have been superior to average returns in public securities due to all of the reasons listed in the first part of this book: Privately held business owners have always struggled with treating their businesses like investments. They also have limited resources to attract capital and talented, professional managers. Private business owners struggle to maximize their investments. This results in inefficiencies in the private business marketplace that are captured by investment groups that inject capital and appropriate management into otherwise inefficiently run businesses. The end result of the combination is described next.

> The results-oriented focus imposed by a leveraged capital structure, pay-for-performance compensation that aligns owner and manager interests, and superior monitoring and strategic oversight by active investors have all contributed to a strong growth in corporate productivity and profits.[2]

Private equity groups are groups of investors who purchase majority (and some minority) ownership stakes in privately held businesses with a high return expectation for their investments. Because these groups are comfortable with the risks these private businesses offer, they are formidable players in the private marketplace.

WHAT IS A RECAPITALIZATION?

Every business has a capital structure. Many business owners believe a capital structure is simply their ability to repay the bank before losing the rights to their homes, which were pledged as personal guarantees. In fact, however, the company's combination of debt and equity are what combine to form its capital structure.

A private equity group recapitalizes the exiting owner's company by replacing that owner's equity in the business with its own mixture of debt and equity. The owner's stock—equity—is turned into cash for personal diversification and postexit lifestyle concerns. The private equity group becomes an owner of the business, executing, as partners, on the exiting owner's growth strategy.

Note: Like most business combinations, the agreement amongst the parties and the manner in which the company is run after the transaction can vary greatly. The combination discussed here of professional capital with privately held businesses is the traditional form of a recapitalization. In this traditional recap, the owner stays on and continues growing the business in concert with his new private equity partners. In many cases, the private equity group will take the lead in designing the overall growth strategy for the business.

KEEP OPERATIONAL CONTROL, SELL STRATEGIC AND FINANCIAL CONTROL

Exiting owners who score low on their mental readiness to stop working can consider a private equity group recapitalization transaction as a substitute for selling the business. Here the exiting owners will stay on board to execute the growth strategy that the equity group is interested in pursuing.

Typically, private equity groups look to purchase 80% of the shares of a target company from exiting owners. Then the groups offer the owner multiyear employment agreements to continue running the day-to-day operations of the business in return for salary and bonuses. In addition, the owner maintains a percentage of the business—here, 20%—so that the exiting owner's interests are aligned with those of the new financial owners.

TWO BITES AT THE APPLE

Under the traditional scenario, private equity groups have a five- to seven-year holding period for their investments, after which they will look for an exit at synergy value. At this time, the exiting owner gets a second bite at the apple (an industry term indicating that the owner will get a second liquidity event at a later date when the entire company is sold again) selling their remaining shares along with the private equity groups' shares. Under an ideal scenario, the value of the exiting owners' 20% stake in the second transaction is worth more than the 80% that was recapitalized in the original transaction. Recapitalizations work to everyone's advantage because exiting owners would not have had the financial and professional ability to achieve that level of growth in their business without the assistance of private equity group partners.

The benefits of such wealth accumulation are illustrated through an example in Chapter 8.

VALUE MEASUREMENT

The value measurement used under a private equity group recapitalization is investment value. This is the value of a business's cash flows multiplied by a trading multiple (the risk in the transaction), without the synergies.

In a typical private equity group recapitalization, the equity group cannot achieve synergies from the transaction so the value is lower than a sale to a competitor (synergy value). The key difference here is that a private equity group adds additional capital to fund the expansion plans for the business, allowing the exiting owner to potentially achieve an overall superior value for the combined transactions.

LIBERATOR OR OCCUPIER OF YOUR BUSINESS?

Let's take another look at some of the characteristics of a recap transaction that make it a successful financial transaction for all parties involved. Some of the benefits that an exiting owner expects when going through a recapitalization transaction are listed below:

- Results-oriented focus
- Imposed by a leveraged capital structure

- Pay-for-performance compensation that aligns owner and manager interests
- Superior monitoring and strategic oversight by active investors
- Achieve growth in corporate productivity and profits

Why wouldn't every business owner choose this option? After all, you get to keep your job, shift the business risk to your new partners, and see your growth objectives fulfilled in your business and industry while still participating in the future value of the business. Well, let's focus again on reality. Is this how you currently run your business? Is this how you want to run your business? If you stick around for five years on an employment agreement, is this how you want to be managed? Do you want to go through the cultural changes that a recapitalization would impose on your business to get these results? These are the important questions that only you, the exiting owner, can answer.

Again, no exit strategy is perfect for everyone. In fact, each exit option has pros and cons that need to be carefully measured. This book presents an objective look at each option to engage you in thinking about refining your exit strategy plans. From a strictly capitalistic and profit-maximization viewpoint, the private equity group transaction can be an ideal solution for the exiting owner with a low mental readiness to leave the business who is open-minded regarding changes that are required to achieve profit-related goals. We reexamine these considerations in Chapter 8 as we compare the sale of a business to a recapitalization and an employee stock ownership plan.

In other words, if you view your business as a job and not an investment, you may not be comfortable making the changes to generate more profits. You need to reflect on your ability to work with new, high-performing partners before seriously considering a private equity group recap transaction. Don't be swayed by the personal liquidity that such a transaction brings. Rather, keep in mind that the private equity group has annualized return expectations from the investment in your business of anywhere from 20% to 40%, depending on the industry and the stage at which the equity group invests in the business. (Note: Your business does not need to be growing at this rate to qualify. The private equity group will use leverage in the recap transaction to achieve its return expectations. For more information, visit www.exitingyourbusiness.com.) If you are more interested in the lifestyle that your business provides than the attainment of superior levels of wealth, the private equity group transaction may not be for you. However, if your company is qualified (discussed next) and the recapitalization appeals to you, Chapter 8 explains how it may further enhance your exit strategy planning goals to protect and grow your personal wealth.

MARKET REALITIES AND YOUR EXIT STRATEGY PLANNING

The reality of the marketplace today is that if you are going to exit your business via a sale transaction, private equity groups are going to be invited into an auction process to make offers on your company. If your mental readiness to leave the business is high, that equity group will discuss the feasibility of replacing you in your role as day-to-day operator of the business.

This market reality holds true because the recent explosion of capital flowing into the coffers of private equity groups has created an imbalance of demand for good companies to invest in relative to the supply of exiting business owners who can meet the return expectations of the private equity groups. Put another way, private equity groups are eager buyers of well-run, profitable companies, and you are well served in knowing this as you look to grow and protect your wealth.

WHICH COMPANIES QUALIFY FOR A RECAP?

As an exiting owner, your personal financial and mental readiness to exit your business are clearly not the only factors contributing to the exit path that you choose. For example, in order for you to receive a check for your business sale, there needs to be an interested buyer in an external transaction.

To interest private equity groups, your business should ideally be in a growing industry (or one that is ripe for consolidation). If your company does not have historical profits of at least $1 million or does not have a future projected growth path, it may not qualify for private equity investment, and this exit option may not be available to you.

You can also measure your qualification for private equity investment through your earnings, or EBITDA (earnings before interest, taxes, depreciation, and amortization). EBITDA is used in the deal world to reflect a normalized earnings stream. The variables of interest expense, tax rates, and noncash deductions such as depreciation and amortization expenses are added back to reflect the normalized cash flows of the business. This EBITDA figure should be in excess of $1 million (at the low end) for private equity groups to consider a recap transaction for your business. In very general terms, the low end of your investment value (the total value of your company) must be approximately $6 to $8 million to qualify for a private equity group transaction. Private equity groups are reluctant to participate in recap structures much lower than this value floor.

BILL'S SCENARIO APPLIED TO A RECAPITALIZATION TRANSACTION WITH A PRIVATE EQUITY GROUP

We again return to our exiting owner, Bill.

This time around Bill believes that he is ready to continue working (his mental readiness is low) and ideas for future growth are brewing in his entrepreneurial mind. Bill would like to monetize a large part of the illiquid wealth in his business, and he is willing to accept a partner in order to achieve the dual goals of growing his business while diversifying his personal wealth.

Bill is approached by a private equity group with the idea of executing a recapitalization of his company. Under the proposed structure, Bill will sell the private equity group 80% of his ownership interest in the business while retaining 20%. The folks at the equity group are very up front with Bill about why they want him to keep 20%: They want his interests aligned with their financial interests. And by offering Bill an opportunity to potentially cash out his remaining 20% at a higher level than the 80% sold in the original transaction, the equity group is betting that Bill's profit motivation will continue to drive his performance as the continuing operator of the business. In fact, Bill receives a generous employment agreement, including salary and bonuses for achieving the profitability targets.

As we see in Exhibit 6.2, Bill exchanges his ownership for cash and keeps his job—what a deal!

Bill's mental readiness to exit the business was low and his financial readiness to leave the business was also low. The recap exit option satisfies both of these personal needs. Bill gets liquidity and diversification and keeps his job. Bill also now has partners with high performance expectations. Bill also has access to growth capital to expand the business.

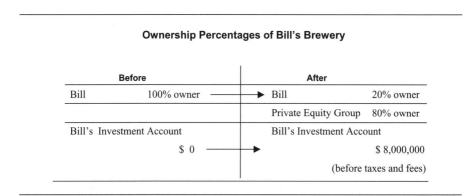

Ownership Percentages of Bill's Brewery

Before		After	
Bill	100% owner	Bill	20% owner
		Private Equity Group	80% owner
Bill's Investment Account		Bill's Investment Account	
	$ 0		$ 8,000,000
			(before taxes and fees)

EXHIBIT 6.2 TRANSACTION 1: RECAPITALIZATION TRANSACTION

DIVERSIFICATION AND WEALTH ACCUMULATION

From a financial perspective, Bill is theoretically in the best position. He achieves personal liquidity by selling the majority of his stock to the private equity group; keeps his job, salary, income, and perks; and also retains some equity in the business, which promises to be worth a significantly greater amount in the future. Such future equity participation is generally unavailable in a traditional sale to an industry buyer.

On a personal level, Bill has achieved his monetization goal of converting his illiquid business wealth into cash and putting that cash to work for him in an investment account. He can get comfortable with being a liquid millionaire while still keeping his job. Bill now has a powerful stream of passive income that can provide him with financial security, regardless of the fate of the business that he just recapitalized. In other words, Bill has kept his job but shifted the majority of the risk of business ownership to his new partners.

Bill satisfies his desire to keep working and to bolster his personal financial readiness for retirement. At age 56, he can continue working and begin to look ahead to his projected retirement date while watching over his now-flush investment account.

REVIEW

We have reviewed the sale of a business, illustrating how an exiting owner gives up strategic and financial control of the business and also likely loses his/her job, salary, income and participation in the future value of the company. In exchange, that exiting owner can receive the highest value for the sale of shares, synergy value.

With the private equity group recapitalization, the exiting owner is able to sell the majority of their business, surrendering strategic and financial control, but retain operational control through an employment agreement. Along with continued employment—i.e., keeping her job—the owner gets to continue doing what he/she enjoys doing, continue receiving income and participate in the future value of the business through an anticipated later sale of the business, or receive a second bite at the apple.

But, many owners know enough about themselves to determine that having partners in the business is not attractive. As entrepreneurs, most of their decision making in growing their business has centered around maintaining control of their own destiny and not answering to anyone else for their decisions. What if an owner wanted to achieve personal diversification without bringing in an outside partner?

We segue into the next chapter by asking a very insightful question that gets the attention of many exiting owners:

Can you take some money out of your business, avoid taxes and double Lehman–type fees, and still keep your job and control of your business?

Yes, you can. The tool to do so is an ESOP.

NOTES

1. John L. Chapman, "A Vital Engine of Economic Growth," *The American*, October 23, 2007, http://www.american.com/archive/2007/october-10-07/a-vital-engine-of-economic-growth
2. Ibid.

7

EMPLOYEE STOCK OWNERSHIP PLANS AS EXIT VEHICLES

Nobody spends somebody else's money as carefully as he spends his own. Nobody uses somebody else's resources as carefully as he uses his own. So if you want efficiency and effectiveness, if you want knowledge to be properly utilized, you have to do it through the means of private property.

—*Milton Friedman*

As we have seen, there are a great number of business owners in the marketplace today who have prudently saved for their personal financial security and are now reaching retirement age. These Baby Boomers are beginning to think about exiting their businesses but are not yet ready to retire; these owners score high on financial readiness but low on mental readiness to exit.

Exhibit 7.1 illustrates where this well-off-but-chooses-to-work exiting owner fits on our exit quadrant chart.

If you fit this profile, you are the opposite of a get-me-out-at-the-highest-price exiting owner. You have been a very good saver and are not ready to stop working. It is likely that you are highly involved in the day-to-day running of your business, and you may or may not have a successor in mind. High

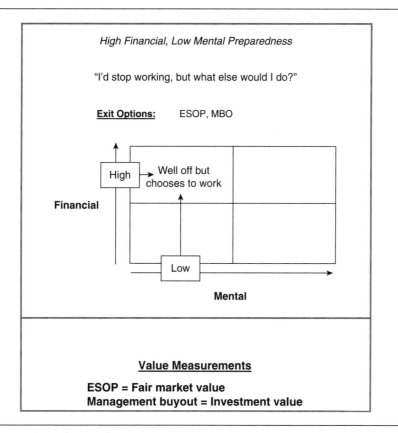

High Financial, Low Mental Preparedness

"I'd stop working, but what else would I do?"

Exit Options: ESOP, MBO

Financial — High → Well off but chooses to work — Low — Mental

Value Measurements

ESOP = Fair market value
Management buyout = Investment value

Exhibit 7.1   Well-Off-but-Chooses-to-Work Exiting Owner

financial readiness is relatively easy to understand. You can walk away from the business today because you are not dependent upon the income or value of the business for your retirement. Many options are available to you to accomplish the exit that you desire.

Here, however, you scored low on the mental readiness part of the exit assessment. A low mental readiness means that you do not want to leave your business; you choose to keep working even though you have personally saved enough money not to need to work. When this situation occurs, your exit strategy planning should include internal transfer strategies and the value that you can get, over time, by transferring to insiders. Insiders include family members, employees, such as key management groups and co-owners. In this case, you are going to continue to run and control the company in the short run while putting into place an exit strategy that will be executed over many years. And, as this book has stated a number of times, your readiness to leave the

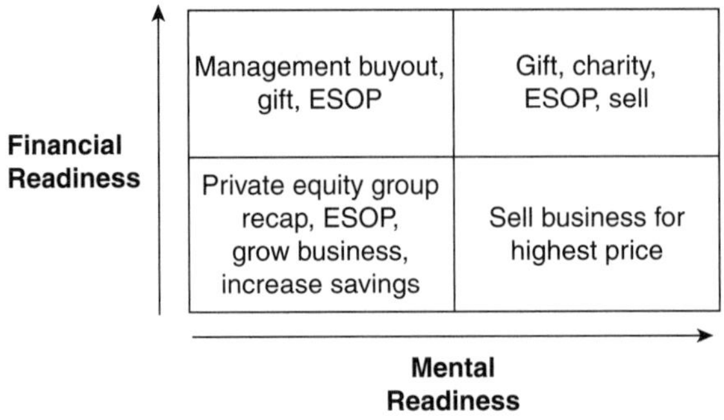

	Management buyout, gift, ESOP	Gift, charity, ESOP, sell
Financial Readiness	Private equity group recap, ESOP, grow business, increase savings	Sell business for highest price

Mental Readiness

EXHIBIT 7.2   EXIT OPTIONS CHART

business should be the determining factor in establishing an exit strategy to protect your wealth.

Exhibit 7.2 repeats the exit options chart, illustrating the options that can be considered by an exiting owner who is well off but chooses to work.

EXIT OPTIONS AVAILABLE

- Management buyouts

- Employee stock ownership plan (ESOP)

- Gifting programs

Two major insights are worth noting:

1. Once you decide not to exit your business via a sale to a third party, you almost certainly forgo the opportunity to achieve synergy value.

2. Although synergy value is not available, you can potentially achieve a higher level of net proceeds from your exit by avoiding/minimizing taxes; keeping your job, income, benefits, and perks; and participating in the future upside value of the business. This financial outcome is illustrated through our hypothetical business owner, Bill, at the end of the chapter.

USING AN ESOP IN YOUR PLANNING

The ESOP actually fits within the three exit quadrants other than "sell business for highest price". In this chapter we explain the ESOP option and illustrate how utilizing an ESOP instead of a sale transaction customizes Bill's exit strategy over a number of years and actually increases his total wealth while accommodating his low mental readiness to stop working. Bill keeps his job, continues running the business, diversifies his personal wealth, and nets a higher amount in the end.

Let's see how this works.

ESOP BASICS

An ESOP is a qualified retirement plan that is allowed to buy your company's stock. ESOPs have been in existence for over 30 years; currently more than 11,000 ESOPs exist nationwide. Despite the many misconceptions about ESOPs, they are very flexible tools for assisting with the design of an exit strategy plan. After all, who would guess that a retirement plan for the company could provide a monetization strategy for an exiting owner? The ESOP is not, however, a panacea for your exit dilemma. Many factors contribute to successfully installing an ESOP into your business. Well-informed exiting owners study the pros and cons of ESOPs in order to determine if this type of exit strategy will help them meet their personal goals. Once again, entire books are written solely on the topic of ESOPs. Here, however, we present you with the basic concepts so you can consider this potentially valuable tool in designing your exit strategy plan.

CREATING A BUYER FOR YOUR COMPANY STOCK

Most business owners enjoy the aspect of control that they have over their businesses and lives. After all, the likely reason that you are in business for yourself is to have control over your destiny. Selling your business for the highest price requires that you give up strategic and financial control of your business. However, by establishing an ESOP, you can create a buyer for the shares of your stock without involving an outsider in the transaction; thereby you can maintain control.

Many business owners have heard of ESOPs but do not recognize what powerful planning tools they truly are. It is an unfortunate reality that many business owners fail to utilize an ESOP for their exit strategy planning because they do not understand its benefits; instead, many stay focused on the burdens of ESOPs. In fact, installing an ESOP is not a simple process; it includes a good amount of thought and planning as to what you are trying to achieve with your exit. Setting up an ESOP involves advisory fees, a valuation that, as we will see, is likely lower than the value that can be achieved with the sale of your business, and an ongoing obligation for the business to one day repurchase the ESOP shares, effectively cashing out the employees who retire or leave the company. Why would you consider a lower initial valuation and this somewhat burdensome plan? Because you can maintain control of your business, achieve personal diversification, and enjoy these benefits:

- Creation of a market for the purchase of shares
- A low-cost savings plan for the exiting owner
- Keeping your job, salary, and company perks
- Flexibility to sell any number of shares to the ESOP at a timing of your choosing
  Owners can customize their personal planning by selling some shares today to achieve some liquidity and some at a later date.
- A vehicle for cashing out minority shareholders
- Opportunity to achieve your chosen level of diversification today while still benefiting from future growth in the business
- Potential to increase business cash flows through reduction of taxable income due to annual, elective ESOP contributions
- Potential to defer or avoid capital gains taxation on the sale of shares (if your business is a C corporation and the ESOP owns more than 30% of the company shares, and you follow the rules in the tax code, Internal Revenue Code section 1042 (discussed later in this chapter))
- Potential to improve performance by instilling a culture of ownership among employees without having to disclose financial or other confidential company information to them
- Ability to sell the entire company at a future date

ESOP EXPLAINED

The most compelling feature of an ESOP is that you can literally create a buyer for the shares of stock in your business. The mechanism that allows you to create this buyer is the ESOP laws that empower this special type of retirement plan to purchase the shares of your business.

The ESOP Association offers this description of an ESOP on its Web site (www.esopassociation.org/about/about_use.asp):

> Many closely held companies have no plans, or incomplete plans, for business continuity after the departure or retirement of the founder or major shareholder. If the company repurchases a retiring or departing owner's shares, the departing owner sells his or her stock to another company, the proceeds will be taxed as ordinary income, or as capital gains if certain requirements are met, and, finding

a buyer is not always easy even for a profitable closely-held company. Even if possible, it is not always desirable; furthermore in a family business, a retiring owner may face an unpleasant choice between selling to a competitor or conglomerate, or liquidating.

An ESOP can provide a market for the equity of a retiring owner—or any interested major shareholder—of a closely held company, and provide a benefit and job security for employees in the process.

An ESOP "can provide a market for the equity of a retiring owner" through a trust that is established, and funded, to purchase an exiting owner's company shares. If you are an exiting owner who is not ready to leave your business, the creation of a buyer means that no outsider buyers need to be contacted to purchase the shares. This allows you to maintain a certain level of privacy in your dealings while still receiving cash for the sale of your shares. This aspect of personal diversification is an important component of wealth protection and the overall theme of this book. Therefore, we next discuss the common misconceptions surrounding ESOPs, explain a few more details regarding ESOPs, then turn to our hypothetical exiting owner, Bill.

MISCONCEPTIONS ABOUT ESOPS

Many business owners dismiss the idea of establishing an ESOP because they do not understand the manner in which ESOPs work. A few of the more common misconceptions are listed next.

Common Misconception	Actual Relevant Facts
I need to be a C corporation.	No, ESOPs are for S or C corporations.
I need to borrow money.	No, ESOPs are highly flexible and do not require an exiting owner to borrow money.
I need to sell 30% to the ESOP.	No, any amount of stock can be sold to the ESOP (the 30% requirement is only a part of utilizing IRC 1042—discussed later)
My employees become partners.	No, the employees are "beneficial" owners of stock in the ESOP trust, not partners.

The laws of trusts apply to the functioning of an ESOP. Under trust law, two types of ownership exist for assets: equitable ownership, which comes with a certain amounts of rights to the trust property, and beneficial ownership, as in a beneficiary of a trust. The beneficial level of ownership has very few actual decision-making rights to the trust property; rather, beneficial owners participate in its equity value. Therefore, as beneficial owners, your employees will not have the full complement of rights that a partner would have in your business.

These misconceptions often prevent exiting owners from considering ESOPs in their exit strategy planning.

In short, the tax laws allow a business owner to sell company shares to an ESOP trust and receive cash for those shares so long as, over time, those shares go to the benefit of the employees, the beneficiaries of the ESOP trust. Accordingly, the ESOP trust holds the shares that an owner sells to the ESOP, in trust, for the benefit of the employees who are beneficial (not equitable) owners of shares. Because they own only a beneficial interest, employees cannot demand to see the books and records of the company or exercise any control over its daily operation. The shares that they receive go into a retirement account, and the employees are entitled to an annual accounting of the value of their shares.[1]

An ESOP can be used to design an owner's exit while keeping the focus on the owner's equity and how it can be turned into cash to benefit his or her personal planning. The flexible nature of ESOPs allow them to be used as tools, immediately or over many years, to customize owners' exit strategy plan. ESOPs also can be used in conjunction with other planning methods, such as gifting programs and management buyouts, to achieve a highly customized strategy for exiting business owners. Their flexibility is why ESOPs fit into three of our four quadrants. In addition, ESOPs do not preclude an owner from later selling the entire business at the highest price.

WHERE DOES THE CASH COME FROM?

The term *leveraged ESOP* refers to the ability of an ESOP to borrow money to fund the purchase of company shares. As just mentioned, an ESOP does not have to borrow money in order to purchase company stock. In fact, an ESOP can be established as a savings vehicle, where each year employee contributions are made to the ESOP trust and that money is accumulated according to a plan to later purchase the company's shares. This is referred to as a prefunded ESOP plan. Or, alternatively, the owner can take back a note for the sale of some or all of the shares of stock to the ESOP trust, charging interest on the note, thereby serving as the bank for this transaction. Or your company can contribute shares of nonissued, treasury stock to the ESOP trust in order to take advantage of valuable tax deductions without a cash outlay.

All of these different potential scenarios reinforce the flexible and potentially confusing nature of ESOPs. In our example at the end of this chapter, our exiting owner, Bill, is installing a leveraged ESOP in his company through a multistage sale of stock. As we will see, Bill achieves financing for this transaction from his current bank, which understands ESOP transactions and is willing to lend the money to his company. Bill does not want to borrow too much money at once, so he decides to stage his stock sales over a number of years.

This ESOP structure allows Bill to exchange his shares of stock for cash today while not burdening the company with overly high levels of debt. After a number of years of repaying this initial loan, Bill envisions selling the balance of his shares in a second transaction. This creative exit strategy plan is coordinated with Bill's personal retirement plan to provide cash both today and in the future to fund his retirement expenses.

1042 ELECTION

Internal Revenue Code section 1042 permits the deferral of capital gains taxes for a sale of stock to an ESOP if:

- That corporation is a C corporation

- More than 30% of the company's stock has been sold to the ESOP

- The cash that is paid for that stock is reinvested in *qualified replacement property* (as further defined in the code)

- There are specific reinvestment rules for qualified replacement property that extend beyond the scope of this chapter's coverage of ESOPs but can be located on our companion website at www.exitingyourbusiness.com

The opportunity to have a tax-free transaction is very appealing to many exiting owners. And, if your business is a C corporation, it is certainly a viable option. However, many new ESOPs today are S corporations, where the 1042 election for tax deferral is not permitted. Further, with the capital gains tax rate at a relatively low level, 15%, the financial incentive is not as great as it once was under other tax environments. Nonetheless, this deferral of taxation on the sale of a block of stock can provide the ideal scenario for some exiting owners. After all, who enjoys paying taxes?

We now examine Bill's use of an ESOP for his exit strategy. Then, in Chapter 8 we compare and contrast the benefits of this exit strategy to sale and recapitalization transactions.

APPLICATION OF AN ESOP TO BILL'S EXIT STRATEGY PLANNING

Bill, as you recall, is 56 years old and considering an exit from his business. He has given some additional consideration to his exit, and now he realizes that he is an entrepreneur at heart and does not want partners in his business and is not ready to go cold turkey on working. He now wants to stay with the company for at least a few more years and perhaps benefit from some additional future growth in the business's value. He wants to keep his job, his perks, and his standing in his community. In addition, he does not want the competition to even think that he is considering getting out of the business.

Bill wonders if there is a way in which he can achieve some diversification to meet his personal goals today, while still maintaining control of the brewery.

CUSTOMIZED EXIT STRATEGY USING AN ESOP

Bill decides that he is going to establish an ESOP to serve as the cornerstone of his exit strategy planning.

COMMITMENTS THAT COME WITH AN ESOP

Bill agrees in advance to adhere to a few requirements of this ESOP planning. First, he must incur the expense of conducting annual valuations of the business. Annual statements are how share values are reported to employees who benefit under this structure. And Bill, as head of the company, must decide each year what amount will be contributed to the ESOP as an employee contribution. Bill also needs to consider the future obligation of the company to repurchase the shares from employees. This is a distant consideration, as many of his employees are younger than he, but he still recognizes that this future liability will be a part of his business planning.

After achieving a comfort level with this list of requirements, Bill sees that the burdens of ESOP planning are far fewer than the benefits to him and what he is looking to accomplish with his exit strategy plan. He has already calculated the net benefit of selling his business to Jim, his competitor. He uses this net benefit of a sale transaction as a comparative benchmark to see how an ESOP would improve his exit strategy planning. Because Bill is not mentally ready to exit the business but would prefer to stick around for the next few years, he wants to analyze the advantages of designing a customized exit strategy plan with an ESOP.

ESOP ADVANTAGES

Bill takes note of a few immediate advantages to utilizing the internal transfer strategy that the ESOP provides:

- He does not need to let others in the industry know his intentions for planning his exit.

- The projected advisory fees for the sale of his business can be greatly reduced relative to a sale transaction and its double Lehman formula.
- The projected taxes that Bill would have to pay for the sale of his business can be greatly reduced or eliminated.
  - Bill can sell 30% of his stock to the ESOP and, because he is a C corporation, he can make a 1042 election to defer taxation on the transaction.
- Bill gets to keep his job, salary, and perks.
- He can structure an exit that meets his personal schedule for retirement.
- His total estate will be diversified, thereby creating passive income from his investments—a new income stream for Bill.

Based on Bill's low mental readiness to exit the business, the ESOP provides an incredibly flexible tool for him to sell shares of his company to the ESOP in a manner and time period that most accommodates his personal goals.

CUSTOMIZED PLAN

The ESOP allows Bill to control his exit, selling just the amount of shares that he wants to achieve personal liquidity and diversification. Bill is also able to incorporate the ESOP strategy into his retirement plan from the business. He puts the plan in place in 2008 and details this schedule for his personal exit from the business:

Year	Age	Action
2008	56	Establish ESOP.
2009	57	Sell 30% of stock to ESOP, make 1042 election.
2013	61	Sell remaining shares of stock to ESOP or to an outside buyer, retire.

Bill has now established a customized exit strategy from his business that will occur over five years. It will provide him personal diversification today; allow him to keep his salary, benefits, and perks; and give him a sufficient amount of time to transfer responsibility to his future successors or sell the business at a future date. The sale of his stock to the ESOP gives him a tax-deferred transaction (utilizing IRC section 1042) and allows him to benefit from any business growth over the next five years with his remaining equity interest.

Bill forecasts what his company's stock is likely to be worth over the next 5 years to assess the value of retaining a future stake in the business (as opposed to selling all or most of it today to another buyer). By working closely with his financial advisor, he sees that the sale of stock over time will coordinate nicely with his desired retirement date and, with the projected growth rate of the business, he believes that this customized strategy will yield him a greater return—with greater control—over the next exit 5 years.

Another benefit to Bill is that of certainty. The ESOP strategy has the benefit of certainty of execution whereas the sale of his business is largely dependent on many variables, including the economy, the business life cycle, demands of outside buyers, and Bill's own personal timeline. The ESOP is a more controllable transaction, providing Bill with diversification today and many options for the future. Again, with a low mental readiness for an exit, Bill is protecting his wealth today while retaining the ability to consider additional exit options in the future.

LOWER VALUE

One drawback to the ESOP decision is the loss of opportunity for synergy value that was available under the sale transaction. ESOP valuations fall under the developed valuation standard discussed in Chapter 4. Let's see how this lower standard of value will impact Bill's financial goals.

FAIR MARKET VALUE STANDARD

Sales of stock to an ESOP require using the fair market value standard for the pricing of the shares, as most internal transfers do. Exhibit 7.3 provides a reminder.

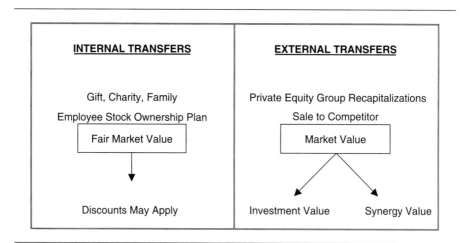

EXHIBIT 7.3 INTERNAL VERSUS EXTERNAL TRANSACTION VALUATIONS

Although Bill has achieved a tremendous amount of flexibility with his exit strategy planning by using the ESOP, he realizes that the fair market value standard likely will produce a lower offering price for his shares than the external transfer values, including investment and synergy value. Recall from Bill's sale transaction that he was going to argue that Jim should be paying him additional amounts of money for the synergy benefits that Jim will realize from owning Bill's Brewery. With the fair market value appraisal technique, these synergies are not necessarily going to increase the price of the shares.

Discounts also will apply to the initial block of stock that Bill is selling to the ESOP. Remember, a 30% sale of stock to the ESOP represents a minority holding that lacks marketability or control over the business. As stated in Chapter 4, discounts can work for or against you. In this case they are working against Bill's exit strategy goals of getting the highest price for his shares.

How can Bill reconcile this lower value and the discounts that are being applied with the ever-so-tempting synergy value that awaits him if Jim buys his business?

Bill puts the figures into his exit strategy plan to make an objective comparison. By engaging in the exit strategy planning process, Bill can think clearly and objectively analyze each exit option. (See Exhibit 7.4.)

Note that the sale of the business results in fees (double Lehman formula) and taxes paid that reduce the net amount that Bill keeps for himself. By the same token, the reduced value of the shares in the ESOP sale is mitigated by the fact that Bill did not pay taxes on the transaction today because of his tax-deferred election under IRC section 1042. Furthermore, Bill retains his job, salary, perks, and benefits so that he continues to receive income and control of the business.

To assess whether the ESOP will meet Bill's financial goals, he measures his wealth picture after the ESOP is installed, taking into account his new

Sale	
Gross proceeds from the sale	$ 10,500,000
Transactional service provider fee	($ 410,000)
Federal taxes	($ 1,575,000)
State taxes	($ 525,000)
Bill's Net Proceeds	**$ 7,990,000**

ESOP	
Fair market value of company	$ 7,000,000
30% of stock sold to ESOP	**$ 2,100,000**
Discount for minority stake (25%)	$ 525,000
Value on a minority, marketable basis:	$ 1,575,000
Discount for lack of marketability (10%)	$ 157,500
Adjusted indicated value	**$ 1,417,500**

EXHIBIT 7.4 FINANCIAL COMPARISONS OF A SALE VERSUS AN ESOP

---

1. <u>Passive income from reinvestment of sales proceeds from recapitalization</u>

   $ 1,417,500   earning 6% income (pre-tax)   = $ 85,050

2. <u>70% remaining interest in company, expected annualized growth of 10%</u>

Year 1	Year 2	Year 3	Year 4	Year 5
$ 7,000,000	$ 7,700,000	$ 8,470,000	$ 9,317,000	$ 10,248,700

3. <u>Salary, benefits, and bonuses from his job</u>

   $ 225,000 annual salary

   $ 100,000 annual perks

Exhibit 7.5   Diversification Using an ESOP Strategy

liquidity, his continued income and perks, as well as his continued ownership in his business, which is growing at a rate of 10% per year (Bill's continued interest is measured at investment value because of his option to sell to an outside buyer at age 61). Exhibit 7.5 details his net worth picture and assumptions.

At first, it may appear that Bill is giving away too much value when using the less favorable fair market valuation standard. However, he is recouping that lost value from a few sources. Namely, he is continuing to draw salary and perks from the company for the next five years. He is also avoiding the payment of capital gains taxes on the sale of his stock to the ESOP. And the cash flow of his business is increasing through the application of annual deductible employee contributions to the ESOP plan. In addition, Bill continues to benefit from the future growth—and higher value—of the business by continuing to own a majority (70%) of the stock.

WHY ESOP PLANNING WORKS DESPITE THE LOWER INITIAL VALUE AND DISCOUNTS

When Bill's mind-set changed away from selling control of the business through an outright sale or from bringing in partners such as a private equity group, he started thinking about internal transfer strategies. Bill chose an ESOP and created a highly customized exit strategy plan that allowed him to continue working and to exit in a controlled and phased manner. Much of the

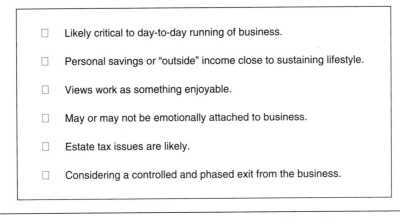

☐   Likely critical to day-to-day running of business.

☐   Personal savings or "outside" income close to sustaining lifestyle.

☐   Views work as something enjoyable.

☐   May or may not be emotionally attached to business.

☐   Estate tax issues are likely.

☐   Considering a controlled and phased exit from the business.

Exhibit 7.6   Attributes of the Well-Off-but-Chooses-to-Work Exiting Owner

value that he lost through the fair market value standard was recouped by the taxes and fees that he saved by choosing the ESOP over a sale. In fact, over time, his total net worth increased because he kept his salary and benefits and participated in the future growth of the business. Recall Bill's readiness for an exit to see how the ESOP benefits his planning. (See Exhibit 7.6).

To put these figures in further perspective, the next chapter compares the ESOP transaction to the sale and the recapitalization options, highlighting the short-term and long-term benefits of each exit strategy to Bill's total wealth.

REVIEW

Bill assessed all of the financial pros and cons and concluded that the benefits of the ESOP strategy as the cornerstone of his exit strategy planning far outweighed the drawbacks. He has created a customized internal exit from his business that keeps him in control. And, because Bill's mental readiness for an exit was very low, he was able to engineer an exit strategy solution without having to sell the business.

As we can see, an ESOP is a powerful planning tool for the business owner who is not ready to give up control but would like some diversification and liquidity today. Recall from Chapter 1 that most business owners have the majority of their wealth tied up in their businesses. Achieving diversification and liquidity today while maintaining control over the business is a powerful option for Bill. The financial benefits, over time, outweigh the reduced sales price that he would have received under a sale transaction, once the advisory fees and taxes had been paid. And recall that Bill does not lose the option to sell the entire company at a later date to an industry buyer at synergy value.

As an overall review so far we see that Part I of this book used the exit quadrant chart to have exiting owners discover how ready they are for a business exit.

Part II has explained and applied three different exit options to our hypothetical exiting owner, Bill. Each option has a different value, but depending on Bill's changing motives, each one helps him achieve his personal goals for his exit. In each of these three cases, Bill was able to receive cash for the sale of his stock (or assets).

Let's now compare these three exit options to each other so that you can see which, if any, will suit your exit strategy planning goals.

If you are ready to see how the sale transaction, the recapitalization, and the ESOP compare to one another, turn to Chapter 8.

NOTE

1. See www.exitingyourbusiness.com for more information on ESOPs.

8

SALE VERSUS RECAPITALIZATION VERSUS ESOP

A sly rabbit will have three openings to its den.

—*Chinese proverb*

This book has reached a critical juncture. Three different exit options that can turn your shares (or assets) into cash have been presented. Here we need to offer a clear perspective on how and where you can apply them to reach the personal goals you established in Chapter 2.

Your financial and mental readiness for an exit are the strongest indicators of which exit option best suits you. The planning work that you did earlier will be your guide to choosing the transaction that helps you meet your personal goals. Bear in mind that every business and business owner is different; each has its own unique set of opportunities, challenges, and circumstances. This book is written from the perspective of a business owner who would like to protect her wealth but does not know how to begin the process. Perhaps she mistakenly believes that an exit is the same thing as selling the business. Now you know that other options exist. The key is to choose the one that is best for you.

The core tenet of this book is that by being proactive with exit strategy planning, owners should be able to avoid losing the wealth that has accumulated in their privately held business. Let's return to our exiting owner, Bill, to see where this proactive approach helps him meet his personal goals.

BILL'S THREE CHOICES

When we introduced Bill in Chapter 3, he believed that selling his business to a competitor would be the fastest, most profitable, and least painful manner in which he could exit. Without much forethought, Bill approached Jim about buying the business. Our story ended in Chapter 3 with a failed transaction. The weakness in Bill's process was mostly attributable to his improper mind-set and a lack of preparation.

Now Bill has considered three major transaction alternatives, each of which met his different objectives as we modified his motives and financial goals. A review of Bill's financial outcomes from each type of transaction will be helpful in understanding how Bill can best optimize his wealth with the exit option that he chooses. We remain focused on Bill's net proceeds from each transaction and how the different options provide various levels of flexibility for Bill to meet his personal goals.

OPTION 1: SALE OF THE BUSINESS

In the sale transaction, Bill successfully exited his business through a sale to his competitor, Jim. The after-fee, after-tax net amount of proceeds was sufficient to generate enough passive income to support his postexit lifestyle. Bill received synergy value for the shares of his business—the highest value available—because his acquirer was able to reduce a number of duplicate expenses. The combined entities are also stronger than the individual entities competing with each other. Bill was able to negotiate for and capture a fair percentage of the synergies created in the transaction, thereby driving the price higher than any other value available.

Did Bill make the right decision?

Bill's financial readiness was low and his mental readiness was high. He was ready to go. Bill was able to negotiate for a sharing of the synergies in the sale transaction to his competitor. Let's assume that Bill achieved a 20% sharing of those synergies in the gross proceeds from the sale (see Exhibit 8.1).

Although Bill gets an additional $500,000 in his selling price because he negotiated effectively for the sharing of synergies with his buyer we see that most of this increase in sales price goes to taxes (as we will see in detail in Chapter 11) and the fees of his transactional service provider.

In the typical business sale of this size, a double Lehman formula applies. Federal and state taxes will further reduce Bill's net proceeds from the sale (Exhibit 8.2).

Is Bill's personal value gap closed?

Cash flow: $ 2,000,000 × 5:	$ 10,000,000
Annualized Synergies: $ 500,000 × 5:	$ 2,500,000
Synergy value	$ 12,500,000
Value of synergies	$ 2,500,000
20% sharing of synergies	$ .20
Value of shared synergies to Bill	$ 500,000
Gross proceeds from the sale to Jim	**$ 10,500,000**

EXHIBIT 8.1   FINANCIAL ILLUSTRATION OF BILL'S SYNERGY VALUE

Transactional service provider fee (based on double Lehman formula) $ 410,000
Then 2 levels of tax are paid: Federal capital gains taxes and state taxes
Assume that Bill received capital gains treatment for the sale of his stock
Federal level (assuming the basis in his company is near $ 0): 15% tax rate $ 1,575,000
Bill is also subject to state level taxes; let's assume a state tax rate of 5% $ 525,000
Bill's fees and taxes: **$ 2,510,000**
As a percentage of transactional value, this equals: 24%   Ouch!

- Bill writes the checks for the taxes in April when his taxes are due.
- He pays the advisory fees at the closing of the sale transaction.

Bill's net, after-fee, after-tax proceeds: **$ 7,990,000**

EXHIBIT 8.2   BILL'S AFTER-FEE, AFTER-TAX NET PROCEEDS FROM THE SALE TRANSACTION

Bill's financial advisor runs a scenario where Bill's investable, liquid proceeds are able to generate, on a pretax basis, nearly 6% dividend and interest income from the nearly $8 million base of assets. This income replacement strategy will generate approximately $480,000 in annual pretax income for Bill on a going-forward basis. Bill is pleased because his salary and perks drawn from the business were less than this amount. Since he does not plan on increasing his lifestyle expenses after the exit, he can afford to execute this exit strategy plan and generate enough passive income to meet his postexit personal expenses without drawing from the principal sum of his investable assets.

At age 56, Bill appears to have achieved the American dream. He can now slip into retirement, walking away from the business, devoting more time to his family, and living happily ever after.

But can Bill survive as a retiree?

Chapter 3 illustrated that business owners don't easily transition into retirement because they are addicted to their businesses. We should therefore ask: "What if instead of retiring, Bill decided that he was young enough to pursue the dream of greatly expanding his business but he did not want to risk his personal capital?" If his mental readiness was low instead of high, Bill may in fact stand to achieve a higher degree of wealth through a private equity group recapitalization transaction.

A shift in mental readiness produces a new set of exit options, as shown in Exhibit 8.3.

OPTION 2: PRIVATE EQUITY GROUP RECAPITALIZATION
We now see that Bill is actually more interested in staying with the company for a number of years but does not want to continue to place his personal wealth at risk or put additional personal proceeds into the business. He did

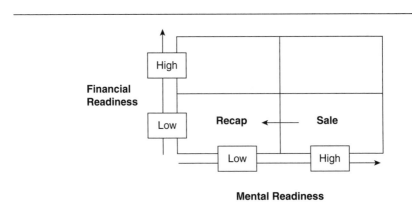

EXHIBIT 8.3 SHIFTING MENTAL READINESS OPENS THE DOOR TO NEW OPTIONS

not want to make further personal guarantees to his bank for expanded credit lines. After all, Bill will be relying on his savings for his retirement in the not-too-distant future.

Bill constructed a financial exit from the business through a private equity group recapitalization (recap) transaction. In this instance Bill sold 80% of his shares of the business, thereby monetizing that interest. The private equity group bought the business as an investment in Bill's projections for growth and profitability. The value that the private equity group used is investment value. In this case, investment value is not as high as the synergy value that Bill could have experienced in a sale to an industry buyer, but Bill still owns the 20% that the equity group did not buy. (Note: Technically, Bill is able to/required to reinvest back into his business with the equity group in the leveraged transaction. The result is the same, Bill continues to own 20% of the same business.) Bill is also able to maintain operational control of the business through a five-year employment agreement that will continue to pay him a salary. This salary is in addition to the earnings on his now-liquid investments. Also, because Bill's mental readiness to leave is low, he gets to keep his job. The financial illustration of Bill's transaction is represented in Exhibit 8.4.

This net proceeds figure of $6,160,000 is substantially less than the $7,990,000 amount received in the sale transaction. However, an exit strategy is a process, not an event. In this case, Bill is just beginning a new chapter of wealth protection and creation in his life. With a partnership that supports his aggressive growth plans and a remaining 20% holding in his business, Bill now has three significant piles of wealth working for him (Exhibit 8.5). By contrast, a sale transaction does not allow Bill to participate in the future value of the business or to continue receiving a salary and benefits.

Investment value for Bill's Brewery	$ 10,000,000
Sale of 80% of stock to private equity group	
Gross proceeds	$ 8,000,000
Advisory fee (3%)	($ 240,000)
Federal taxes	($ 1,200,000)
State taxes	($ 400,000)
Bill's Net Proceeds after transaction 1	**$ 6,160,000**

Exhibit 8.4 Bill's After-Fee, After-Tax, Net Proceeds from His Recapitalization Transaction

1. Passive income from reinvestment of sales proceeds from recapitalization

   $ 6,160,000   earning 6% income (pre-tax)   = $ 369,600

2. 20% remaining interest in company, expected annualized ROI from PEG = 30%

Year 1	Year 2	Year 3	Year 4	Year 5
$ 2,000,000	$ 2,600,000	$ 3,380,000	$ 4,394,000	$ 5,712,200

3. Salary, benefits, and bonuses from his job

   $ 225,000 annual salary

   $ 150,000 expected annual bonuses.

EXHIBIT 8.5 THREE PILES OF WEALTH

Liquidity and a New Era of Wealth Creation

A key component to the recapitalization transaction is that Bill remains motivated toward achieving the annual return on investment (ROI) objective of his private equity group partners. If the growth projections are met (here, we assume 30% annualized), Bill's remaining stake in the business (20%) is projected to grow to $5.7 million (pre-tax and pre-fee) over the next five years. At age 61, five years after his original transaction, Bill will sell his remaining shares along with his private equity group partners as they collectively execute the larger exit strategy at a substantially higher value. At this time, the 20% equity that Bill owned after the first transaction is worth nearly as much (5.7 million) as the original 80% that he sold five years earlier (8 million). This is the second bite at the apple that was referenced in Chapter 6. This is a win-win situation for all parties, as Bill was reluctant to pursue this growth strategy because of his limited financial resources at the time of the original transaction.

As we see in Exhibit 8.6, over a five-year period, Bill is substantially better off from a financial perspective when he partners with the private equity group on his recap transaction.

By staying with the business and successfully executing on his growth strategy plans with his new partners, Bill increases his total wealth by more than $4.4 million—a 55% increase—over the five-year period following his original recap transaction.

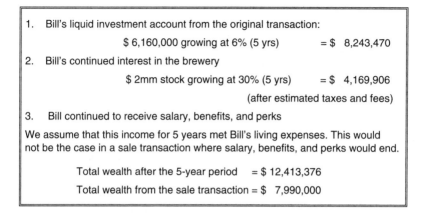

1. Bill's liquid investment account from the original transaction:

    $ 6,160,000 growing at 6% (5 yrs)   = $ 8,243,470

2. Bill's continued interest in the brewery

    $ 2mm stock growing at 30% (5 yrs)   = $ 4,169,906

                                    (after estimated taxes and fees)

3. Bill continued to receive salary, benefits, and perks

We assume that this income for 5 years met Bill's living expenses. This would
not be the case in a sale transaction where salary, benefits, and perks would end.

    Total wealth after the 5-year period   = $ 12,413,376
    Total wealth from the sale transaction = $ 7,990,000

EXHIBIT 8.6   BILL'S WEALTH GROWS OVER FIVE YEARS

Is the Recap the Best Option?

With such a tremendous disparity in wealth accumulation, why wouldn't every business owner act this rationally and enjoy the riches that such a partnership can bring?

Because of the profitability and growth projections mentioned in Chapter 6, not every business qualifies for this type of transaction. But a more interesting answer lies in Chapter 3 and the mind-set of the typical owner-operator. The habits of running your own business and answering only to yourself are extremely difficult to break. It is often said that business owners do not make good employees.

What then does Bill really sacrifice to achieve the riches of the recap deal?

It's his autonomy—or bluntly put, his pride. After the private equity group deal, Bill becomes an employee to his new owners. At some level, Bill will need to watch his creation molded into a more efficient and profitable money machine. If the culture of his business is lost in the process, so be it. In this game of capitalism, the ends justify the means, and cash flow is the ultimate pursuit. In addition, Bill needs to report and answer to his new owners—a tough pill to swallow for most entrepreneurs.

Do private equity group recaps work?

Yes, they do—when business owners can reconcile in their minds that they are no longer in control of the business. In order to achieve this higher level of profitability and personal net worth, exiting owners need to let go of the emotional trappings of their privately held businesses. Higher levels of earnings require that new processes be employed in the business. However, stretching to reach this new level of earnings requires change, and change can be quite uncomfortable.

A Mind-Set Change

Change is massively difficult for most exiting owners. At some level, most owners know this. Their unwillingness to change manifests itself in a manner similar to Bill's original approach to his competitor Jim and the attempted sale proposal that followed. In Chapter 3, we saw that Bill's approach towards selling his business to his competitor Jim demonstrated a subconscious pattern that created resistance and confusion in the selling process. Bill set a get-out price in his mind and took a shot at achieving it in as quick and as painless a manner as he believed possible. His actions reflected a mind-set that subconsciously resists change. As we saw, resistance in the mind manifests as doubt, then fear, then hesitation—and ultimately a failed exit.

However, if Bill had been able to make those changes and adapt to new situations and partnerships, the financial rewards could be tremendous.

Application to Your Exit

You can preserve and/or expand your illiquid business wealth through the lessons Bill learned. Across the United States today, there are millions of Baby Boomer business owners who do not want to change. As Chapter 1 indicated, the majority of their wealth is tied up in their businesses. They simply do not want to adjust to the new global economy as they continue to look to the past to create solutions for the future. Their competitors are teaming up with international partners and with private equity and creating a more competitive business landscape. Those business owners who will not make the necessary changes should strongly consider protecting the wealth that is already built in their businesses before it is lost to the competition.

This book illustrates the benefits that can accrue to exiting owners who can view their businesses as investments, not as jobs. The exercise in Chapter 1 asked: What is the current return on investment for your privately held business? You may discover that your business wealth ultimately would be better protected in a significantly less risky portfolio of liquid assets instead of in your slow-growing—or shrinking—privately held business. Protecting that wealth by recognizing your exit options and today's business environment is the point of this book.

When change is embraced, great wealth can be created. When change is rejected—as it all too often is—alternative solutions need to be formed to protect existing business wealth.

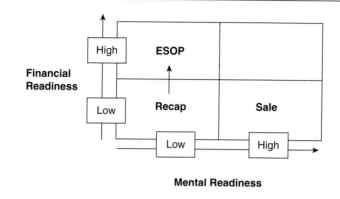

Exhibit 8.7   Shifting Financial Readiness Opens Yet Another Door to New Options

We now return again to Bill, our exiting owner. Here he is resolved not to include other partners in his business. In this case, the business shows a promise for the future and Bill now wants some personal diversification without outside buyers or investors while maintaining his low level of mental readiness for an exit.

An employee stock ownership plan (ESOP) will allow Bill to diversify and maintain strategic and financial control of the business, as shown in Exhibit 8.7.

Here we review again the *internal* transfer technique of employee stock ownership planning (ESOP) to see the financial rewards and flexibility of installing an ESOP as the primary exit strategy option.

OPTION 3: EMPLOYEE STOCK OWNERSHIP PLAN

In Chapter 7 we saw that Bill did not engage an outside industry buyer or choose a private equity group recapitalization. He also did not want anyone to know that his business was for sale. He chose instead to keep things private and decided to pursue an internal transaction that allowed him to sell some of his stock to an ESOP trust, thereby monetizing his investment in his privately held business. This transaction provided personal diversification for Bill. He also maintained control of his business, keeping his job, salary, and perks. Most important, Bill avoided having new partners and was able to own the higher future value of his company's shares.

Bill's decision to pursue an ESOP as his primary exit tool was also based in part on his capable management team and the promise that one day they would be in a position to succeed him in the business. Bill felt strongly about the loyalty of his employees and their contributions in making him a wealthy man. At some level, he wanted to give something back to those employees. Bill is balancing protecting his wealth—taking some chips off the table—

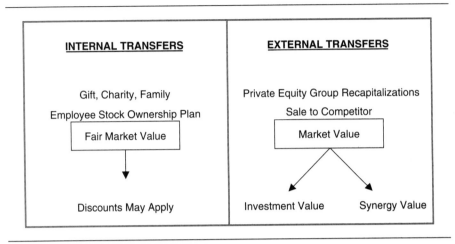

EXHIBIT 8.8 INTERNAL VERSUS EXTERNAL TRANSACTION VALUATIONS

while also setting up a scenario for his management team to take over the business in the future. If Bill's management team cannot take over, the installation of the ESOP will not prevent Bill from later selling the business to an outsider.

When choosing the ESOP option, Bill had to value the shares of his business under the fair market value standard. He also had to apply discounts to the value of those shares, further reducing the amount of cash that he received in exchange for his shares sold to the ESOP trust. Bill's initial sale of stock to the ESOP was a 30% block.

Exhibit 8.8 reproduces our valuation chart from Chapter 4.

The ESOP is an internal transfer. Moreover, because the ESOP is subject to the ERISA (Employee Retirement Income Security Act) laws, the fair market value standard is mandated for this type of transaction.

The lower value for Bill's company and the discounts are illustrated in Exhibit 8.9.

By applying the fair market value (with discounts) to the shares sold to the ESOP, Bill receives $1,417,500 for his $2.1 million block of stock. He loses 32.5% of the fair market value because of discounts to the shares through a sale to the ESOP.

Why would an exiting owner agree to this lower value?

Mitigating the Valuation Discounts for ESOP Transactions
TAX SAVINGS
The first reason that Bill would consider these ESOP metrics is that his corporate formation is a C corporation and the transaction will qualify for a

Fair Market Value of Company	$ 7,000,000
30% of stock sold to ESOP	$ 2,100,000
Discount for minority stake (25%)	$ 525,000
Value on a minority, marketable basis	$ 1,575,000
Discount for lack of marketability (10%)	$ 157,500
Adjusted indicated value	$ 1,417,500

Exhibit 8.9 Bill Gets Some Liquidity While Maintaining Control and Majority Ownership

tax-deferred election under Internal Revenue Code section 1042. Qualifying for the 1042 election makes Bill's transaction eligible for tax deferral. Therefore, he gets back 15% of the value that would have been lost to the payment of capital gains taxes under either a sale or a recapitalization transaction. It is also possible to avoid state taxes in this transaction, further increasing the savings to Bill's tax liabilities.

Note: If Bill's company was an S corporation, an ESOP would still be an effective exit strategy with some tax advantages. In this case, the earnings on the shares of the company that were sold to the ESOP would not be taxed, further increasing the brewery's cash flow, making the business more competitive in the marketplace. This competitive advantage further potentially contributes to an increased share price for Bill's remaining shares (70% of the company's shares).

Lower Advisory Fees

In addition to deferring taxes, advisory fees in an ESOP transaction are generally much lower than in a sale or recapitalization. When you consider that advisory fees in a sale transaction to an outsider—such as an industry buyer or a private equity group—cost a seller anywhere from 3% to 10% of the gross proceeds (depending on where the transaction falls in the double Lehman formula), the avoidance or reduction of these fees is very meaningful to Bill's net proceeds from this transaction.

Between the taxes and advisory fees that can be saved, the valuation discounts to the ESOP stock are suddenly not so great. There are, however, additional benefits to installing an ESOP in the business.

Bill Stages His Exit

One of the greatest benefits of the ESOP is the customization that comes with the flexible nature of the exit strategy. In Bill's case, he is able to sell as much or as little of the stock to the ESOP as he desires. Bill does not have to commit to future sale transactions,[1] and the ESOP does not preclude him from selling the business at a later date. His exit strategy plan is customized to meet his personal timeline and desire for an exit.

Additional Benefits of an ESOP

Remember that Bill keeps his job, salary, and perks with the ESOP transaction. And since he still owns 70% of the business, he also benefits from the increasing value of the business going forward. Bill is able to keep control of his company and provide a partial monetization strategy for himself that will allow him to diversify and jump-start his retirement planning.

Increased Business Cash Flows

The leveraged ESOP in Bill's case also benefits the cash flows of his business. Each year the company decides whether to make elective employee contributions to the ESOP plan. When these contributions are made, a deduction is created for the business, thereby reducing taxes and, in effect, increasing the cash flow of the business.[2] Since Bill is still the majority owner of the business, this increased cash flow will benefit his total wealth.

TEAM CULTURE AND ESOPs

Bill also educates his management team and workforce so that they will appreciate the value of the shares that they will be receiving in their retirement accounts. This process aligns their retirement plan balances with the growth and prosperity of the business. Since the employees are receiving shares in their retirement accounts, they are more motivated to behave as owners of the business. The ESOP education encourages them to defend the company's profitability and to find more purpose in their work.

CONCLUDING ESOP THOUGHTS

Bill was particularly pleased that he was able to complete an internal transfer and avoid the complexities of letting other parties know that his business was for sale. Bill also valued the preservation of the corporate culture that took years to build and maintain.

As an exiting business owner, you must recognize a few critical points:

- Not every business is salable. If your business is not salable—either to an industry buyer or to a private equity group—the consideration of an ESOP becomes rather significant.

- Chapter 9 examines management buyouts as another internal transfer strategy to consider if the enterprise cannot attract outside buyers.

- Business owners like control.

- In both a sale and a recapitalization, owners lose strategic and financial control of their businesses. An exiting owner can never be certain of a buyer's intentions and plans for the business after the transaction. For this reason, an opportunity to maintain a legacy is also lost in a sale or recapitalization transaction.

- When feelings for employees—often they are family members—get in the way of objective financial projections, the decision-making process often turns to a balance between owners not wanting to lose their wealth while still maintaining the look, feel, culture, and profitability of businesses they built over many years.

- When objective wants and subjective feelings collide, it is nice to know that options exist for your exit strategy planning.

Those three main exit strategies—sale, recapitalization, and ESOP—were derived from slight alterations in Bill's hypothetical motives. When his financial and mental readiness shifted, his choice of exit options also changed. This book opened with the idea that business owners have options for exiting their businesses that will protect their wealth. We now have seen how three options for exchanging shares for cash can work, what valuation process is attributed to each, and how each different option goes towards suiting the mental and financial readiness to exit the business and achieve personal goals. Exhibit 8.10 helps to compare the different transaction alternatives.

The common denominator of these transactions is that exiting owners trade their stock (or assets) for cash.

This book is focused on how business owners can protect their wealth through an understanding of various types of exit strategies. So far, we have discussed exit strategy options that can convert your illiquid stock into cash. We now survey two transaction types—management buyouts and gifting programs—that likely produce significantly less up-front cash but provide a flexible and customized approach to a business exit that is executed over many

EXHIBIT 8.10   COMPARING SALES VERSUS ESOPS VERSUS RECAPS

	Sale	Recap	ESOP
Value	Highest (synergy)	High (investment)	Low (fair market value)
Keeping/Losing Control	Strategic: Lose Financial: Lose Operational: Lose	Strategic: Lose Financial: Lose Operational: Keep	Strategic: Keep Financial: Keep Operational: Keep
Taxes	Full	Full	Some/None?
Advisors	• M&A • Tax • Legal • Financial • Insurance	• M&A • Tax • Legal • Financial	• ESOP • Financial • Legal • M&A (if capital needs to be raised)
Legal Agreements	• Letter of Intent • Purchase and sale • Earn-out • Non-compete	• LOI • P&S • Employment agreement • Non-compete	• P&S • ESOP trust • ESOP
Deal Structure	Cash and notes?	Cash (80% or stock) Employment	Flexible—can sell any % of business to ESOP
Continued Income Streams	• Investment returns • None (buyer buys cash flows)	• Investment returns • Continued salary under employment agreement	• Investment returns • Full • Keep job and control of the business
Legacy	None	None?	Full

years in order to achieve the personal goals of transferring ownership to your management team or executing a plan of distribution to your heirs and/or charities.

As mentioned, many businesses will be precluded from a sale transaction, from a recapitalization, or from installing an ESOP simply because they are too small or the marketplace will not produce a buyer who meets the exiting owner's expectations. Or, alternatively, a business may be eligible for these exit options but the owner won't pursue them because they would not advance his or her motive of transferring the business to family members and/or employees.

ISSUES SURROUNDING MANAGEMENT BUYOUTS AND GIFTING PROGRAMS

One of the primary challenges facing internal transactions is the fact that the intended successors, or beneficiaries, are not paying full price—or any price—for the shares of the stock. In the case of management buyouts, the management team may be able to invest some of their personal savings into the buyout, but most of the transaction's proceeds will likely be structured by paying the exiting owner over time. An additional issue here is management's skill level in running the business while the exiting owner desires to step away.

The primary motives for gifting programs are estate planning concerns—generally around estate tax issues (see Chapter 12)—and the philanthropic desire to give some wealth to charity. In both family gifting and charitable gifting, the exit strategy is coordinated with a larger plan to reduce or eliminate taxes while the business wealth ends up in the hands of the intended parties.

VALUATION OF INTERNAL TRANSFERS

The valuation chart in Exhibit 8.11 shows us that internal transfers, except for management buyouts, generally are valued with the fair market valuation standard.

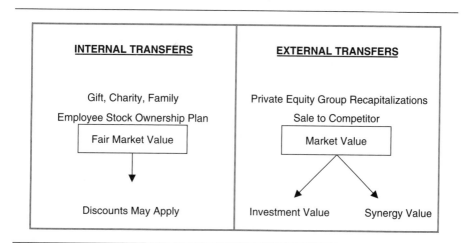

EXHIBIT 8.11 INTERNAL VERSUS EXTERNAL TRANSACTION VALUATIONS

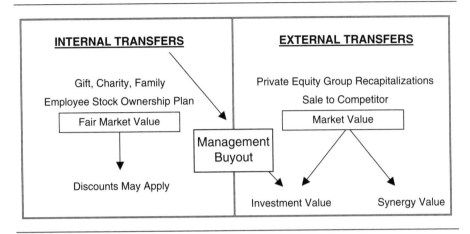

EXHIBIT 8.12 MANAGEMENT BUYOUT VALUED AS AN EXTERNAL TRANSACTION

Management buyouts are internal transactions but not subject to the fair market value standard (Exhibit 8.12). Managers will act as market players to produce a value for the business that represents their actual expected returns from the investment.

When stock was sold to the ESOP, the lower fair market value standard produced a result that worked against the exiting owner as discounts to the share value reduced the amount of cash the owner received. In the case of gifting programs, a lower value benefits the exiting owner's plans. Let's see why.

LOWER VALUATIONS CAN ASSIST WITH YOUR PLANNING GOALS
In the case of gifting strategies to family members or charities, the objective is to get a low valuation of company shares so that a greater amount of wealth can pass within the limitations of the gifting laws. The objective here is to transfer large amounts of wealth out of the exiting owner's name in order to reduce estate taxation. It is important to point out that a high financial readiness generally is required to give away assets in this manner.

HIGH FINANCIAL READINESS REQUIRED
There are two reasons why the best candidates for internal transfers are those who rank high for financial readiness on the exit quadrant chart:

1. First, an exiting owner may lose the loyalty and trust of a management team if a management buyout conversation does not produce the results that the employees were expecting and the future payments are contingent upon the continued success of the business (see Chapter 9).

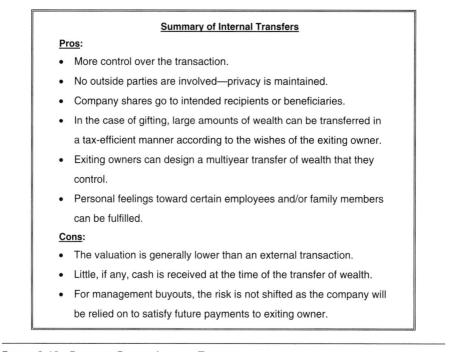

Summary of Internal Transfers

Pros:

- More control over the transaction.
- No outside parties are involved—privacy is maintained.
- Company shares go to intended recipients or beneficiaries.
- In the case of gifting, large amounts of wealth can be transferred in a tax-efficient manner according to the wishes of the exiting owner.
- Exiting owners can design a multiyear transfer of wealth that they control.
- Personal feelings toward certain employees and/or family members can be fulfilled.

Cons:

- The valuation is generally lower than an external transaction.
- Little, if any, cash is received at the time of the transfer of wealth.
- For management buyouts, the risk is not shifted as the company will be relied on to satisfy future payments to exiting owner.

EXHIBIT 8.13 PROS AND CONS OF INTERNAL TRANSFERS

2. Next, an exiting owner cannot gift away that which is needed for his or her own financial security (see Chapter 10).

In both cases, an exiting owner should have a strong personal financial standing to be able to withstand the consequences of either of these negative outcomes. Exiting owners who do not have enough money saved to support their postexit lifestyle today should be cautious about undertaking these internal transfers.

STRUCTURED PAYOUTS

In most cases of management buyouts and gifting programs, the exiting owner is establishing a multiyear payout or transfer of ownership (see also Chapter 11). These structured payments will be either cash payments received by the exiting owner from the management team or annual gifts made over many years to intended beneficiaries. These multiyear approaches to designing an exit strategy fit perfectly with retirement and estate planning objectives.

We now proceed to Chapter 9, management buyouts, where we begin our discussion of these important issues that surround internal transfers.

NOTES

1. Unless he takes a premium price for the shares, he will need to sell more to the ESOP at a later date.
2. Used for (1) treasury stock contributed to ESOP and (2) leveraged ESOPs, where cash is used to repay loans—visit www.exitingyourbusiness.com for more information on how to use ESOPs creatively as a tool of corporate finance.

9

MANAGEMENT BUYOUTS

Today, a skilled manager makes more than the owner. And owners fight each other to get the skilled managers.

—Mikhail Khodorkovsky

In real estate, it's "location, location, location." In business, it's "management, management, management."

—Joe Durnford

There are a great number of business owners who have prudently saved for their financial security and are now reaching retirement age. For many reasons, these Baby Boomers do not want to sell to outsiders but would rather give their management team an opportunity to purchase the business. These owners are beginning to think about exiting their businesses but are not yet ready to retire.

Here the motive driving the choice of exit options is a desire to pass the business to a management team through a management buyout (or, alternatively, the exiting owner has exhausted other options) Exhibit 9.1 illustrates where this exit option fits in the exit options chart. It also highlights the concept that, for reasons to be discussed in this chapter, a high financial readiness is recommended when considering management buyouts.

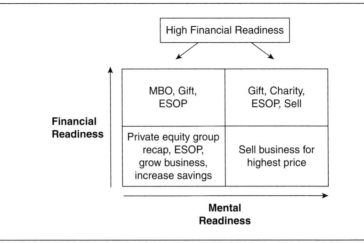

Exhibit 9.1 Exit Options Chart

MANAGEMENT BUYOUTS

As we open our discussion regarding management buyouts (MBOs), an exiting owner needs to answer two primary questions:

1. Can your employees think and act like entrepreneurs?
2. Does the vitality of your organization require this type of continuing entrepreneurial thinking?

These two questions represent the foundation for deciding if an MBO is viable as part of your exit strategy plan. Too many exiting owners begin with their employees' lack of capital as the primary obstacle in considering an MBO. This is important, but not nearly as important as your assessment of the employees' ability to run the business in your absence.

If your employees do not show an ability to blossom into entrepreneurs, you must give careful consideration to the implications of turning over the reins to them. This is particularly true if your business is going through many changes and requires constant fresh thinking and ideas. Alternatively, if your industry is more stable and your business is more of a cash cow, this entrepreneurial skill set may not be as necessary.

MBOs can be extremely rewarding to an exiting owner, or extremely frustrating. They do, however, provide an opportunity for management to experience the ultimate promotion: future ownership of the business. Making certain that your wealth is not compromised in the process is the point of this chapter.

COMMON DENOMINATORS

All businesses are different, so the potential outcomes from management buyouts will vary. However, some common denominators can be identified in virtually any MBO:

- Your employees don't have the money to buy your business.
- Your managers do not take risks the way that you do.
- Your relationship with your managers will change from employer/employee to partners.
- You are negotiating with the people who work for you.
- The business will likely need to serve as collateral for the exit to function properly.

Why head down this road?

There are benefits to the exiting owner who chooses to work with his management team as the primary exit strategy plan:

- The managers know the business, so value can be maintained through continuity of business operations.
- It is a controlled exit that can occur over many years, providing a flexible deal structure and tax situation (see Chapter 11).
- An internal transaction does not require an outside party.
- There is an affinity toward this group who helped grow the business and your wealth.

CAVEAT ABOUT MANAGEMENT BUYOUTS

An MBO is the most flexible but most difficult exit option to analyze on a comprehensive basis because it is so highly dependent on the business, the exiting owner, the management teams (sometimes a single person) as well as the facts and the personalities of all involved. Exiting owners will want to determine what they are most interested in getting out of the exit and then consider how much time and energy they are willing to commit to succeeding with this exit option. Again, since future payments likely depend on the continued success of the business, you, the exiting owner, cannot completely step away from watching over the business's continued success.

The viability of an MBO as an exit option depends on the business, its industry, and its sector. For example, many entrepreneurs are just that, entrepreneurs, not managers. Some industries are in constant states of change and require dynamic and forward-thinking leadership in order to keep abreast of these changes. Other industries are more mature and are less in need of the specialized skills of the entrepreneur after the business has reached adolescence. Therefore, some businesses will require managers to think and act like entrepreneurs in order for the exiting owner's wealth to be protected; others can have managers serve as capable stewards to continued prosperity in the absence of the exiting owner.

Only you, the exiting owner, can determine the skill sets required from your managers to continue running your business in a profitable manner without you.

LITTLE CASH AT CLOSING

Unlike the sale, recapitalization, or ESOP (as presented), these internal transactions do not necessarily provide cash at closing for the exiting owner. The reason for this is a bit obvious: Your employees either don't have, or won't risk, the money that is required to purchase your business. In addition to this lack of liquidity, they also likely are unable to attract equity partners who can take over and run the business profitably. Much of your manager's lack of ability to attract investment capital to provide you with an up-front payment for the business has to do with the fact that financing sources will quickly assess that you are the rainmaker in the organization. Again, this is highly fact- and case-specific, but, as a general rule, the attributes, and perhaps proven track record, of the exiting owner are what outside investors will be interested in backing. This fact makes it difficult for your managers to put together a financial package that will allow you to achieve any significant cash at the closing. From a wealth management perspective, this is not great news for the exiting owner; in order to receive value from the exit, the business needs to continue to produce profits into the future. The risk has not really been shifted; the exiting owner is not really diversified away from the business risks. This is why we opened this chapter by reminding you that a high financial readiness is recommended when attempting a management buyout.

DEFERRED PAYMENTS

When considering an MBO as an exit option, exiting owners must understand that a fairly significant percentage of the sales price likely will be structured as future—deferred—payments that will be received when the business produces profits. In this respect, exiting owners may have been liberated from day-to-day operations of the business, but the risk still belongs to them as future payments are contingent on the continued success of the business under its new owners.[1]

The good news about deferred payments is that they can be structured to complement a customized retirement plan as a means for meeting postexit expenses. The bad news, as mentioned, is that these payments are effectively contingent on the businesses' success. In other words, you may not receive these payments, so you are not diversified and you have not reduced your risk exposure.

VALUATION METRICS

Exhibit 9.2 illustrates that although an MBO is an internal transfer to a management team, the valuation methodology falls within the external transfer world of investment value. From a valuation standpoint, this means that your management team will want to know that their return on investment (ROI) is appropriate, given the level of risk that they are inheriting. (As many exiting owners remind their managers, it is the risk that they helped to create as contributors to the business.)

INVESTMENT DECISION

Exiting owners find themselves in an interesting position when they need to defend the viability of the business as a suitable investment to the very people who have been assembled to make it so. Nonetheless, an objective assessment

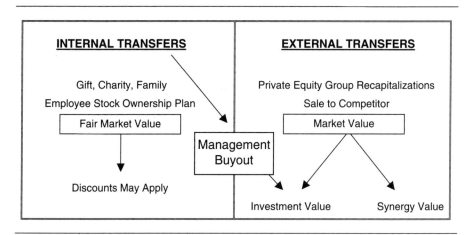

EXHIBIT 9.2 MANAGEMENT BUYOUT VALUATION

of a management buyout reveals the fact that the managers are investors just like anyone else. And given the opportunity to invest in alternative vehicles, these employees/would-be owners require that the business should produce a superior ROI.

As an exiting owner, you need to remember that your successors, like any buyers, have options for investment of their personal capital. The better job you can do to explain the benefits of the business to your successor(s), the higher your probability of success with your exit strategy plan.

In this case, your management team is acting as an investor in the business. This can be very good news for you as your value actually may be enhanced over some of your other exit options. Alternatively, you may not qualify for a sale, recapitalization, or ESOP transaction; sale to your management team may be your primary exit option.

Whether the management buyout option is elected or effectively mandated for your situation, the same analytical criteria apply. You need to view your employees as future owners and convince them of the value of the business going forward. After all, once you are gone, they will need to execute on that vision in order for you—and them—to get paid.

ACCELERATING YOUR GROOMING PROCESS

The flexibility of an MBO allows you to install incentives and equity bonuses into talks with your management team about buying you out and taking over control of the business, thereby accelerating your grooming process. Your financial readiness should be high because these negotiations can prove to be a very slippery slope. For years your employees have toiled under your rule. Now you want to empower them to fund your exit. It is best if you have a solid financial foundation to support you as the outcomes can vary widely.

An additional consideration in establishing an MBO is to coordinate certain milestone achievements with the receipt of ownership in the business. A useful strategy is to define the responsibilities that a management team will assume over time. Then, as time passes, you measure the success of these assumed responsibilities.

The key is to write down the responsibilities and the manner in which they will be evaluated. By setting this plan in writing, you are taking some of the subjectivity out of the process and defining clear expectations of the managers who want to become owners. Clear direction and a process that managers can use to measure their results is a critical component to the success of this type of transfer.

Again, every company and situation will vary; however, it is worthwhile to repeat the need to write down your plan before we delve deeper into management buyout issues.

ULTIMATE IMPASSE

Successful MBOs focus on the employee mind-set and gets managers to shift to an entrepreneurial mind-set. After all, if your employees could easily assume the head job at the company: (1) they probably would not be working for you, and (2) your risk in the transaction would be low enough to accept virtually any form of deferred payment.

In fact, your employees have followed direction from either you or another authority for most of their professional lives. Now they are being asked to make a significant change to their thinking and begin behaving like owners. You are asking them to rise to the challenge of being strategic-thinking entrepreneurs after years of training them to serve subordinate, tactical roles. It is a large leap. Only you, the exiting owner, can assess whether your illiquid business wealth will be safe in their hands.

ENTREPRENEUR'S TRIANGLE

Exhibit 9.3 represents a simplified version of most organizational structures. It will help us in understanding the new role that managers are being asked to assume in an MBO. Again, this exhibit is general in nature. You must consider your own specific circumstances when applying it to your exit strategy plans.

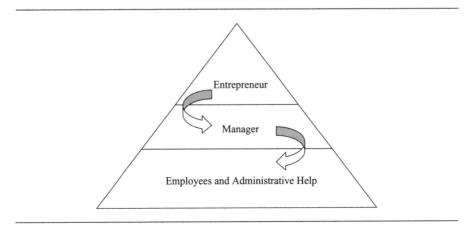

EXHIBIT 9.3 ENTREPRENEUR'S TRIANGLE

BASE

At the base of this triangle are the lower-wage employees and the administrative staff. They take care of the day-to-day functions within the business. The decision-making authority for staff members at this level is very limited. Hence, creativity and imagination are not required for success in these positions. These are the most tactical, least strategic-thinking positions within your organization.

QUALITY OF YOUR MANAGEMENT TEAM

The next level in the triangle represents the managers. The managers in your organization watch over the employees and administrative staff, making certain that the tasks are performed properly. This special group helps to shape and monitor your vision for the business by turning your ideas into actionable projects for the employees and administrative-level people to execute. In many small businesses, managers free up the entrepreneur by managing tactical tasks and providing summarized reports of progress within the business to you, the owner. In other organizations, managers play a critical role in the growth of the business because the business has matured beyond the entrepreneur's skill set. The former group of managers make questionable management teams for a buyout; the latter provide a solid foundation for the exiting owner to consider building an exit strategy plan around.

ENTREPRENEUR'S CREATIVE LEVEL

The pinnacle of the triangle is where you, the owner, live. The creation of ideas that keeps the business moving forward rests on the shoulders of the person in charge—you. Achieving this position is a tremendous accomplishment and a sizable responsibility. Think back to all of the good and bad decisions that you made building your business. You needed a great deal of creativity and ingenuity to get to where you are today. Likely no one else in your organization possesses that sort of drive and commitment.

The good news is that the business is beyond the start-up phase and much of the initial survival risk has been removed. The bad news may be that your business is changing all the time and creativity may remain its lifeblood. Depending on the dynamics of your business, your managers may or may not be able to assume your responsibilities at the head of the organization. Again, whether or not your managers can take the reigns is the ultimate question that you need to answer when considering an MBO for your exit strategy plan.

LEAP: EMPOWERING YOUR MANAGEMENT TEAM

Will your managers be willing to make the business an investment of their own? Or will they be permanently relegated to the employee mind-set?

Will the managers be able to exercise their creative faculties to guide your business to continued profitability in your absence?

Ultimately, how much of your wealth would you like to stake on this assessment of your managers' abilities?

Since you will likely be receiving only a small percentage of your company's value with the initial transfer of ownership, you will likely need to protect your wealth through contracts that allow you to take back control if the managers fail to make the deferred payments. (See Chapter 13.)

MANAGEMENT BUYOUTS AND FINANCIAL BACKERS

The main assumption in this discussion is that your management team will not be able to pay you, the exiting owner, a substantial amount of cash for the initial transfer of the business. This, in fact, may not be the case if your management team can partner with a private equity group (or another financial sponsor/investor) to buy out your ownership stake all at once. This scenario is not outside the realm of possibility. In this case, the transaction and conversation would shift from focusing on your managers' limited resources and how a deal can be structured with deferred payments to getting an up-front payment from the financial partner, given that its resources are presumably deep and such an up-front payment to you will not compromise the continued health of the business. It is now the private equity group that is helping your managers determine the return on investment criteria. Your negotiations change as the ability to receive up-front payment for your business increases. Your exit strategy planning may be well served by helping your managers meet and partner with financial sponsors who believe in the growth of your business.

BUSINESS AS COLLATERAL

In the absence of a financial backer to the transaction, many management buyouts rely on the business's existing assets as collateral for a loan for an initial down payment to the exiting owner. You will want to reduce your risk with the MBO by requiring that the management team produce *some* cash at closing. Managers often have little equity aside from some personal savings and perhaps the ability to borrow against their home equity line of credit. In order to supplement this relatively low level of equity, they may pledge assets of the business as collateral for the transaction.

The company's balance sheet will indicate the value of the assets that can be used as collateral for the loan to the MBO. Generally, the tangible assets of the business, such as plant, property, and equipment are added to the accounts receivable to form an asset base that supports this initial loan. A meeting with your banker will tell you the viability of such a loan. When you are seriously considering an MBO, you also should give the managers an opportunity to develop their own relationship with your loan officer. The sooner this process can begin, the better.

SELLER FINANCING

Regardless of the amount of the initial payment, you will most likely be required to take back some paper, which means that you will have to be paid out of future profits of the business. When an exiting owner is willing to be paid over time, he or she holds a note against the management team. The stock in the business can be pledged as collateral. Sometimes an exiting owner will also look to personal guarantees to secure the payments.

EXIT OVER TIME: LOW MENTAL READINESS

One of the primary benefits of an MBO is that it can evolve and mature over time. Responsibilities for managers can be increased on an incremental basis. A process of testing and measuring results can occur over many years to assess how the managers are adapting to their new roles. This process of increasing responsibilities is consistent with the natural progression of an employee's standing in the business. These promotions can be formalized to support each party's desire to define the process by which you, the exiting owner, will be leaving the business.

As mentioned, these calculations are very fact specific and will vary just as personalities and circumstances vary with any management buyout. As the exiting owner, you will need to assess both the quality of your management team and the viability of your business in their hands. If the managers are successful, you can achieve a high value because the managers will make payments for a longer period of time, which add up to a higher total return to you. These payments can also include continued perks for you and perhaps some continued salary and other negotiated benefits.

Again, each case is different, but you have the flexibility to negotiate with your managers the amount and timing of the payments that you receive. This flexibility has the added benefit of giving you, your accountant, and your financial advisor an opportunity to measure the anticipated taxation of those revenues. A complete exit strategy plan will forecast those payments—both gross and net of tax—into your postexit financial plan (or retirement plan). With proper structuring the MBO payments can be managed for tax-efficiency, with continued payments from the company going into retirement and other tax-advantaged vehicles (assuming that you are continuing as an employee and providing value to the company).

TOOLS TO ASSIST WITH MANAGEMENT BUYOUTS

It may take a number of years for the MBO transaction to take shape. The managers may want some time to raise capital for a down payment, and they may also want to test the waters with the notion of ownership prior to assuming control of the business. Three tools that can facilitate a gradual transfer of responsibilities and ownership are:

1. Right of first refusal agreements
2. Right of first opportunity agreements
3. Setting schedules and milestones

RIGHT OF FIRST REFUSAL

A right of first refusal is a written agreement given to managers that empowers them with the contractual right to match or beat the terms of any other offer that is made for the purchase of the business. In this case, the exiting owner is assuring the managers/employees that their future succession of the business is guaranteed if they can match another offer for the purchase of the business brought by an outside party.

This right of first refusal indirectly limits the exiting owner's ability to offer the business freely to the marketplace. Potential outside buyers will be informed that the right of first refusal exists with the manager(s) and may think twice about purchasing a business where their offer may be trumped or the managers believe that they will one day own that business. Because those managers are likely critical to the operations of the business, a certain amount of value is likely to be lost once their expectations of one day owning the business are disappointed. Potential buyers will give this heavy consideration.

The right of first refusal is a useful tool for an exiting business owner to give an early but uncommitted expression of interest in turning managers into future owners.

RIGHT OF FIRST OPPORTUNITY

An agreement that can further encourage managers toward future ownership of a business is the right of first opportunity. This right empowers employees to preempt the market for offers for the business by having the opportunity to bid first. This type of arrangement is an affirmative statement by the exiting owner that the managers are the primary candidates for taking over the business in the future.

Typically this type of agreement is made with an eye toward a transfer of the business at a future date. To this end, a price for the business is oftentimes determined at the time that the right of first opportunity is granted to the managers. Managers typically pay a nominal amount of money for this right. The amount that is paid is generally symbolic of the intention of the parties to move towards a formal agreement in the near future. The managers will have a certain period of time—generally one to four years—in which to coordinate a formal offer, including financing, for the purchase of the business, after which the right expires.

Managers who hold a right of first opportunity are most often moving toward making a formal offer for the business. Similar to the right of first refusal, most likely the exiting owner is not actively seeking another buyer. However, this exiting owner is also not assuming that the management team will be able to achieve the financing necessary to meet his or her terms. The agreement does, however, provide a clear signal that the managers are valued in the organization and have somewhat exclusive rights to attempt a buyout over a certain period.

SETTING SCHEDULES AND MILESTONES

A written schedule of responsibilities and milestones that acts to transfer ownership to a management team is one of the easiest and most effective tools to begin planning the MBO. When establishing this schedule and milestones, the exiting owner and the management team are dividing the future responsibilities of running the business amongst themselves, allowing the management team to take more responsibility while the exiting owner bows out of certain tasks. The milestones within this schedule indicate how the business needs to be performing in order for the transfers of ownership to continue.

Exiting owners who execute an MBO generally find themselves involved with the business for quite some time as they continue to watch over their investment. These exiting owners need to protect their wealth by monitoring the grooming and succession process on an ongoing basis. If a milestone is not reached, the parties meet and discuss the failure and reevaluate the viability of the MBO process. Also, you will want to have triggers in your agreements with your management team that allow you to recapture the ownership and shares in the business if you do not receive future payments.

APPLICATION OF A MANAGEMENT BUYOUT TO BILL'S SITUATION

Our exiting owner, Bill, has now taken a new approach toward his exit strategy planning: He is going to negotiate with his management team to buy him out. Bill's management team consists of three key employees who have worked for him for an average of 12 years. This team has executed on Bill's vision for the business over the years, and, from time to time, they have demonstrated leadership qualities above and beyond the stated responsibilities within their roles as managers. In fact, one manager has routinely impressed Bill with ideas about the direction of the business and the industry and has offered insights as to how the brewery could be better positioned to capitalize on these trends going forward.

Bill has a low mental readiness to leave the business but a high financial readiness. He has saved diligently in his retirement and personal savings accounts over the years, forecasting that his exit strategy plan would be better served by doing so. Bill does not need to get top dollar for his business, and, as was stated in Chapter 3, "he would rather work until he's 75 than see the business suffer under the wrong ownership. (Clue: Getting the highest price suddenly does not seem like Bill's underlying motive—he actually cares about who takes over the business)."

Bill decides that he will have a conversation with his three-person management team regarding the possibility of them purchasing the business from him. He understands that his managers do not have the type of liquidity that would enable them to buy him out right away. Instead, he wants to discuss a structured payout from the business, whereby he would get some money up front, with the balance of the payments coming on an interest-bearing note that he would provide to make the transaction possible. In other words, because Bill's management team is not bankable, he will be the bank.

As we saw, the craft beer industry has matured over the years, reducing the dynamic changes that occurred in the early years. As a result, Bill's skills as an entrepreneur have not been as necessary as they once were. In fact, Bill has found that his managers' skill sets far exceed his in terms of hiring (and firing) staff members and maintaining the business operations. He believes that he can begin to gradually remove himself from the business operations while giving more and more control to his management team.

To assist Bill with this conversation with his managers, he reviews a right of first opportunity agreement. Bill understands that if this conversation goes well, he will want to demonstrate his seriousness for this exit strategy by offering this agreement in return for a nominal payment—say $5,000. With this plan, the management team will make a commitment to the process with a token amount of money but with a significant psychological indication that they are interested in owning the business.

Also in preparation for this meeting, Bill reviews his financial situation with his local banker. Bill believes that the assets on the balance sheet of his business can serve as good collateral for his managers to use as an initial loan to pay him a $2.5 million down payment for the business. Bill's banker is in general agreement with this assessment and indicates that Bill's management team should begin to form a relationship with him, the lending officer, as a first step toward a multiyear transfer. Once direct communication begins, the banker can make a qualitative judgment about the managers' ability to repay the loan in Bill's absence.

Bill resolves himself to the fact that he is only going to receive $2.5 million for the down payment and that his $7.5 million note (remember our value measurement is investment value: 10 million) will be received over time and will be subordinated to the bank's loan to the business. With the $2 million in cash flow from the business, Bill's accountant helps project estimates that the management team can afford to repay the loan to Bill—as well as repaying the bank loan—over a seven-year period without compromising the strength of the business. Bill is going to ask for a 7% rate of annual interest on the loan.

Bill establishes a schedule for the transfer of ownership to the management team. This schedule calls for the achievement of certain operational and profitability milestones in the first few years prior to shares being transferred. Bill's loan agreement that empowers the managers to take over the business will also include a pledge of the stock against that loan. If the loan is not paid, then Bill takes back a percentage of the stock and retains the rights to reclaim control of the business.

Bill is confident that his management team is up to the task and will be excited about the prospect of owning the business. He understands that he will be negotiating with his employees about the price and terms of the buyout but believes that his team is mature enough and the business is stable enough—and his financial readiness is high enough—to withstand a good deal of failure in the process. Bill remembers that his managers will now be looking at the ownership of this business as an investor would. Therefore, he is going to stress not only the return on investment criteria but also the ancillary benefits, such as his willingness to finance the transaction and their ability to make significantly more money once their loan obligations to Bill and the bank have been satisfied. Bill will impress upon his managers that long-term thinking and the desire for creating wealth for themselves are the foundation for doing this MBO.

Bill reflects on the other exit options that are available to him and decides that his management team deserves the opportunity to own the business. His involvement in watching over his illiquid wealth—which is now represented as a note against the business—is easy enough to allow him to enjoy his phased entry into retirement. Bill schedules the meeting with his management team, expecting a positive response and outcome from this choice of exit strategy plan.

REVIEW

We have now seen that Bill was able to meet his exit strategy planning goals by including his management team in the process. He thought through the concerns of his managers and understood the complexities of his business and industry before determining that his managers would be good owners for the business. Bill's financial readiness was high, so he was able to afford the risks that come with this type of exit strategy and to allow the management team to structure a majority of the purchase price as deferred payments.

In this case, Bill felt an affinity toward his management team and wanted to conduct an internal transfer that, he believed, would allow the business to continue to be run the way that he had always wanted. Bill was able to consider his own departure from the business in a phased manner, thereby also providing a solution to his low mental readiness for his exit.

Now that we have covered the major ways in which a business can be traded to another party, we can move onto a special set of internal exit strategies, which include giving away illiquid wealth in order to achieve both philanthropic and estate tax-planning goals. If you are ready to learn about gifting strategies as a part of exit strategy planning, turn to Chapter 10.

NOTE

1. The owner's note will likely be subordinated to the bank loans to the company, further reducing that owner's ability to control the future payments that come from the business.

10

GIFTING STRATEGIES FOR EXITING BUSINESS OWNERS

My father used to say "You can spend a lot of time making money. The tough time comes when you have to give it away properly." How to give something back, that's the tough part in life.

—Lee Iacocca

I resolved to stop accumulating and begin the infinitely more serious and difficult task of wise distribution.

—Andrew Carnegie

Our final exit strategy option is actually a grouping of many options that fall under the general term "gifting." When exiting owners reach a point in life where they want to give something back, they turn to gifting programs to satisfy that urge. Almost always—or at least it should be—the urge to give, not the tax incentives, motivates the implementation of gifting programs. Gifting programs are a study unto themselves, encompassing volumes of written work and constantly changing tax code sections and tax court rulings. Here we cover the essentials of gifting, including the benefits of valuation discounts, before applying these basic concepts to our exiting owner, Bill.

The initial questions that exiting owners need to ask prior to establishing a gifting program are:

- To whom do I want to give my wealth?
- Can these transfers of wealth benefit my exit strategy plan?

We will see that with a desire to give comes the potential for a few tax benefits that sweeten the feelings associated with philanthropic gestures.

EXECUTE YOUR ESTATE TAX PLAN, NOT THE GOVERNMENT'S

Many exiting owners, after meeting with their estate planners, will be both impressed and depressed about the amount of estate tax exposure that exists in their lives. The tax laws of the United States levy taxes against your wealth either during your lifetime or at your death. Two primary forms of taxation:

1. **Gift taxes** are applied against lifetime transfers that exceed certain dollar limits.
2. **Estate taxes** are applied to transfers at death that exceed certain dollar limits.

If assets are in your name, and if they exceed a certain dollar amount (discussed in this chapter and in Chapter 12), they will be subject to a federal tax whether you part with them during your lifetime or at death. These tax rates are both currently 45% (2008 rate)—that's 45 cents out of every dollar, above the stated limits—that go towards lifetime gift taxes or estate taxes. In addition, there are individual state estate tax rates (varies state by state) added to the federal rates just mentioned. Gifting programs are useful because each dollar that is removed from your estate can protect your wealth against this 45% estate tax pinch.

One very healthy way to avoid estate tax exposure is to transfer assets out of your name by establishing a gifting program. This chapter demonstrates that you can combine philanthropic desires and apply some special rules for valuing privately held business shares to get you further toward your dual goals of philanthropy and reducing your estate taxation. In particular, if you are transferring your business to family members or employees, gifting programs can supplement nearly any exit strategy plan.

In short, your lifetime objective of accumulating wealth may very well be compromised by a tax system that will not let it leave your possession without the imposition of a stiff tax. Exiting owners who are forward-thinking about protecting their wealth will build a plan that utilizes these tax laws so that assets can pass to others in the most tax-efficient manner possible; often a multiyear time period is required (in addition to these types of plans, life insurance can be purchased to pay the estate taxes due, see Chapter 12).

Remember that if you do not do your estate tax planning, the government will do it for you. It is more likely that your plan, not the government's, will produce the results that you want for your hard-earned money.

HIGH FINANCIAL READINESS

You may come to realize that with a high financial readiness for your exit, you likely no longer need all of your wealth to meet your personal expenses. It now may make sense to begin gifting some of it away to the beneficiaries and charities of your choice.

Exhibit 10.1 indicates where these internal transactions best fit.

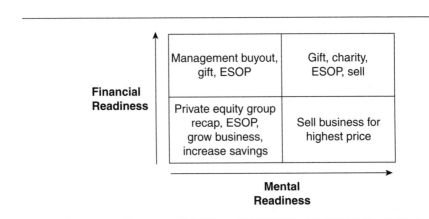

Exhibit 10.1 Exit Options Chart

FLEXIBILITY

Gifting programs are often used in combination with other strategies, such as employee stock ownership plans (ESOPs) and management buyouts (MBOs), to get additional amounts of company stock into the hands of your desired successors. For example, you can use an annual gifting program, which allows you to transfer $12,000 per year (2008 limit) in value to an unlimited number of individuals, over many years to transition ownership in your business to your desired successors. In addition, exiting owners can use their $1 million lifetime gifting limit to transfer more than $1 million worth of stock because of the discounting that is allowed for this type of transaction. (This topic is explained in the section "Planning over Time, Using Discounts" later in this chapter.)

NO CASH FOR YOUR SHARES

Each of the four exit options that we have examined up until this point—sale, recapitalization, ESOP, and MBO—have included projections of when exiting owners would get paid for the transfer of the equity in their businesses. For example, although MBOs provide little to no cash initially for exiting owners, they will produce a stream of income for owners to receive in the future to satisfy postexit expenses.

With gifting, however, our exit strategy objectives vary. When gifting away stock, exiting owners are interested in getting their wealth into the hands of others, such as employees, heirs, or charities, without receiving cash in exchange. What exiting owners receive is the fulfillment of their desires to be generous or philanthropic with their success. The "payment" back to these owners is not in the form of cash but rather in the feelings associated with touching the lives of other people. However, as we will see, certain transactions allow for income streams back to exiting owners as well as current-year tax deductions that financially reward exiting owners for the assets that have been gifted away.

TAX BENEFITS

The government uses the tax code to both incentivize and prevent certain behaviors. For example, the entire world of employee stock ownership plans (Chapter 7) is a good representation of what tax benefits can create in the way of business owner behavior.

One of the behaviors that the government promotes through tax benefits is the gifting of assets, including company stock, to charities. In this case, an exiting owner who feels philanthropic can transfer wealth to a charity—

through a charitable trust—while receiving a current tax deduction and a stream of income in return.

Many exiting owners with a desire to give, looming estate tax issues, and a high financial readiness for an exit should be proactive and deliver wealth to the people they care most about rather than to the government. Along the way, they can seek out tax breaks to complement their generosity.

GIFTING TO FAMILY, EMPLOYEES, AND CHARITIES

Exiting owners generally consider two types of gifting programs when contemplating wealth transfers to other parties:

1. Programs that gift to individual beneficiaries, such as family and employees

2. Programs that gift to causes, institutions, or charities

Each of these gifting programs has tax and planning attributes that impact an exiting owners' goals for their wealth. Before moving into the specific planning options that are available for each of these transfers, let's once again review the valuation standard that is used with gifting and charitable transfers.

FAIR MARKET VALUE STANDARD

Shares that are transferred via gifting strategies will be valued using the fair market value standard. Again, the fair market value standard is the standard that the Internal Revenue Service and the courts recognize for measuring the value of a privately held business transaction for gifts and ESOPs. Again, these assessments are made by trained experts in business appraisals. They consider many of the factors that drive valuation in the marketplace for the sales of business but follow specific steps for making the valuation conclusion. This process is defensible against the Internal Revenue Service or the tax courts for any future contest by the government regarding the value attributed under this fair market value standard (for a review of this standard, see Chapter 4.)

Exhibit 10.2 illustrates the valuation standard used for different types of transactions.

PLANNING OVER TIME, USING DISCOUNTS

When we first reviewed fair market value in Chapter 4, we saw that discounts were allowed, and sometimes required, in certain transactions involving minority blocks of shares that were sold (or transferred) to another party. We

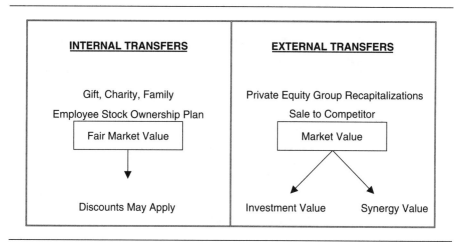

EXHIBIT 10.2 INTERNAL VERSUS EXTERNAL TRANSACTION VALUATIONS

then saw in Chapter 7 that ESOPs included the sale of stock to an ESOP trust and were mandated to use the fair market value standard. In the case examined, the exiting owner was interested in receiving a high amount of money for the shares that he was selling to the ESOP. Because discounts were applied to the value of those shares, the exiting owner got less money than he wanted. In other words, discounts applied to the sale of stock to the ESOP frustrated that exiting owner's objective of achieving the higher value for those shares.

By contrast, when discounts are applied to gifting transactions, they work in favor of the exiting owner's planning goals because those discounts decrease the value of the shares and allow for a greater amount of wealth to exit the estate—thereby minimizing future estate tax exposure. Again, these discounts are permitted because minority shareholders in any privately held business have no decision-making authority over the strategic or financial operations of the business. It is therefore recognized that the shares represent a discounted value to what would otherwise constitute some form of control over the business. It is also recognized that these blocks of stock have no ready market (i.e., no liquidity) for the transfer or sale of shares, so further discounts are permitted.

For example, let's assume that our exiting owner, Bill has been a good saver and has liquid wealth that far exceeds any amount of money that he will need for his illiquid business lifestyle on a postexit basis. In this case, he is interested in transferring his illiquid business wealth to his family and charities through a plan that, over many years, will assist in avoiding (not evading;

Fair Market Valuation of Company Stock:	**$ 7,000,000**
Assume that a minority stake (1.5%) will be transferred:	**$ 105,000**
Discounts applied:	
Lack of control discount @ 30%	**– $ 31,500**
Value of shares before discount for lack of marketability	**$ 73,500**
Lack of marketability discount @ 20%,	
Based on the discounted value of $ 73,500	**– $ 14,700**
	$ 58,800

$105,000 in company stock is discounted to under $ 60,000 in value, allowing over $105,000 to leave Bill's estate and go to his chosen beneficiaries.

EXHIBIT 10.3   TWO DISCOUNTS HELP IN TRANSFERRING GREATER AMOUNTS OF WEALTH TO BENEFICIARIES

there is a big difference: One is legal, the other is not) estate and gift taxes. Bill establishes a program to begin transferring shares of his company's stock to five different family members.

Under a straight application of gifting laws, Bill could transfer $60,000 per year ($12,000 per person times five recipients). Utilizing the discounts, however, Bill discovers that he can transfer $105,000 of illiquid business wealth each year in a tax-free manner. This figure is $45,000 higher than the straight application of the annual gifting limits of $12,000, allowing Bill to remove more assets from his estate and protect his wealth against onerous gift and estate tax rates. Let's see how this occurs through the example in Exhibit 10.3.

Over a 10-year period, Bill is able to transfer $1,050,000 in company value to his intended heirs, on a tax-free basis.

At an estate tax rate of 45%, this annual gifting program reduces Bill's federal estate taxes by $472,500, protecting more of his hard-earned wealth.

The stock ends up in the hands of the people Bill wanted to give it to. And Bill gets the dual pleasure of transferring these assets while he is alive and can enjoy the good feeling associated with these gifts while also knowing that he saved nearly $500,000 in estate taxes.

LIFETIME EXCLUSION

In addition to an annual gifting program that utilizes the $12,000 annual exclusion amounts, every individual in the United States is allowed to transfer $1 million worth of assets, in his or her lifetime, free of gift taxation. This $1 million lifetime exclusion is a one-time event for an individual, and the amount that is gifted reduces the amount that can be excluded from estate taxation at death (see Chapter 12).

An important topic that will get brief mention here but should be examined in any gifting plan that includes private business interests is that once gifted away, the growth of those gifted assets occurs outside of the estate of the exiting owner. This is a significant point, particularly for growing privately held businesses. In many cases, the growth—or fast growth—of a privately held business compounds the estate tax problems that already exist for assets held in that owner's name. When utilizing your lifetime exclusion of $1 million, you are able to remove a sizable amount of wealth from your estate and allow it to continue to grow in another vehicle or to be owned by a desired heir or beneficiary.

When calculating the amount of growth that occurs outside of an owner's estate, the estate tax savings become rather sizable. This fact emphasizes the main point that when an exiting owner takes the time to make an exit strategy plan, options for protecting wealth increase dramatically.

ANNUAL GIFTING PROGRAMS

Our first, and simplest, transfer of company stock to a family member can be executed via a gifting transaction. The annual gifting program that we just reviewed demonstrates the power of utilizing discounts to transfer larger sums of assets out of an exiting owner's estate. These programs are used most effectively when they are conducted over a number of years—systematically transferring the assets out of your estate at discounted rates.

An exiting owner can also utilize a gifting program in conjunction with an MBO or an ESOP. Remember, the annual gifting rules are not restricted to transfers to family members only. Rather, exiting owners can gift away $12,000 to any number of people, related or unrelated, in any given year. This would therefore also include employees. And there is no limit on the number of people to whom these annual gifts can be given. Therefore, an exiting owner who is interested in gifting some stock to her management team as part of the exit strategy plan under an MBO or an ESOP is free to do so. Additionally, if she is feeling generous toward nonmanagement employees, she can gift other shares to them. In fact, the gifting of shares can assist in creating a culture of ownership within a business. This can be particularly important in protecting an exiting owner's wealth in an MBO situation, because the future profits of the business are where that owner's note payments are coming from (see Chapter 11). A stronger business should—all things being equal—lower the risk level of those future payments, making for a more sound exit strategy plan and retirement.

GIFTING SHARES TO CAUSES, INSTITUTIONS, AND CHARITIES

The second major form of gifting is to causes, institutions, and charities. Gifts to charitable trusts are the most common forms of these wealth transfers. There is a vast array of vehicles in this charitable category. They include both charitable remainder trusts and charitable lead trusts (both of which offer different features, depending on how income is distributed).

The primary benefit of these transfers is that they fulfill a philanthropic desire. A close second in terms of benefits is the avoidance of capital gains taxation because these not-for-profits entities are not subject to taxation. In the most basic case, exiting owners can transfer shares of privately held stock that have a very low cost basis (i.e., founder's shares from many, many years ago). When this stock is later sold by the charitable trust, the proceeds are diversified into liquid investments; that cash flow can be used to make the income payments that these trust structures promise. The key point here is that no tax is paid on the sale of the stock. This transfer to the charity also has the benefit of a current tax deduction to donors/exiting owners.

Exiting owners need to know that these transfers are irrevocable, meaning you give up ownership and control of the asset when it is transferred to the trust. Even though you avoid capital gains taxes, get a stream of income in return, and get a current-year tax deduction, you do lose control of this wealth. After a set period of time, the assets will stop yielding income to the donor, and the remaining balance transfers permanently to the charity to which it was donated.

Why would owners of privately held stock effectively disinherit their heirs by giving wealth to a charitable trust? Because there is an easy remedy for the replacement of that wealth: life insurance. We visit the concept of an irrevocable life insurance trust (ILIT) in Chapter 12 when we turn our attention to moving assets out of our exiting owner's estate as part of a larger estate tax plan. Briefly, an ILIT can be established to purchase a life insurance policy—called a wealth replacement trust—so that assets will pass to beneficiaries tax-free. Also, since the insurance policy is not held in the exiting owner's name, the proceeds of the insurance payout are not subject to the decedent's gross estate tax calculation.

This book will not delve more deeply into the alphabet soup of charitable trust planning strategies. Simply understand that the application of each strategy is very fact- and case-specific and is not something that should be attempted without the guidance of experienced advisors.

FAMILY LIMITED PARTNERSHIPS

For owners who want to gift business assets to their children but do not want to give up control of those assets, the family limited partnership (FLP) is a strategy that can be incorporated into an exit strategy plan. An FLP is a formal partnership, with its own tax identification number, that effectively allows the exiting owner to serve as the general (i.e., controlling) partner while children serve as limited partners.

If structured properly, FLPs allow for the reduction in value for wealth transfer purposes while also delivering business cash flows to the children, who are now limited partners in the business. The exiting owner achieves a transfer of wealth out of her name, allows future growth in the business to occur outside of her estate, and provides a stream of income to her chosen beneficiaries while still controlling the business.

As with other complex estate planning strategies, you need an experienced planning specialist to give updated guidance on structuring family limited partnerships.

GRANTOR-RETAINED ANNUITY TRUSTS

For owners who want to gift assets to their children while also addressing estate tax issues, grantor-retained annuity trusts (GRATs) can be effective tools. A GRAT allows exiting owners to remove a block of stock from their estates through a transfer to a trust. In exchange for this transfer, exiting owners receive an income stream back from the GRAT for a set number of years. After that period has passed, the remaining assets in that trust transfer to the beneficiaries, generally the children of the exiting owners.

With GRATs, assets are removed from the estate and wind up in the hands of intended beneficiaries in a very tax-efficient manner. GRATs work best for businesses that have a growth rate that exceeds the rate of interest payments that the trust must make back to the exiting owners. Exiting owners also must make cash distributions from the business interests, in order to satisfy the income requirement. (Note: Technically, shares of stock can come back to exiting owners, but this negates the purpose of removing this wealth from the owners' estates.)

Unlike with an FLP, here owners lose control of the assets that are contributed to the GRAT. Therefore, exiting owners need to consider how an estate tax planning strategy can be combined with an effective wealth transfer strategy that allows them to remain in control. If controlling the contributed shares of stock is not a major issue for you, a GRAT may well serve your planning needs.

Once again, an experienced advisor is required for this level of planning.

APPLICATION TO OUR EXITING OWNER, BILL

Our exiting owner, Bill, has a new outlook on his exit strategy plan: Now he wants to gift away some of his wealth. Bill's three children will also play a role in his gifting strategy. Bill understands that his total net worth far exceeds his applicable exclusion amount of $2 million and that he needs to be proactive in addressing his looming estate tax issues or lose a substantial portion of his wealth to the government. Bill realizes that he needs a complete and comprehensive strategy for his entire estate and wealth picture.

Bill has been an extraordinary saver and preserver of wealth over the years. He has, in fact, many real estate investments that provide substantial monthly income to him, liquid stock and bond investments, as well as some rare artwork and a few racehorses that occasionally provide him some return on his investment. The brewery represents a small percentage of Bill's total net worth.

Bill has a high financial readiness for his exit. He also has been thinking that he would like to spend time in his postexit phase giving back a percentage of the wealth that he has accumulated throughout his life. Bill's mental readiness to leave the business is average. The brewery business remains his passion, but his thoughts are turning to his next phase of life.

Bill also envisions his family members participating in the process of gifting some of his wealth. What is very important to Bill is that his children are not spoiled by the inheritance that they will one day receive. This is not a small issue for Bill; he realizes that although he needed to work very hard to achieve his wealth, his children already show signs that they are not fiscally responsible. A large inheritance may, in fact, do them a disservice as they squander their newfound wealth on self-indulgent activities.

Bill would also like to make a charitable donation—something by which he can begin to give back to his community and also to establish a legacy for himself and his family.

GIFTING USING DISCOUNTED VALUES

Since Bill is now considering gifting strategies, he decides to have his business valued by a professional appraiser. The appraiser uses the fair market value standard for valuing the brewery business. Bill tells the appraiser that the purpose of the appraisal is for a gifting program. The appraiser understands that Bill's objective is to achieve a lower value for the transfer of his wealth. This is true because he wants to move more of his wealth out of his estate at the discounted rates. In addition, the appraiser reminds Bill that minority blocks of shares of the brewery that are transferred out of his name will qualify for lack of control and lack of marketability discounts. (Review Chapter 4 for discussion of these concepts.)

ANNUAL GIFTING PROGRAM

Bill begins his gifting program by transferring shares of his company stock to his three children under an annual gifting program. Each year Bill intends to transfer $12,000 worth of discounted share value to his children. This amounts to $36,000 per year of wealth that is transferring out of his estate. The value of these shares, prior to the discounting, was closer to $50,000. Bill expects that over a 10-year period, he will be able to move over $500,000 in business stock value out of his estate. However, because his company continues to grow, the shares that are gifted will grow in value outside of Bill's estate, thereby further assisting Bill's overall goal of moving wealth out of his estate. In other words, if the company stock remained in his name, as the company became more valuable, his estate tax situation would only get worse. Here, the growth occurs outside of his estate because the shares are owned by the children.

TRANSFER OF STOCK TO A CHARITABLE REMAINDER TRUST

In addition to the annual gifting program, Bill also decides that he is going to transfer some shares of his stock to a charitable remainder trust (CRT). He is motivated to conduct this transfer primarily because of his feelings associated with a particular charity. Bill's primary motive is not to achieve a tax break, but rather, to experience the good feelings associated with providing for the charity of his choosing.

Although the tax incentives were not the driving reason behind this transaction, Bill does get a handsome tax benefit for the charitable transfer. Bill receives a tax deduction today for the value of the shares transferred to the trust and he also will get a stream of income, for 20 years, back from the CRT. Bill takes the projections of income that will come back to him and places them in his retirement plan that he has been building with his financial advisor. With this transfer, Bill also removes more assets from his estate, which again allows the value of the business for those allocated shares to grow outside of his estate.

The trust will be able make the cash distributions because Bill will declare dividends for all shareholders each year. In the future, he expects that if his mental readiness for an exit turns to high and he sells to an outside buyer, he will avoid capital gains tax on the sale of shares within the CRT, and the new diversified portfolio of liquid investments will continue the income stream to him for the balance of the term.

What has Bill achieved in the way of wealth protection and preservation?

So far, Bill recognized that, like most privately held business owners, a large piece of wealth was tied up in his illiquid business. In Bill's case he had many other assets outside of the business that contributed to his estate tax issues. However, because of the discounts that are allowed for the value of shares of privately held businesses, he found the business stock the best asset to begin his gifting to charitable causes and to his family.

Bill receives a number of benefits because of this strategy. First, he gets to move more assets out of his estate because of the discounts. Second, because the brewery is still increasing in value, Bill avoids the compounding effect of his current estate tax issues by holding more of a growing asset in his name. He is able to transfer the illiquid shares of business stock which represent value, but not cash, to his family members, avoiding the problem that he foresaw in providing his children with large sums of liquid wealth that they could spend at their leisure (and likely to their personal detriment). In addition, certain tax benefits also went along with this strategy.

Bill recognized that getting rich was only one part of the puzzle. Equally challenging is the process of staying rich, or in this case, avoiding the payment of large estate tax bills due to a lack of planning. Bill has protected his wealth and has also provided for his family and the causes that he cares deeply about.

REVIEW OF PARTS I AND II

We now see that exit strategy planning is not the same as selling your business. Exiting owners have options and the ability to customize their exit strategy planning to meet their personal goals.

An owner's financial and mental readiness is the guide to assessing her ability to meet personal goals with the appropriate exit options.

Understanding the range of values concept is a critical component to most exiting owners' abilities to meet their financial goals. Simply, if an internal transfer occurs to family, an ESOP, or to charity, then a fair market value measurement is taken to represent the value of the business. If, however, an outsider, such as a private equity group or competitor (synergistic buyer), is considered for the exit transaction, then the likely value that an owner will receive will be in the world of investment or synergy value. The exception to this rule is the management buyout which is technically an internal transfer but measured as if the managers were objective, outside buyers/investors.

At this point, we have seen the shortcomings of not setting exit goals and not understanding your readiness to exit. We have also illustrated why your buyer is directly linked to the value that you receive.

Let's reexamine how Bill will change his exit strategy to accommodate what has been learned so far.

First, Bill gives serious consideration to what he wants from his business exit. He excludes nothing from consideration at this stage and is limited only by his imagination.

Next, Bill ponders his readiness to leave the business. What will replace the time that he spends in the business? What will replace the feelings of satisfaction that he derives from the business?

Then Bill takes a look at the myriad ways that a business can be transferred and decides that there are a few options that are available to him based on his financial situation.

Bill considers the pros and cons of each of these transfer options and the value that will be received from them. He concludes that he can reach his goals and afford to consider many options that include him continuing to work in the business and, in fact, building a stronger business for a larger sale at a later date.

Bill's exit strategy planning has come a long way. The hard-earned wealth that he built into his business is getting closer and closer to being protected.

Bill has one more very important hurdle to clear in completing his exit strategy planning. He needs to understand some of the technical components of an exit strategy plan so that he can measure the net results that he will achieve after taxes and advisory "fees" are applied against each of his exit options. Bill also has to figure out who is going to be his "quarterback" in taking care of this exit strategy planning because both running a business and handling this exit strategy is too much for almost any entrepreneur.

These are the topics that will be covered in Part III. So, if you are ready to turn the corner and learn about the technical components of a business exit and how they impact the net amount that an exiting owner receives, turn to Chapter 11, which begins Part III.

III

PLANNING YOUR EXIT, PROTECTING YOUR WEALTH

So far this book has provided tools for an exiting owner to begin establishing an exit strategy plan from her business. The process began with a survey of today's marketplace of exiting owners, including insights into the current marketplace of advisors and how exit strategy plans currently are designed and executed. We discussed setting exit strategy planning goals related to postexit lifestyle and the type and timing of business exit that would most closely align with those objectives.

We then proceeded to assess your financial and mental readiness for an exit. Within this discussion, the exit quadrant chart helped us identify with one of four types of exiting owners. The chart was filled with options that empowered us to begin planning for the option most closely aligned with our goals. Each of these options was illustrated through an example of our exiting owner, Bill. In each case, the benefits of the chosen exit strategy helped Bill determine the pros and cons of each type of exit. We studied valuations that are applied to each strategy and how discounting the value of your shares of stock can work for you (in the case of gifting strategies) or against you (in the case of sales of stock to an ESOP). Throughout all of the discussion, the focus remained on protecting your illiquid business wealth and achieving the exit goals established in Chapters 2 and 3.

Exhibit III.A illustrates the steps in this process again.

We now conclude our exit strategy planning process by turning our attention toward developing the written plan for your exit strategy. First, however, we address some common obstacles that get in the way of virtually every exit strategy plan. Those obstacles include:

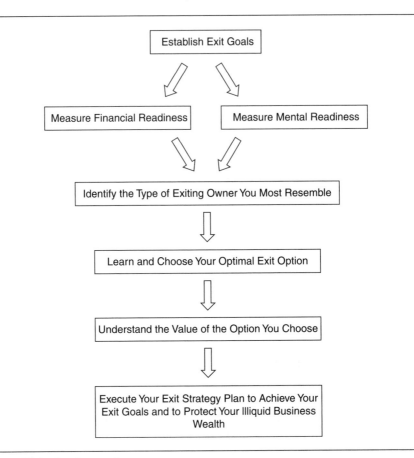

EXHIBIT III.A   EXIT PROCESS STEPS

- **Transfer taxes.** These taxes are tied directly to deal structuring.
- **Estate taxes.** These taxes are the leading contributor to estate shrinkage.
- **Legal agreements.** We show you how to make sure that your deal is what you think it is.
- **Advisory team.** We also show you how to put the right players in place.

These final chapters of the book conclude with a step-by-step example illustrated through our exiting owner, Bill, on how to establish a complete exit strategy plan from your business that focuses on you meeting your goals, using the options that have been presented, and building the advisory team that you will need to clear the hurdles that may stand in your way.

11

DEAL STRUCTURING AND TAXES

It's Not What You Get but What You Keep that Counts

A corporation's primary goal is to make money. Government's primary role is to take a big chunk of that money and give it to others.

—*Larry Ellison*

You tell me the price, I'll tell you the terms.

—*Anonymous*

In any exit strategy transaction, an owner needs to see that the price that is received (or value of shares) and operational control are important but, equally important are deal structuring and taxes. All too often, owners do not invest enough time learning about taxes and deal structuring and wind up having to understand these very challenging, interrelated concepts at a time when the execution of the exit strategy transaction is well under way. It does not benefit an exiting owner to increase the selling price of a business through tough negotiations only to give back those gains to higher tax rates due to structuring that favors the buyer.

Exiting business owners benefit from knowing about tax burdens early in the exit strategy planning process. This way they can focus on the net proceeds that they will keep from the transaction rather than on the ego-boosting price that they may want to get for the business. Accordingly, as the chapter subtitle states, it's not what you get but what you keep that counts.

The more that exiting owners know about the basics of deal structuring and taxes, the better they will be able to ask the right questions that lead to the protection of the net proceeds that meet their postexit goals.

WILL UNCLE SAM KILL YOUR EXIT STRATEGY PLAN?

Many exit strategy plans fail because exiting owners do not realize early enough in the transaction what exactly is being offered to them and how it will be taxed. Consequently, the size of the checks that need to be written to Uncle Sam (and others) often offend exiting owners to the point that they allow the proposed transaction to die. Those tax payments, relative to what exiting owners need to satisfy their postexit lifestyle, are simply too much money to part with after a lifetime of success in business. At this unfortunate juncture, many exiting owners conclude that it is simply easier for them to continue running their business; hence a failed execution of the exit strategy plan.

Can this be avoided?

Yes, many of these issues can be anticipated early in the transaction with a basic understanding of deal structuring and taxation. And with enough forethought, exiting owners will choose an exit option that leaves them in better control of the transaction and helps them to meet their exit strategy goals.

FOUR STEPS TO UNDERSTANDING DEAL STRUCTURING AND TAXES

Taxes and deal structuring are a necessary component to every exit strategy transaction. To simplify this otherwise complicated topic, we offer four steps to understanding deal structuring and taxes:

Step 1. Taxation of your exit strategy transaction

Step 2. Deal structuring

Step 3. Your corporate structure

Step 4. Making it all fit

After we explain and apply these four basic steps to a case study, this chapter concludes with some additional thoughts surrounding deal structuring and taxes.

STEP 1. TAXATION OF YOUR EXIT STRATEGY TRANSACTION

The Constitution of the United States gives the government the power to tax. As a result of this power to tax, legislation from time to time is passed and codified inside of the Internal Revenue Code (the Code). The Code controls the first and largest level of tax, federal-level taxation (state taxes also apply to many exit strategy transactions, and they should not be overlooked. Here we focus on federal-level taxes to illustrate the largest exit strategy planning issues regarding taxation.)

There are different levels of tax within the Code. Some dollars in an exit strategy plan will be taxed at a high rate, say 35% (corporate and top income tax rates), and some may be taxed at the more favorable, lower rate of 15% (capital gains tax rate 2008). By understanding these issues, exiting owners can design an exit strategy plan that achieves a lower tax rate. This naturally means that exiting owners get to keep more of what they get.

How a transaction is characterized for tax purposes determines how it is taxed. Tax characterizations are tied to how transactions are structured. Therefore, understanding deal structuring becomes critical to knowing the tax liabilities of your exit proceeds.

STEP 2. DEAL STRUCTURING

The tax rates of an exit strategy transaction are determined by its deal structuring. The term *deal structuring* simply means the specific manner in which exiting owners relinquish ownership of their businesses, including how and when they will get paid. Sometimes all of the business is sold or transferred at once; other times the business is sold in a series of transactions. Also, payment for the transfer of the business may occur all at once or over a period of time.

CRITICAL QUESTION

Will the structure of my transaction subject the proceeds of my exit to the 35% federal tax bracket or the more favorable 15% tax bracket?

Asset versus Stock Transactions

Exiting owners should know that a buyer or successor can purchase the *assets* of a business and not its *stock*. Purchasing the assets of a business has the same effect on the transfer of ownership as a stock purchase. In both cases, the buyer purchases the business from the exiting owner. Do not take the term *asset purchase* too literally. It means that the purchase price that is agreed on will likely exceed the value of the assets of the business. In this case the additional compensation is allocated to goodwill (explained at the end of this chapter).

Asset purchases are very common. In fact, the majority of transactions that occur in the smaller deal space—under $10 million in transaction value—are structured as asset deals.

What is the difference between an asset purchase and a stock purchase, and why is this a critical part of your exit strategy planning?

Buyers Buy Assets and Sellers Sell Stock

As a general rule, buyers or successors want to purchase assets while sellers (or exiting owners) want to sell their stock. Exiting owners will want to have the proceeds that they receive taxed at the lower tax rate of 15%. The easiest way to achieve this more favorable tax rate is to sell the stock of the business, not the assets. For stock sales, capital gains treatment will most likely apply to the gain in the stock over your original cost, or *basis*, allowing for the lower tax rate of 15%.

Why won't buyers simply acquiesce to an exiting owner's desire and purchase their stock?

The most common answer to this question from buyers is that they do not want to assume the known and unknown liabilities of the acquired business. When buyers purchase the stock of a business, they get every piece of that business, good or bad. The contracts, rights, and obligations of that business now transfer hands to the buyers. Technically, this transfer of ownership is *by operation of law*, meaning that buyers or successors inherit all parts of the acquired company.

Buyers or successors will also be motivated to purchase the business assets, and not the stock, for a very specific tax reason: namely their ability to write up the basis of the assets acquired (*writing up* the basis in an asset means that the buyer can account for the asset that is purchased at its purchase price, as described in the next section). Buyers who purchase an exiting owner's stock do not get this tax benefit.

Writing Up the Assets

When a buyer purchases the assets of an exiting owner's business, the basis of those assets can be written up to reflect the purchase price. As a result, the new basis in the assets subsequently can be depreciated over time, providing a noncash deduction to the business. This results in increased cash flow through

Exhibit 11.1 Comparing Asset and Stock Deals in S versus C Corporations

	S Corporation	C Corporation
Stock Deal	15% capital gains	15% capital gains
Asset Deal	Highest individual tax rate* or capital gains	Highest corporate tax rate, plus a second tax on the distribution of proceeds from corporation to selling business owner

*The rate depends on how the assets are characterized.

reduced taxation. Buyers are reluctant to give up these valuable deductions because their improved cash flow contributes directly to their return on investment in purchasing your business.

STEP 3. YOUR CORPORATE STRUCTURE

A final point in the navigation of deal structure and taxation is the form of entity in which your business currently exists. Each type of corporate formation is treated differently for tax purposes. Many businesses are structured as traditional C corporations. Today, however, far more entities are being structured as "flow-through" entities such as S corporations.

Exhibit 11.1 will help with an initial understanding of the interplay of these concepts.

We see that stock deals are characterized as capital gains transactions and are awarded the more favorable tax rate of 15%. Asset deals, however, may subject the exiting owner to higher tax rates and possibly two layers of taxation, as is seen with an asset sale from a C corporation. Again, this is why sellers want to sell stock—to get the more favorable 15% tax rate.

STEP 4. MAKING IT ALL FIT

To navigate this complex area, you must:

- Understand that there are different levels of tax for exit dollars received.
- Understand that what a buyer or successor is offering—a stock or an asset purchase—will have tax consequences to both parties.
- Examine your corporate structure.
- Determine how the taxation of your payments will impact your written goals for your exit strategy plan.

Simply put, you need to know the answer to this question:

When you receive your check(s) from the exit, how much are taxes going to shrink it?

Once you can determine how taxes will affect your net proceeds, you need to ask two follow-up questions:

1. Can I make changes to my deal structure to improve my tax situation?
2. Will my buyer/successor accept those changes?

(Note: At this point in an exit strategy, exiting owners are advised to seek the counsel of experienced tax and deal-structuring professionals. Creative ideas are the lifeblood of a successful deal-structuring negotiation. The absence of creative ways for dealing with taxes often results in a poor tax outcome for exiting owners and a failed execution of an otherwise viable exit strategy plan. Investing in experienced advisors at this point can determine the success or failure of your exit.)

CASE STUDY

We return to our exiting owner, Bill, to examine deal structuring and taxes. Bill approaches his competitor, Jim, about purchasing the business. Jim agrees to purchase the business and is willing to share some of the financial benefits resulting from synergies in their transaction. The price is roughly agreed on. Bill feels good about the value that he negotiated.

Jim sends a letter of intent (see Chapter 13) to Bill, stating his interest in purchasing the business, including the price and terms. The structure of the offer is for the purchase of the assets, not the stock in Bill's business.

LEVELS OF TAX, DEAL STRUCTURING, AND BILL'S CORPORATE FORMATION

Bill knows that there are many levels of taxation in the code, and, before the transaction moves too far along, he wants to know how his exit proceeds will be characterized for tax purposes. Recall that his business is a C corporation. Therefore, Jim's offer to purchase the assets (not stock) of the business will almost certainly negatively impact Bill's net proceeds from the transaction. (See Exhibit 11.2.)

When Jim purchases the assets of Bill's business, there is a tax at the corporate level for the receipt of income due to the sale of those assets. Bill's corporate tax rate is applied to this initial transaction. The proceeds of that asset

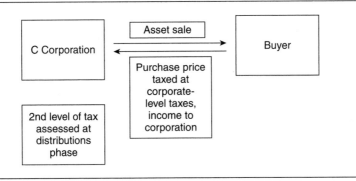

Exhibit 11.2   Asset Purchase Is Being Offered

sale remain in the corporate account of Bill's company. They do not yet belong to Bill as his company is a C corporation, not a pass-through entity like an S corporation. In order for Bill to get those proceeds, there will be a distribution from the corporation. A second tax will be assessed to the exit proceeds when Bill receives them. These two levels of tax greatly reduce the net amount that Bill receives from the sale. The fact that he was able to get a higher selling price for his business is quickly negated by the fact that he needs to pay two levels of taxation in order to receive those exit proceeds.

CONVERTING THE EXIT TRANSACTION TO A STOCK DEAL

If Bill could convince Jim to purchase the stock in his company instead of the assets, Bill could move from the dual taxation of his exit proceeds and into a single level of tax at the favorable 15% capital gains tax rate. (See Exhibit 11.3.)

In this case, Bill has simply sold his stock in the business to Jim. The tax that will be applied to this transaction is a capital gains tax for the gain in the sale of the stock—one level of tax, and at a more favorable level.

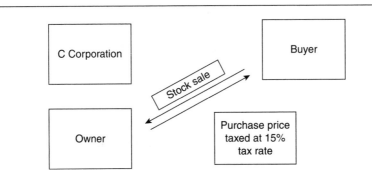

Exhibit 11.3   Stock Purchase Is Being Offered

WHY WON'T JIM GRANT BILL THIS FAVORABLE DEAL STRUCTURE?

Naturally, Bill would prefer the lower (and single) tax rate of 15%. The easiest way for him to achieve this outcome is to have Jim amend his offer by converting the asset purchase into a stock purchase. Jim, however, will be reluctant to purchase the stock of Bill's business for two primary reasons:

1. When Jim purchases Bill's assets, Jim gets a tax benefit because he gets to write up the basis of those assets. This will allow Jim to depreciate these assets later. Since depreciation is a noncash deduction for the business, a valuable tax opportunity exists that Jim will not willingly surrender. If Jim were to purchase Bill's stock, he would inherit the basis in that stock and lose the tax benefits associated with the purchase of the assets.

2. Jim does not want to inherit all of the known and unknown liabilities of Bill's business through a stock transaction. When a buyer purchases the stock of a business, all of the known and unknown liabilities of that business transfer to the buyer *by operation of law*. In this type of purchase, Jim will now own Bill's problems—all of them.

WILL UNCLE SAM KILL THIS DEAL?

When Bill realizes that up to 50% of his exit proceeds (35% tax at the corporate level and a second tax for the distribution) could be lost because of the two layers of tax in the C corporation/asset deal structure, he is likely simply to reject Jim's offer. Those checks are simply too much for Bill to write to the government after a lifetime of hard work as a successful business owner. This is where buyers and sellers must negotiate to reach parity in the treatment of taxes in a sale transaction.[1]

BEYOND THE BASICS: MORE THOUGHTS ON TAXES AND DEAL STRUCTURING

As we saw in Chapter 1, most exiting owners believe that selling is the primary means of exiting a business. By now you see that there are many ways to exit a business. And each of these ways of exiting depends on your primary objectives and your opportunity to build an exit strategy that protects your wealth.

The financial object of exiting a business includes not necessarily achieving the highest price but rather achieving the greatest sum total of all payments for your business. The largest obstacle toward netting this favorable result can be the payment of various levels of taxes. When exiting owners can see the entire picture of how a potential transaction will be structured and taxed, they are better prepared to anticipate problems. Having your tax awareness raised may lead you to look harder at other structuring or transaction alternatives to avoid paying large amounts of taxes.

INTERNAL TRANSFERS AND SMALLER DEALS

Chapter 1 stated that the vast majority of businesses in the United States today are small businesses—worth less than a few million dollars. It went on to say that exit strategies for smaller businesses are more difficult to execute than those for larger businesses. The primary risk in transferring a smaller business relates to the fact that exiting owners have made personal involvement a critical part of the day-to-day running of the business. As we saw, these owners typically consider their business more of a job than an investment. Consequently, in their absence, the viability of the business is called into question. For this reason, smaller business exit strategies are structured with many deferred and contingent payments.

DEFERRED PAYMENTS AS A RESULT OF "BUYER PROTECTION"

Certified public accountant and 20-year veteran of deal structuring Monty Walker of Walker Advisory Associates explains these deferred arrangements:

> A deferred sale is a transaction which allows for the payment of the transaction over a period of time. This can be beneficial for both the Buyer and Seller. A Buyer is able to utilize cash flow generated by the business to apply toward the purchase price instead of being required to have the entire purchase price in the form of cash on the date the business transaction is officially closed. A Seller is able to delay the payment of taxes because income is recognized as payments are being received. Since income recognition is being deferred to future periods, it is possible for a Seller to pay less tax if the income is recognized in periods where he/she is in a lower tax bracket.

APPLICATION TO MANAGEMENT BUYOUTS

Monty goes on to say:

> This form of structuring is especially beneficial in key employee and management buyouts because key employees and management teams often do not have large accumulations of excess cash for the purpose of buying a company, and they also have difficulty procuring the necessary financing [see

Chapter 9]. Thus, if a key employee or management team is identified as a viable acquisition candidate, utilizing some form of deferred sale strategy can be what enables the deal to close with this type of [buyer].

Some form of deferred sale is likely to be a part of most smaller deals and internal transactions because buyers generally expect sellers to provide some form of seller note or other deferral as a part of the negotiated transaction.

A deferred sale generally can be broken down into two primary categories:

1. Installment sale/deferred payments
2. Earn-out

INSTALLMENT SALE/DEFERRED PAYMENTS

An installment sale (or installment method) is a sale in which at least one payment occurs in a year after the year of sale. The benefit to the buyer of receiving proceeds from the exit transaction in the future is that it enables that taxpaying owner to spread the recognition of gain on the sale of the property over the payment period.

As was stated in Chapter 9, one of the benefits of a management buyout—one of the more common areas where deferred payments arise—is the flexibility that can be used in constructing the payouts. With proper deal structuring from the deferred payments, an owner can benefit by deferring the payment of taxes and by perhaps receiving income at a lower tax bracket in the future. These combined strategies stand to yield the exiting owner a higher net amount of proceeds by agreeing to receiving payments into the future. (However, as mentioned in Chapter 9, the risk is not, shifted away from the exiting owner.)

EARN-OUTS

An earn-out is the portion of the purchase price of a business that is contingent on the occurrence of some future event. For example, if a buyer and seller cannot come to terms on the validity of existing data to support the seller's asking price, a lower price may be accepted with a contingency that if the business performs at a level to support the asking price, then the difference between the asking price and agreed-on price will be paid to the seller. The actual events to trigger an earn-out obligation vary, but most are based on some target matrix, such as sales, earnings, cash flow, and so on.

An earn-out can be an excellent way to provide upside opportunity to the seller while mitigating risk exposure to the buyer. If the business performs, the seller benefits from the additional earnings. If the business does not perform, the buyer is not exposed to additional purchase price requirements.

Installment sales/deferred payments and earn-outs are important parts of structuring a transaction. They allow buyers or successors to make payments in the future while also permitting exiting owners to receive the value that they would ultimately like to receive, but postponing payment into the future. We revisit both of these deferred payment concepts in Chapter 13 under the discussion of legal agreements.

Exiting owners need to work with their tax advisors to determine the net proceeds that will be received from these deferred payments. Financial advisors and legal advisors are also needed to estimate how secure those payments will be and whether they are enough to meet the exiting owners' postexit expenses.

A NOTE ON GOODWILL

Many exiting owners initially are confused by the concept of an asset purchase as it relates to the price that a buyer or successor will pay. They will look at the balance sheet of their business and see that the actual assets of the business are not, in fact, worth anywhere near what the buyer is willing to pay. How can this difference be reconciled?

The difference between the value of the hard assets of a business (and other items defined as assets, such as accounts receivable) and the price that is being paid often is categorized as goodwill. The term *goodwill* is used to reflect the going-concern value of the business as an entity, independent of the individual assets within the business.

A buyer does not get to depreciate goodwill but rather amortizes the goodwill payments over a 15-year period. This amortization schedule for goodwill does not have the same short-term impact as the more favorable scales for depreciating assets, but it is nevertheless still a valuable noncash deduction for the business every year, which helps to further increase the buyer's cash flows.

REVIEW

You are establishing your exit strategy plan, recognizing that it will not be easy. There are many options to consider and a few hurdles that you need to clear before you can declare your exit strategy plan a success.

You begin the process with a price in mind that you would like to get for the business. As Chapter 1 taught us, it helps the process if this price is somehow supported by data points, such as a professional valuation or comparable sales of similar companies. In other words, can you make a strong, cogent argument for the price that you would like to get for your business?

You now understand that you may not get all of your money at the closing. Rather, some money may be paid to you at a future date. The natural response is to get as much as you can at closing to reduce the risk that you will not receive the future sums. But how much of that closing amount, and future payments will you keep? This is the key question because this net amount will need to replace the income that you drew from the business. To a larger extent, it is the measure of your success in exiting the business. Remember that the price is only half of the equation. The terms of deferred payments and the tax characterization of the payments are equally, if not more, important to making your exit strategy plan a success.

We now see that the myopic concept of price that consumes exiting owners' minds is really only a piece of the overall deal structuring and tax puzzle that leads to what they keep in an exit strategy deal. Most owners are familiar with the levels of taxation that are levied against the money that they have received for most of their lives. What they are less familiar with is the deal-structuring components of a transaction and how those factors can negatively contribute to the characterization and taxes owed in an exit strategy plan. Understanding these issues early in the exit strategy planning process is critical to goal achievement. Being able to anticipate and deal with issues such as deferred and contingent payments assists exiting owners with envisioning the process they will need to undertake to convert their illiquid business wealth into cash that can be used for retirement expenses. Careful deal structuring, with an eye toward taxes, will assist in protecting a large amount of illiquid business wealth.

The next form of tax that we look at for an exiting business owner is estate taxes. Estate taxes, along with transaction (i.e. lifetime) taxes, are another leading contributor to estate and wealth shrinkage for many business owners.

NOTE

1. Visit www.exitingyourbusiness.com for more information on deal structuring and achieving tax parity among the parties.

12

EXIT STRATEGIES AND ESTATE TAX PLANNING

Protecting Your Wealth with Some Estate Planning Strategies

The politicians say "we" can't afford a tax cut. Maybe we can't afford the politicians.

—*Steve Forbes*

There's an old saying that the government is your partner from birth, but they don't get to come to all the meetings.

—*John Malone*

After paying taxes on your personal income, your business income, and on all of the goods and services you have purchased throughout your lifetime, the government taxes you once again, essentially for dying with wealth that exceeds certain limits. Actually, it is more appropriate to say that the government taxes your heirs because you are, of course, dead. Whether business owners feel that it is their patriotic duty to surrender their hard-earned wealth to estate taxes is beyond the scope of this chapter and, for that matter, this

book. However, business owners rarely, if ever, seek to surrender more of their wealth to the government.

Unfortunately, too few business owners consider the estate tax consequences of their business success. In other words, without knowing the value that
the Internal Revenue Service (IRS) will place on your business at your death,
you are leaving your wealth exposed to onerous estate tax rates. In addition,
by not including your business in your larger estate planning objectives, you
may compromise its succession and survival.

Adding to the already complex nature of estate planning is the fact that the
estate tax laws are in a constant state of flux, with Congress threatening to
alter them each year. Vaugh Henry of Henry & Associates summarizes this
situation nicely:

> Despite the posturing by politicians advocating "tax relief" and the elimination
> of the death tax, the reality is that by changing the rules and moving the goal
> posts so frequently, Congress has created a tax environment that results in
> taxpayer paralysis.

Addressing the small business owner, Henry specifically states:

> While business owners acknowledge the risks of neglecting their transition
> programs, they doom their business to failure because they will not take the
> necessary steps to minimize the "easiest tax to avoid" with just a little
> planning.[1]

Because this book is about exit strategies and protecting your wealth, it
would be incomplete without a basic overview of estate taxation and how it
can impact your illiquid business and wealth.

THE GOVERNMENT HAS AN ESTATE PLAN FOR YOU; YOU PROBABLY WON'T LIKE IT

Business owners survive many challenges to succeed. As Chapter 3 showed
us, these success habits are ingrained in business owners' minds, and success
breeds more and more success. Businesses grow, profits flow, and a nice lifestyle is built around the business.

We have seen that being proactive with exit strategy planning is difficult
because owners have many emotional ties to their businesses. Likewise, being
proactive with estate planning can be difficult. Many exiting owners do not
want to confront the issues surrounding estate planning because of the psy-
chology of considering the end of life. As this book has tried to convey, you
should view an exit strategy not as leaving something behind but rather as

stepping into something new and exciting that lies ahead. By the same token, you should plan your estate not to challenge your thoughts of immortality but rather in recognition of the fact that the government has set the rules of the game and you can end up on the losing end if you do not make your own plans for your inevitable death. In the absence of some planning on your part, you may die intestate (without a will), or you may not have your assets titled properly. In either event, the default rules of probate courts and the estate tax laws will deliver a plan for your hard-earned wealth that you, in all likelihood, would not have come up with yourself. Again, the government has an estate plan for you; it's your choice as to whether your plan or the government's will determine what happens to your wealth.

THE BASICS

What you need to know about the estate tax laws is that (at a federal level), all assets above a certain dollar amount will be taxed at a 45% tax rate (2008 figure). Again, 45 cents out of every dollar above the applicable exclusion amount goes to the government—and that money is due nine months after the date of your death (unless the Internal Revenue Service allows an alternate payment plan to delay payment of this tax). Also note that even though your business value is likely the main contributor to the estate taxes you will owe, due to the illiquid nature of your business, it likely will not be able to provide the cash necessary to pay that estate tax bill. The need to sell a business to pay estate taxes results in lost wealth. If you do not know the value of your business today and your current estate tax exposure, you should set a meeting with your estate planners right away because a great deal of your hard-earned wealth is likely at risk of loss to the government.

APPLICABLE EXCLUSION AMOUNT

What is the applicable exclusion amount, or the limit under which assets can pass without tax and over which the 45% tax rate applies? Technically, the applicable exclusion amount is the credit that is applied against an estate at death. In 2008, the equivalent dollar amount that can pass without tax is $2 million per person. This $2 million effectively transfers to your heirs, or to any other party, person, or entity, tax free. Anything over this $2 million will be taxed at the 45% estate tax rate. Today's limits are listed next, but it is important to note that Congress is preparing to make changes to these amounts.

Year	Applicable Exclusion Amount	Tax Rate
2007	$2.0 million	45%
2008	$2.0 million	45%
2009	$3.5 million	45%
2010	No limit	No estate tax
2011	$1.0 million	55%

In 2010, this legislation is repealed, and there is no limit and hence no estate tax for someone who dies in that year. This is what is known as a sunset to the current estate tax laws, which were overhauled in 2001. This looming repeal of estate taxes—and, hence, a serious loss of revenue for the government-explains why Congress is currently rethinking and redesigning the estate tax laws. Furthermore, in 2011, the applicable exclusion amount is reduced to $1 million and the estate tax rate is increased to 55%.

STATE EXCLUSION AMOUNTS

In addition to the estate taxes that the federal government imposes, most states apply separate levels of estate taxation. In many cases, the applicable exclusion amounts, per state, are lower than the federal government (known as *decoupling* from the federal limit), thereby subjecting a greater amount of wealth to estate taxation at the state level.[2] Exiting owners need to understand the implications of both federal and state estate taxes and consult with estate planners to see how their wealth is exposed to the separate levels of taxation.

In addition to the amounts of wealth that can transfer at death without taxes, there are also limits to lifetime transfers. Exiting owners need to know two important dollar limitations: the annual limit and the lifetime gifting limit.

ANNUAL LIMITS

The $12,000 annual gifting limit is the amount of wealth that can be transferred, via gift, in any and every year, to any number of other individuals without incurring gift taxes (and the recipient does not pay taxes for receiving the wealth). This means that every calendar year, any individual can gift away $12,000, per person, to any number of people. This is a use-it or lose-it policy. If you do not make the gifts in one calendar year, you cannot later make those gifts on a retroactive basis; the opportunity is lost. This is a major reason why gifting programs that begin early and last for many years are more effective in transferring wealth in a tax-efficient manner than those that are delayed.

Note: There are a few interesting exceptions to the limitations just discussed that are unrelated to business exit strategies: Healthcare payments are unlimited, and education payments are unlimited provided the payments are made directly to the educational institutions, not to the student. (See www. exitingyourbusiness.com for more information.)

LIFETIME GIFTING LIMIT

Exiting owners also need to know about the $1 million lifetime gifting limit which is in addition to the annual gifting limit of $12,000 per person. Any individual can use this $1 million at any time in their lives to transfer assets out of their names. When this $1 million is used, it is debited dollar for dollar against that exiting owner's ability to use the full $2 million applicable exclusion amount at death.

For example, an exiting owner who transfers a $500,000 block of (discounted) stock to a family member during his lifetime (not including any additional annual gifts) has a reduction of an equal amount applied against his applicable exclusion amount at death. This means that this exiting owner's estate tax limit for assets that can transfer is reduced from $2 million to $1.5 million. Alternatively, this donor may choose to pay the gift tax today for this transfer, thereby protecting the full exclusion amount at death.

TOO MANY INCOMPLETE PLANS

Many business owners believe that their estate planning is complete because they met with an attorney a number of years ago and had their will and perhaps a trust or two completed. Estate planning is a far more complex process than simply executing a few documents. In fact, many fortunes have been lost due to a lack of awareness or preparation for estate taxation.

KEY QUESTIONS FOR EXITING OWNERS REGARDING ESTATE PLANNING AND TAXATION

- Does your estate plan include an accurate and updated value of your business?
- Are you aware of the applicable exclusion amount limits and the current status of your estate tax exposure?
- If your estate exceeds the applicable exclusion amount:
  - Have you reviewed how your assets are titled to take advantage of your exclusion amount(s)?
  - Have you discussed this estate tax exposure with your risk management or insurance advisor to arrange for the payment of the estimated estate taxes?
  - Have you started a gifting program that can move assets out of your estate in a tax-efficient manner to avoid large estate tax exposure?
- Do your estate planning documents detail the succession for your business?

BUSINESS VALUATION

The value of your business is a critical piece of your estate. You should be aware that the value of your business may drive your gross estate over the limits of the federal applicable exclusion amount. Once this threshold is crossed, the 45% tax rate applies to all assets beyond this figure.

Let's take a look at the next case study so we can better understand estate tax implications to a business owner's estate.

Your gross estate, at your death, will include all of the assets titled in your name. For example, our business owner, Bill, dies while owning these assets:

Personal residence	$ 1,000,000
Brewery	$ 7,000,000 (fair market value, IRS)
Portfolio of liquid assets	$ 500,000
Term life insurance in Bill's name	$ 2,000,000
Total assets	$ 10,500,000

Let's assume for now that Bill is not married. His applicable exclusion amount is equal to $2 million (2008 rate). This simply means that Bill's estate can reduce the total amount of assets exposed to estate taxes by this $2 million before assessing the 45% tax rate. The calculation:

Total wealth at death	$ 10,500,000
Less: Applicable exclusion amount	− $ 2,000,000
Gross estate tax exposure	$ 8,500,000
Federal estate tax rates (2008)	45%
Tax due for Bill's estate	$ 3,825,000

Bill's total estate at death is $10.5 million, and the applicable exclusion amount that passes tax free is $2 million. In 2008, when Bill dies, the 45% estate tax is applied to the taxable estate after the exclusion amount. A federal estate tax of $3,825,000 is owed on the assets that are exposed to this estate tax rate.

Paying more than $3.8 million in estate taxes after working all his life to amass wealth is an unfavorable outcome, to put it lightly. Also note that the $3.8 million in tax that is owed is paid primarily from the investment portfolio of $500,000 and likely by whomever was the beneficiary of the life insurance policy.

The business, worth $7 million, and the home, worth $1 million, are by definition illiquid assets. Cash, however, is what the government is looking for to satisfy the estate tax liability payment. Therefore, unless the business and/or the house are sold, the cash will have to come from the liquid proceeds within the estate. This alone can cause a great bit of discord amongst Bill's heirs. This is particularly true if, for example, Bill has three children and one works in the business while two do not. The child in the business may get to keep that illiquid asset while the other children are forced to surrender their liquid inheritance in order to satisfy the estate tax bill. Presumably this is not the outcome that Bill would have liked after a lifetime of success in business and in life.

Note: Estate taxes can be a tremendous burden toward achieving the goal of leaving a legacy and having your wealth transferred to people of your choice.

By being aware of this fact, you may be able to protect more wealth with one meeting with an estate planner than you have earned over many, many years.

WHAT DOES ALL THIS HAVE TO DO WITH EXIT STRATEGY PLANNING?

If you consider that exit strategy planning is about preserving the equity that is tied up in your illiquid business, you will quickly agree that estate taxes can be one of the largest obstacles in protecting that wealth. It is sobering for many exiting owners to realize that their estate tax exposure is large enough to reduce their life's accomplishments to a struggle between their heirs as to who pays what, when, and how. Many exiting owners may say that their heirs are going to argue no matter what they do. This may be true, but that is no reason to allow the government to impose a plan that makes the situation any worse.

THREE STEPS TO ADDRESSING ESTATE TAX ISSUES

For an exiting owner who has wealth exposed to estate taxes, you can seek a few remedies right away. Use the next three steps to assess your estate tax exposure and potentially save you a great amount of hard-earned wealth:

Step 1. Assess the estate tax that you would owe if you were to die today.

Step 2. Figure out how your assets are titled (this means, who actually owns the asset—a significant part of the process).

Step 3. Fix the problem by doing some preexit planning that includes your estate planning.

STEP 1. ASSESSING YOUR ESTATE TAX EXPOSURE

As we have discussed, you should meet with your estate planner and organize your net worth picture to determine your estate tax exposure. Your estate planner will want an accounting of all of your assets and how each asset is titled. As illustrated above, your total net worth will be reduced by the applicable exclusion amount to assess your estate tax exposure. From the amount of wealth exposed, you determine the tax that would currently be due if you died today.

STEP 2. HOW ARE YOUR ASSETS TITLED?

Our second step—after assessing your estate taxes owed—is to figure out how your assets are titled. How assets are titled simply means who owns those assets (i.e., whose name is listed as the owner). This seems like a simple enough question, until you begin to examine how each asset is held.

Asset titling is an important component to any estate. All too often business owners accumulate assets without paying attention to the consequences of how they are owned. Assets are most commonly owned in a way that is convenient for accessing or controlling the wealth, but oftentimes detrimental to achieving an efficient estate tax plan, as we will see.

Example of Asset Titling: Assume a Married Couple

Let's now assume that our business owner, Bill, is married to Jane. Bill and Jane own many assets together. A snapshot of how these assets are held and titled will assist us in understanding the significance of titling assets properly in order to equalize estates and not to forgo the opportunity to use the full amount of each person's federal exclusions (Exhibit 12.1).

BUSINESS ASSET

The business is the largest asset that this couple owns, and it is titled in Bill's name. This means that for estate tax purposes, Bill is the owner of the stock, not Jane. It is likely that when the business started, Bill and Jane were interested only in surviving their first few years. Later on, when the business began to thrive, the asset titling never changed. As a result, Bill's side of the estate is heavily weighted in value because of titling of the business asset. Retitling assets means holding them differently or transferring the ownership to the other spouse in order to address estate tax concerns.

INVESTMENT ACCOUNT

The investment account, worth $500,000, is also titled in Bill's name. This occurred because Bill usually speaks with the couple's investment advisor; it made sense that the account was in his name.

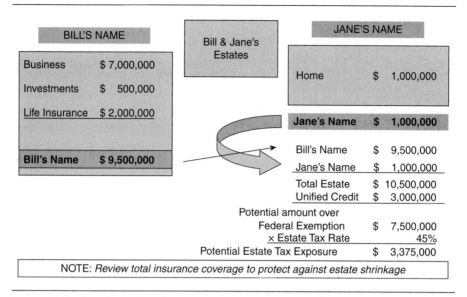

EXHIBIT 12.1   ASSET TITLING IS A CRITICAL STEP IN PROTECTING YOUR WEALTH

LIFE INSURANCE POLICY

Bill's $2 million life insurance policy belongs to him. Jane is listed as the beneficiary of this policy. Having the life insurance policy titled to Bill individually brings the face value of that policy into his gross estate calculation. As we will soon see, there is a better way to title that asset: into an irrevocable life insurance trust (ILIT).

HOME

Thankfully, Bill and Jane put the house in Jane's name. This is the only asset that is in her name, and it is worth $1 million.

ANALYSIS OF ASSET TITLING

The primary problem with the manner in which these assets are currently titled is that neither Bill's nor Jane's applicable exclusion amounts (the $2 million exemptions) will be utilized at the death of the first spouse because the assets are not in trust. This means that the surviving spouse will inherit the assets. The good news is that no tax is owed at the death of the first spouse as transfers between spouses are not taxable events. However, the bad news is that the opportunity to utilize that spouse's credit has been lost, and the assets "stack" in the other spouse's name. (See www.exitingyourbusiness.com for more information.) Consequently, when the next spouse dies, only the single $2 million exclusion is applied against the total estate. With proper planning, a full $4 million could have passed without tax. This is a $900,000 error in today's 45% federal estate tax planning environment.

The second problem with the manner in which the assets are titled is that Bill's life insurance policy is owned by Bill individually. Since Bill owns this policy outright, that $2 million of face value will be added to his gross estate and also will be taxed at the 45% rate.

The third problem with the current estate plan is that there is not enough insurance to cover the estate tax that is due, creating a situation where the business may need to be sold quickly in order for Bill's and Jane's heirs to pay the estate taxes.

STEP 3. FIXING THE PROBLEM, INCORPORATING EXIT STRATEGIES CONCEPTS

Bill and Jane can make a few changes to remedy this estate tax exposure:

- They should consider retitling a number of their assets (explained next).

- They should consider the purchase of additional life insurance to prevent having to sell illiquid assets—the business and the home—in order to pay the estate tax that is due.

- They should consider a gifting program if their desire is to transfer their wealth to their heirs. (Chapter 10 explained the many ways gifting programs could be utilized in an exit strategy plan.)

Retitle Assets

The investment account should be moved into Jane's name and put in a revocable trust account, with limited authority for Bill to execute investment decisions within the account. The house should also be put in a revocable trust. By making these simple ownership changes, Jane now has assets ($1.5 million) to apply against her applicable exclusion amount. Bill should also consider putting his business stock into a trust.

These planning strategies should be undertaken no matter where Bill is with his exit strategy planning. Then, once the basics are taken care of, the exit strategy plan will coordinate with the estate tax plan, to provide a total solution for protecting the business's wealth.

Put Insurance in an Irrevocable Life Insurance Trust

Simply titling Bill's life insurance policy to an irrevocable life insurance trust would reduce his total estate tax liability in the example by $900,000, or 45% of the $2 million face value.

When the insurance policy is transferred to an irrevocable life insurance trust (ILIT), the face value of that policy ($2 million) will be removed from Bill's gross estate.[3] With the ILIT owning the Insurance policy, however, the $2 million face value will not come back into Bill's gross estate.

This very easy change can quickly reduce Bill's and Jane's potential estate taxes by $900,000.

Too many advisors today do not coordinate their advice to business owners in a holistic manner. Simple asset titling errors are made every day. By knowing a few rules and devoting some time to fixing these problems, you can easily avoid these errors and save a great deal of wealth. When considering something as complex as establishing and executing your exit strategy plan, do not forget the simple items, such as an asset titling and estate tax planning reviews with your advisors.

New Estate Tax Exposure

With the retitling of the assets, Bill's and Jane's combined estate tax exposure is reduced by $1,125,000.

Personal residence	$ 1,000,000
Brewery	$ 7,000,000 (fair market value, IRS)
Portfolio of liquid assets	$ 500,000
Total assets	$ 8,500,000
Total wealth at death	$ 8,500,000
Less: Applicable exclusion amount	− $ 3,500,000
Gross estate tax exposure	$ 5,000,000
Federal estate tax rates (2008)	45%
Tax due for Bill's estate	$ 2,250,000

By titling assets in Jane's name and by moving Bill's life insurance policy into an ILIT, the couple's estate tax exposure was reduced from $3,375,000 to $2,250,000. This is a $1,125,000 improvement to their estate tax situation simply by retitling a few assets. How long did it take Bill to earn that $1,125,000? You have seen how quickly it can disappear to estate taxes due to incomplete or poor planning.

PURCHASING LIFE INSURANCE

The final fix for this estate tax problem is rather simple. Bill can purchase enough life insurance through an ILIT to cover the estate tax bill that will be owed upon his death. In this case, Bill should purchase at least another $1 million in life insurance. To keep the face value of the policy out of Bill's estate, the insurance should be purchased by the ILIT. The ILIT can direct this additional insurance to pay any estate taxes that are due when Bill and Jane die. With the estate taxes paid, the assets in the estate can pass to the heirs according to Bill's and Jane's plan, not the government's.

OTHER SOLUTIONS THAT INCORPORATE EXIT STRATEGY PLANNING: LIFETIME TRANSFER BY GIFT

As discussed in Chapter 10, a number of transfer techniques are available to Bill and Jane if they care to begin a gifting program.

Now that we have walked through a detailed example of how estate taxes can negatively impact a business owner's total wealth, it is easier to understand the rationale behind the lessons from Chapter 10. In fact, it would be a good idea to go back and reread Chapter 10 if you would like to protect the wealth in your business through a coordinated strategy that includes estate tax planning and a gifting program to family, employees, or a charity or institution of your choice.

Remember that Bill can transfer a greater amount of his business wealth to his desired beneficiaries because of the discounts to value that are permitted for minority stake transfers. Against the backdrop of the example in this chapter, you can see why transferring larger amounts of assets over many years can serve the dual purposes of reducing your estate tax exposure while also transferring your wealth to your intended beneficiaries. Not to mention the good feelings that you can experience, while you are still alive, of gifting these assets to appreciative heirs.

REVIEW

Exiting owners generally have the majority of their wealth tied up in their illiquid businesses. When the value of these businesses exceeds the federal (and state) applicable exclusion amounts, the owners will be subject to high rates of estate taxation. With a bit of planning and forethought and using some rather basic estate planning techniques, a lot of the wealth that was earned over a lifetime of hard work can be protected.

Like many areas of exit strategy planning, complete estate planning is often times far more complex than has been presented in this chapter. Seek out experienced advisors to assist you with your estate tax planning concerns. And, as Chapter 14 discusses, the sooner you assemble your exit strategy planning team, the better off you will be and the more wealth you will be able to protect.

NOTES

1. Vaughn Henry, "Will Your Family Business Survive to the Next Generation?" http://gift-estate.com/article/continuity.htm.
2. Many states decoupled from the federal limits after changes were made to the federal estate tax laws in 2001. (Prior to that, many states followed the federal limits.) This decoupling created a second layer of analysis in most estate plans, further complicating the process of protecting wealth against these taxes.
3. Three years need to pass from the time Bill transfers this policy from his name to the irrevocable life insurance trust without the asset being pulled back into his estate.

13

LEGAL AGREEMENTS THAT YOU NEED TO KNOW

You Will Sign Agreements; Know Them Before You Sign Them

When I started out in business, I spent a great deal of time researching every detail that might be pertinent to the deal I was interested in making. I still do the same today. People often comment on how quickly I operate, but the reason I can move quickly is that I've done the background work first, which no one usually sees. I prepare myself thoroughly, and then when it is time to move ahead, I am ready to sprint.

—Donald Trump

The most important single central fact about a free market is that no exchange takes place unless both parties benefit.

—Milton Friedman

All exiting business owners ought to know that no matter what their choice of business exit, legal agreements will be required to transfer the ownership (except in the case of gifting). When exiting owners step away from their businesses, legal agreements are what control a good portion of the continued relationship with buyers or successors. And, unlike the sale of a home, the sale of an operating business includes highly customized documentation that gives consideration to the interests of buyers or successors in protecting their investment in the business. The legal agreements also provide the sole area of recourse for business owners to turn to for any default of future payments or performance promised by buyers.

The typical documents that exiting owners will be signing are:

- Letters of intent (to purchase the business)
- Purchase and sale agreement
- Noncompete agreements
- Earn-out agreements
- Seller financing agreements

These legal documents not only memorialize the agreement between the parties, but also provide a road map for sorting out any future issues between the exiting owner and buyer. This is an important point. Exiting owners who want to leave the worries of the business behind should pay attention to the language of these agreements to guard against unnecessary future liabilities that can compromise their postexit lifestyle (in particular, see the section titled "Representations and Warranties" later in this chapter).

LETTER OF INTENT

A letter of intent (LOI) is a written document from a buyer or successor that encompasses the offer for your business, detailing the price, structure, and terms of the proposed transaction (covered in Chapter 5). This letter of intent will outline the fundamental deal points so that the parties can begin to identify the salient points of the proposed transaction and make an initial round of negotiations to determine if the proposal will suit the needs and/or expectations of each party.

The practical significance of the LOI is that it represents the point in time when general conversations ends and the real work begins in executing an exit strategy plan. In fact, if a process for selling a business is undertaken (as described in Chapter 5), the selling business owner will want to have many letters of intent from many different buyers to choose from. Recall that the sales process ideally creates a market for the business sale, allowing exiting owners to choose the offers that best meet their goals and expectations. The selling owner chooses the LOI that is best suited to his financial and personal goals. Remember that a sale transaction is about more than just getting the highest price. Many times an offer will require the exiting owner's continued involvement in the business. In situations where deferred payments are expected, it is important also to heavily weigh the creditworthiness of different buyers.

On an emotional level, the LOI stage is where the exit decision is really made. Many advisors—legal, tax, insurance, and financial—will need to be engaged to move from the LOI stage to a closing, where a host of other documents are signed. This process gets expensive, in terms of both money and time, and most exiting business owners know this. The LOI stage also is a point at which exiting owners may mentally check out of the business, believing that the headaches of running the business now will belong to someone else. A warning to exiting owners: It is never a good strategy to assume that a signed LOI will lead to a successful execution of an exit strategy plan. Stay focused on your business straight through to the completion of the transaction, both to protect your business and wealth and also because you are likely going to attest in the purchase and sale agreement that the business has been running substantially the same as always. In other words, the buyer will not want any surprises as to how the business operations have changed because you were no longer paying attention.

A lengthy and detailed LOI is preferred over a short summary of simply the price and terms that a buyer is offering. The greater the number of issues that can be addressed up front at this stage, the higher the probability that fewer surprises will occur later on in the transaction. Surprises that compromise the execution of an exit strategy plan can become very expensive and unproductive.

The LOI stage is also a time for exiting owners to make initial assessments of the taxes and the structuring (see Chapter 11) of the transaction so that they can understand the full financial implications of what is being offered. This is the optimal time to review the goals that you established in Chapter 2, letting your written objectives—not your subjective feelings about the change that you are undertaking—be your guide through the execution of this exit transaction. Be wary not to let your subconscious resistance affect your decisions at this critical juncture.

SHOULD YOU ACCEPT AN EXCLUSIVITY OR "NO-SHOP" CLAUSE?

As stated in, order to increase your probability of success with an exit strategy plan, you need to be able to see the transaction through the eyes of your buyer or successor. In the case of an exclusivity or "no-shop" clause in the LOI, the buyer or successor is asking you, the exiting owner, not to engage conversations with other suitors for your business while that buyer or successor is conducting a more detailed examination of your business.

Buyers want to invest their time, resources, and capital into examining your business, but they do not want to incur these costs without some assurance that the fundamental aspects of the deal, memorialized in the LOI, have been agreed to and that other parties have now been excluded from the sale process. These buyers are looking for exclusive rights to bring the transaction to a successful completion, without having to continue competing with other offers during the due diligence phase of the transaction.

This is the point at which the negotiating advantages move away from you, the exiting owner, and more toward the buyer. As you eliminate other interested parties from consideration for purchasing your business, you are conceding the leverage that you achieved in your marketing process to one potential buyer. Now the transaction shifts gears and the due diligence process that was discussed in Chapter 5 commences, focusing the parties on bringing the transaction to a close. Re-read Chapter 5 and recall how cumbersome a due diligence process can be—forewarned is forearmed.

PURCHASE AND SALE AGREEMENT

When all of your buyer/successor's questions have been answered to their satisfaction, the process proceeds to a signing of the purchase and sale agreement (sometimes referred to as the definitive purchase agreement).

A purchase and sale agreement is *the* document that articulates the agreement between the parties and allows for the legal exchange of ownership in the agreed-on shares (or assets) of the business. This agreement is generally a very long and detailed document written by legal counsel. It includes all of the details of the transaction and includes all clauses pertaining to the transfer or sale of the assets or stock of the business. (See www.exitingyourbusiness.com for a sample purchase and sale document.) The breadth of this document is extensive, detailing the facts and circumstances specific to each deal.

Recall from Chapter 11 that as a general rule, buyers wants to buy assets and sellers want to sell stock. Your purchase and sale agreement will likely either be a stock purchase agreement or an asset purchase agreement. This is an important distinction. You need to know what the buyer is buying because, as we learned, the tax implications of each type of transaction are different.

A full discussion of a purchase and sale agreement is far beyond the scope of this book. If you are beginning your exit strategy planning, understand that the purchase and sale document protects both you and the buyer by having each party make representations as to the current status of each business. Here we highlight one key area for an exiting owner's consideration: the representations and warranties section.

REPRESENTATIONS AND WARRANTIES

One of the more important sections of the purchase and sale agreement is the representations and warranties. It is here that exiting owners needs to disclose and represent the conditions of the business as they truly are. It is said that "If the truth will kill a deal, then there is no deal." If exiting owners do not disclose the truth of the business as it currently exists, they may be held accountable later for not telling the buyer/successor about any hidden risks of which they were aware at the time of transfer.

You are required to disclose the negative areas of the business in order to fully apprise buyers/successors of what they are buying. Recall from the sale transaction in Chapter 5 that our exiting owner received cash at the closings, paid his fees and taxes, and went on to live happily ever after, meeting his postexit expenses. The representations and warranties section can derail the enjoyment of a successful exit if our owner is later sued for not discussing the true status of the business—as he knew it to be—at the time of the closing.

The representations and warranties section should be negotiated with great care in order to ensure that exiting owners will be able to move into their next phase of life without business problems coming back to haunt them. An aggrieved buyer/successor will look to this section to hold you, the exiting owner, accountable for any omission as to the state of the business, dragging you back into the problems of the business after your exit. Note that individual conversations, where you likely disclosed these problems to your buyer or successor, will not matter. The specific writing of the legal agreement, not ancillary conversations, are where the parties look to determine whether a problem area was disclosed. Work with your legal counsel on the representations and warranties section so that your exit has a degree of predictability that gives you comfort.

NONCOMPETE AGREEMENT

Of primary interest to a buyer/successor will be your continued involvement (or lack thereof) in the business after the transaction. Since you, as the exiting owner, presumably are a critical part of the equation that drives value for the business, the transition away from your control will be a risk factor that any buyer/successor will need to estimate. The formal agreement that reflects your desire or ability to stay with or leave the business will be either an employment agreement (mostly for the case of traditional private equity group recapitalization deals) or a noncompete agreement (where you are exiting the business and not continuing on after the close).

Your financial and mental readiness for your exit will assist you in determining the type of legal agreements you are willing to sign and what protections you are willing to give to your buyer/successor. For example, an exiting owner who has a low mental readiness to exit the business may be reluctant to sign a noncompete agreement that states that he or she can no longer earn a living in the industry (for a reasonable period of time, usually three or four years). Review your answers from the worksheets in Chapter 3 assessing your mental readiness to exit the business prior to deciding whether you want to continue working in your current field.

Legal agreements will also reflect your financial readiness to exit your business. For example, as Chapter 11 stated, many smaller business owners will have a difficult time getting all of the compensation for their exit at the closing. In fact, because those owners are involved in the day-to-day running of the business, the buyer/successor typically (and reasonably) will make a portion of the sales proceeds contingent on certain business not being lost once the exiting owner departs.

These future payments are reflected in seller financing agreements and earn-out agreements.

SELLER FINANCING AGREEMENTS

As discussed in Chapter 11, an exiting owner will often times be asked to receive proceeds from the transaction in future periods, beyond the date of the closing. This is referred to as *seller financing* because the buyer/successor could not achieve enough financing (or perceived too many risks in the business) to pay the agreed-upon transfer price up front. This seller financing usually includes an interest rate that accrues against the amount due.

Seller notes may or may not be personally guaranteed by the buyer/successor. This is a negotiated point in most transactions. Ideally, an exiting owner will want to attract a buyer/successor who has deep pockets and is willing to support the payments of the notes either personally or against a corporation that is in a very strong financial position.

And, as we saw in Chapter 9, management buyouts that do not include a financial sponsor (and in case of smaller transactions), it is common for a high percentage of the sales price to be paid out to the exiting owner over time. Recognize that if other debt, such as bank debt, is included in the buyer/successor's purchase, the seller financing note will likely be in second position or subordinate to the bank debt. For example, the seller financing arrangement illustrated in Chapter 9 with our exiting owner Bill included a pledge of company assets to support a down payment from the management team. Bill also financed the transaction through a seller note. In that example, Bill's note was subordinate to the bank's loan.

Exiting owners should know that deferred payment structures are often necessary to completing a transaction. Many times deferred payments actually are the bridge that helps sellers get the price they want while the buyer/successor is relieved of providing cash at the closing. However, when looking at an exit transaction from a wealth management perspective, it is always better to get more cash at the closing and to get the strongest guarantee possible for any financing that you offer.

EARN-OUT AGREEMENTS

Earn-out agreements (introduced in Chapter 11) state that certain payments will be made to an exiting owner after the closing, depending on how the business performs in the exiting owner's absence. Most exiting owners are disturbed by earn-out clauses, particularly if they have a high mental readiness to exit their business. Most realize that they are going to lose control of the business—and their ability to impact its profitability—once ownership changes. That is why most exiting owners prefer to get more cash up front, at the closing, rather than relying on contingencies that pay them over time only if certain business occurs in their absence. Additionally, there is the practical problem of monitoring the business performance after the closing. In these cases, it is advisable to have a very specific formula and an objective manner in which performance can be measured, to help ensure fairness in the process of determining an earn-out that is due an exiting owner. For example, a buyer/successor should not be able to lower an earnings figure artificially in order to avoid the triggering of an earn-out payment to an exiting owner. Again, since the exiting owner has no control over the business, these areas can be tricky to navigate. The legal agreements that reflect the earn-out should be carefully worded to protect the wealth that is due to the exiting owner in the future.

More important, exiting owners should work with their financial advisors to determine that their financial readiness is sufficient to satisfy their postclosing lifestyle without relying on contingent earn-out payments. Go to www.

exitingyourbusiness.com for sample earn-out agreements that you can review while you are establishing your exit strategy plan.

PRACTICAL TIP ON CHOOSING LEGAL COUNSEL

When the time comes to select legal counsel for your exit transaction, choose someone with experience in transfers of corporate assets. This type of legal advisor typically focuses exclusively in this area.

Many exiting owners reading this book will have a legal advisor with whom they feel very comfortable for their general legal needs. Perhaps this attorney assisted with the original filing of articles of incorporation and was available to answer questions or defend the company against a suit brought by an ex-employee. That type of legal advisor is invaluable to the operations and running of a small business, and usually is a friend to the exiting owner.

Yet when exiting a business, the type of negotiating and structuring involved with the legal agreements is usually very complex. Experience counts. In fact, with the amount of wealth that this transaction must protect, it makes sense for exiting owners to ask questions to determine if legal counsel is up to the job. Do not let ego—yours or theirs—get in the way of selecting legal counsel who have extensive experience with all of the agreements mentioned in this chapter. The ability of these advisors to offer a variety of ideas to the exit strategy process ultimately gets you the exit transaction that meets your personal goals.

REVIEW

Exiting owners should know the types of legal agreements that must be signed for each exit option. They should also understand how the agreements are used to reflect both their mental and financial readiness. Do some homework by reviewing some boilerplate agreements (samples available at www. exiting yourbusiness.com) to see how the terms and conditions work. Doing this will allow you to better communicate with your attorney and help you incorporate ideas of your own into the transaction that will give you more comfort after the close. You are relying on these documents to achieve your exit goals and protect your wealth. Do not let the closing be the first time you see them.

14

FORMING AN EXIT STRATEGY ADVISORY TEAM

Your Agenda Comes Ahead of Your Advisors'

> The best teamwork comes from men who are working
> independently toward one goal in unison.
>
> —*James Cash Penney*

These final chapters on deal structuring, taxes, legal agreements, and estate planning should have you convinced that an advisory team is necessary for the execution of your exit strategy plan. Choose your team wisely. Your wealth is at risk. This chapter discusses who is needed and what you should be looking for in your advisors.

DON'T GO IT ALONE: FIND EXPERIENCED EXIT ADVISORS

Business owners wear many hats in order to handle the challenges of owning and running a business. They often adopt a do-it-yourself philosophy, which can extend to the business exit process. For instance, most business owners know something about the technicalities of exiting their business; they've thought about selling to a competitor or handing the reins to a family member. Owners might know a little something about the technical pieces of a business exit, including accounting, taxation, estate planning, insurance planning, legal preparation, legal documentation, and financial advisory services. But knowing a little bit about something can be dangerous; it can lead to a false sense of control and confidence. Why go it alone?

Time is money, and for the hardworking business owner, time is often scarce. When you consider how much wealth is at stake, it makes great sense to set a budget for your professional advisory team. Now is not the time to be frugal. Each dollar spent may very well be a dollar saved in taxes or in better leverage in your negotiations.

Remember that each advisor will know something about his or her role in your exit, but it is your responsibility to assemble this team of advisors and make sure that they work as a cohesive unit toward helping you achieve your stated exit objectives. Getting an advisory team to "play well in the sandbox" together is a large challenge in the exit strategy planning process.

WHO DO YOU NEED ON THE ADVISORY TEAM?

A team of exit strategy advisors consists of a number of players, each having his or her own role and contributing to the overall execution of the exit strategy plan. The roles of the advisors are summarized.

Attorney. This advisor provides advice on legal agreements in the transaction as well as advice on estate planning documents for titling of assets. (All things being equal, the transfer agreements and estate planning should be divided amongst two attorneys, perhaps from the same law firm.) These attorneys may also provide assistance with negotiations as well as guidance on gifting strategies. As mentioned in the last chapter, experienced M&A attorneys are worth every penny, literally and figuratively—the right idea, at the right time in your transaction, can improve your total wealth substantially.

Accountant. This advisor provides tax assessments for each exit strategy option. The accountant may also be called upon to provide cash flow projections for the company as part of a deferred payment arrangement; this is particularly relevant to a management buyout.

Financial advisor. This advisor provides personal financial retirement projections and an investment strategy for the reinvestment of exit proceeds. This income replacement strategy is critical for exiting owners, who are trading business income for income from investments. This should be one of the first steps that you take in your exit strategy planning: finding out what your value gap is (Chapter 2) and determining if you can fill it with your optimal business exit.

Insurance advisor. This advisor provides recommendations on life insurance policies, key-man policies, business policies, and long-term care policies—risk management tools to protect the owner's wealth. Again, re-read Chapter 12 and review your estate planning with your insurance advisor today, even before your team is assembled – this is a large issue that can be addressed prior to engaging the exit strategy planning process.

Mergers and acquisitions (M&A) advisor. This advisor provides insights as to the current marketplace for sale transactions. The M&A advisor gives real-time feedback on the viability of an external sale, providing pricing comparisons for sales of similar companies as well as whether or not the current marketplace has a demand for purchasing your type of business. He or she may also provide inputs for structuring of internal transactions, such as employee stock option plans (ESOPs) and management buyouts (MBOs).

Valuation advisor. This advisor provides a fair market value assessment of the company for purposes of measuring value and the viability of certain internal transactions. A market value assessment may also be completed by the valuation advisor to be used as a "floor price" this you will accept in an external transaction.

Having a strong advisory team is a critical part of any exit strategy plan. The major hurdles to overcome with any team are competence, attitude, and ego. Assessing these three factors, combined, will help you determine who should be on your advisory team.

Chapter 1 discussed the imbalance between the supply and demand for exit strategy planning advice. Exiting business owners are at a disadvantage in this equation because well-versed exit strategy advisors are in short supply and (increasingly) high demand. Therefore, it is important to seek out advisors who understand exit strategy concepts and are willing to work as a team.

WHOSE AGENDA RULES?

Every advisor has an agenda. After all, like all business owners, they are in business for a profit. However, there is a delicate balance between the agenda that the advisor is promoting and what you need to execute your exit strategy plan effectively. For example, an accountant may have a long-standing relationship with a business owner. For many years, that accountant has provided tax services to both the owner and his business. Now, however, the conversation of exit strategies arises. The accountant's financial incentive is not to have the business owner sell the business because, in all likelihood, that accountant will no longer have the owner as a client, thereby reducing his revenues and creating a need to find a new client to replace that income.

It is not fair to pick on the accountants; the same self-serving motives can be applied to nearly all types of advisors. All advisors have a service that they perform for the exiting owner, and each earns a living delivering that service. When assembling your exit strategy team of advisors, the key is to identify those who understand and have experience with exit strategies and provide holistic and objective advice focused on your goals, not their own.

TEAM MEETINGS

The most effective way to measure competence, attitude, and ego is to require your advisors to attend a semiannual (or quarterly, if necessary) team meeting, where the topic of the meeting is your exit strategy plan and how each of them is contributing towards making it work. These meetings are a very healthy part of the exit strategy planning process for a few reasons.

First, each advisor will need to prepare reports for the exiting owner that will be reviewed by the other advisors. Many advisors see themselves as the most trusted and most important advisor to the exiting owner. Accordingly, their egos may be bruised when they are asked to play on a team and coordinate with other advisors. In the worst case, the advisor will not be open to input from other advisors out of a fear that he or she will be replaced. In most instances, this self-serving attitude becomes a self-fulfilling prophecy; the advisor's unwillingness to participate and share thoughts with a group leads to his or her exclusion from the exit strategy team and, eventually, the end of serving the exiting owner.

The second reason why team meetings can be so effective is that an exiting owner will want advisors talking to each other, not just to the owner. Exiting owners can leverage their time when their advisors communicate with each other. In the absence of this collaborative communication, exiting owners are forced to listen to and interpret all of the information from all of the different practice areas. The exiting owners have to process that information and relay it to the other advisors on the team. Being forced to be the hub in the information wheel further burdens the exiting owner's valuable time. It is far more efficient, and ultimately less expensive, to hold a team meeting where ideas can be exchanged and discussed amongst the advisors while the exiting owner sits and listens, instead of interpreting and trafficking the information.

ASSIGN A QUARTERBACK

There needs to be one "quarterback" for the exit strategy engagement. This quarterback assists the owner with both the design and the execution of the exit strategy plan. Remember from Chapter 2: This plan is a written document that is customized to the exiting owner's needs (again, to see a sample written exit strategy plan visit www.exitingyourbusiness.com).

The written plan lists the advisors who are on the team. Each advisor receives a copy of this plan and is asked to render an opinion, not only on his or her area of expertise but on the plan as a whole. The quarterback's job is to coordinate the team meetings and to consolidate the team members' input into an updated plan. By conducting meetings in this organized fashion, exiting owners have the opinions of team members in writing and coordinated in one exit strategy plan document that they can study and change if need be. The plan is constantly being changed and updated until the exiting owner is comfortable that his personal goals and objectives will be met.

CASE STUDY

We now return to our exiting owner, Bill, to illustrate the roles and significance of each exit strategy advisor on the team.

Bill is building his exit strategy plan and wants to receive input from all of his current advisors to make the plan as efficient as possible. He believes that his current advisors are qualified and willing to help him identify, choose, and execute the exit strategy plan that best meets his personal goals.

Bill's first step in assembling the team is choosing his financial advisor, Michael, to be the quarterback. After all, it was Michael who originally brought the idea of planning for the exit to Bill, and Bill believes that Michael is competent, trustworthy, and has a balanced demeanor that will allow him to communicate well with Bill's other advisors. Michael's incentives are also most closely aligned with what Bill is trying to achieve. In other words, Michael manages Bill's investments for a fee. That fee is a percentage of the total amount of assets that Bill has under management with Michael. Therefore, this exit strategy plan will create additional liquidity that Michael is going to manage (if he can provide the customized solutions required). This will increase the fees that Michael receives. Michael also does not charge Bill by the hour, as an attorney would. However, Bill agrees to pay Michael a flat fee of $7,500 (approximately 3/4 of 1% of the value of his business) for being the quarterback and assembling this plan. Bill realized long ago that in business—and in life—you get what you pay for. He wants Michael to pay very close attention to this exit strategy plan and is happy to invest in seeing that the plan is designed and implemented correctly.

Michael sends e-mails to all of Bill's advisors, informing them of the intention to design an exit strategy plan for Bill and the upcoming meeting to discuss the details. All advisors also receive a copy of the initial thoughts for the exit strategy plan that Michael and Bill have written down (see Chapter 15). The exit strategy team also gets an agenda for the three-hour meeting, detailing the areas for which each advisor will be asked to make a presentation. All of the advisors on the team respond to Michael with their availability, and the meeting is set.

All advisors are in attendance on the day of the meeting, and Bill kicks things off.

Bill announces that he is making a commitment to building an exit strategy plan that will help him with exiting his business and protecting the illiquid wealth trapped inside. Bill goes on to say that he is not ready to leave right away. In fact, he believes that there is plenty of future value in the brewery business but, at age 56, he is open to start planning his exit strategy.

Bill tells his advisors that he will require all of their inputs in order to design the right plan and that the execution of the ultimate plan will be a team effort. To that end, Bill mentions that he has asked Michael to quarterback the process. To assist with the coordination, Bill also asks Michael to establish a secure online forum where the advisors can communicate with each other about the details of the plan and post documents and questions about the process.

FINANCIAL ADVISOR

Michael makes the first presentation of the meeting. He states that Bill's financial readiness to exit the business is fairly low. He explains that this means that Bill has been putting most of his money back into the business over the years and that Bill's accumulated savings cannot currently pay for a high percentage of his projected postexit expenses.

Michael details the exit options being considered for Bill's exit. He delivers a brief description of each exit option and explains the approximate financial impact that each will have on Bill's total wealth. Michael lets each advisor know that their input is critical to assisting Bill in choosing the exit option that is most aligned with his retirement goals. Michael provides Bill's current financial condition as a foundation for continued discussions.

He shares this net worth statement with the team:

Bill's Net Worth	
Individual retirement plan assets	$1 million
Home equity	$1 million
Business range of values	$7 million–$10.5 million

Michael goes on to explain that because Bill does not have an expensive lifestyle, many exit options can be considered. He offers estimates of future income streams (including estimated Social Security payments for Bill), as well as estimated postexit expenses. Michael also shares a strategy for the reinvestment of the approximate amount of the proceeds from each exit option and illustrates how each scenario works toward achieving Bill's retirement goals. He also details the specific asset allocations and the projected income that will be derived from each strategy. He mentions that Bill is particularly interested in the accountant's opinion on the taxability of the various income streams proposed with the business income replacement strategy.

Michael has projected estimates of different outcomes for Bill, depending on the net amount of fees and taxes that the exit proceeds will be subject to, as well as the timing of payments that will be received from the various exit options available. He concludes that Bill can choose the exit option most appealing to him and, in all likelihood, still maintain his current lifestyle postexit.

However, Michael reiterates Bill's comments about not wanting to leave the business right away. Therefore, this team is being asked to make various assessments that will assist Bill in understanding the personal implications of each of the exit options.

LEGAL ADVISOR

Bill's attorney takes the floor next. The attorney states that the business is relatively "clean"; a new owner or successor would not have to resolve very many issues in order to take over the business in Bill's absence. However, the business has not gone through a legal audit exercise, which he recommends. The purpose of this legal audit is to organize and review all of the documents that any buyer or successor is likely to ask for in the due diligence phase of the exit strategy. The attorney goes on to recommend that all of Bill's contracts, files, and vital paperwork be organized in electronic format to provide easy access to the vast amount of information that will need to be shared with any buyer or successor. By instituting the habit of electronically recording of this documentation immediately, the organized approach will reduce the uneasiness often associated with the due diligence information gathering process.

The attorney also shares a document detailing the manner in which all of Bill's and his wife, Jane's, assets are titled. He explains that certain retitling should occur and that trust accounts must be formed to protect Bill's wealth. The attorney mentions to Michael that the titling of Bill's taxable investment accounts should change so that the trusts that he forms will be funded with the investment assets.

The attorney also lists the types of legal agreements required for each transaction being considered as well as the process, time frame, and approximate cost that of each exit option.

The attorney states that be believes that any one of the exit options being discussed will work to protect Bill's wealth and that he is looking forward to working with the team to help Bill achieve his exit goals.

ACCOUNTANT/TAX ADVISOR

Bill's accountant handles both Bill's personal and corporate tax filings. Consequently, she is familiar with the impact that each transaction alternative will have on Bill's total wealth. The accountant shares this information with the team, apprising Michael of the approximate net impact that each transaction would have on Bill's personal income. In other words, she is able to project the amount and timing of the payments that would come from each of the exit options that Bill is considering. The accountant is able to discuss the wealth that would be gained or lost in each transaction, allowing Bill to evaluate objectively how important the outcomes of each transaction alternative are relative to the fluctuation of his net results.

For example, the accountant has taken the valuation estimates from the fair market value assessment and compared them with the value assessments of the synergy value sale of the business to a competitor. This comparison illustrates the cash flows that would result, net of fee and net of tax, to Bill under each transaction. These net figures are combined with the assumptions from Michael, the financial advisor, to further refine Bill's financial readiness and to illustrate his potential total passive income after the exit.

The accountant also reminds the exit strategy team that Bill's corporation is a C corporation and that any transaction which includes a purchase of the assets will be subject to corporate-level taxation as well as a subsequent tax for the distribution of that cash to Bill.

INSURANCE ADVISOR

Bill's insurance advisor reiterates what the attorney discussed regarding the manner in which Bill and Jane's assets are titled. He again offers an assessment of Bill's existing estate tax exposure. Part of this estate tax exposure has been accounted for with the formation of an irrevocable life insurance trust (ILIT), which holds a $2 million life insurance policy on Bill's life. The insurance advisor also walks the team through the key-man insurance coverage for the brewery as well as the other policies that the company owns to prevent a business shutdown—and concurrent immediate loss of wealth—that would occur if Bill were to die or become disabled.

These insurance policies will need to change hands depending on the exit option that Bill chooses. The insurance advisor offers a few alternative suggestions and proposes personal coverage for Bill, including long-term care insurance to prevent his wealth from being shrunk needlessly by any future stay in an assisted-living facility.

MERGERS AND ACQUISITIONS ADVISOR

Finally, the merger and acquisitions advisor offers advice on the different potential deal structures for each exit option. She assesses the difficulties involved with a transfer to a management team as well as the current market demand for good investment opportunities by private equity groups and their recapitalization structure. She mentions that an employee stock ownership plan (ESOP) is likely the most tax-advantaged manner in which Bill can exit the business, then offers some illustrations and cash flow projections regarding the use of the ESOP and avoidance of taxes with the 1042 election. Michael, the financial advisor, will need to source the qualified replacement property and work with the accountant in making the 1042 election.

In addition, the M&A advisor tells the team that a highly leveraged ESOP will require financing beyond what Bill's bank may be willing to extend. She offers suggestions for different types of debt financing and the relative costs of that type of financing, including her approximate fee for attracting this financing to the deal. Those costs help in analyzing the exit option that yields Bill the optimal outcome.

REVIEW

Bill has assembled a competent and collaborative advisory team. The financial advisor Michael has demonstrated a sound ability to handle the quarterback's role. Bill has now heard from his advisory team and likes the options that he is being offered. He can choose the exit option that he is most comfortable with, now that he understands the impact of each transaction on his personal (and corporate) goals. He can also further customize his exit strategy plan as more information is gathered and absorbed.

Since Bill's mental readiness and his financial readiness to leave are both rather low, he can take his time assessing the objective advice and inputs from his advisory team. Whether he decides to stay with the company over the next few years or chooses a more accelerated rate of exit from his business, he will have the information and inputs to make his decision on a fully informed and objective basis. Most importantly, he has all of this information organized in a written document that reflects all of his options, including opinions from all of his advisors.

In the absence of such a team-based approach, exiting owners are relegated to absorbing a vast amount of inputs by themselves, leading to decision making based on imperfect processing and integration of that information. Getting the right advisors is critical to an exit strategy plan. Having these advisors work together is equally important. Exiting owners should give the process of assembling their advisory team heavy consideration. Invest in your advisors. The benefits will pay off immediately as ideas are tossed about among team members who assist you in meeting your exit strategy planning goals.

15

PULLING IT ALL TOGETHER

On average, more than 80 hours are spent writing business plans
while only 6 hours are spent planning an exit.

—Ronen Shefer

*Statistics from a 2007 survey of 500 business owners
in the United States and Canada*

The tools in this book allow owners to customize an exit over any period of time in order to accommodate their next phase of life and, simultaneously protect their wealth. The power to design and control exit strategy plans will help owners adjust to the changes that are just over the horizon, leading millions of exiting owners towards the enjoyment of the fruits of their lifetime of labor as a private business owner.

A marketplace of service providers, who vary in competence, are out there tripping over themselves to meet the needs of exiting owners. You will choose carefully amongst them to be certain that your exit strategy plan is the one being executed, not theirs. Take charge of the exit strategy process with your newfound knowledge of business exit strategy planning so that your options are understood and your timing suits your personal goals. Customize your exit strategy plan to your liking. After a lifetime of success in business, you owe it to yourself to tackle this challenge of cashing in (or transferring your wealth) with the respect that it deserves.

As Chapter 1 indicated, millions of exiting owners are in need of customized planning for their exits. This book is a guide to raising your awareness and following proven steps that lead to a strategy that begins with what you want most from your business exit—and ways to achieve it.

You can put the final steps into action to achieve your goals and protect your illiquid business wealth.

FOLLOW THE STEPS

This book has offered a step-by-step program for protecting your wealth. This is a lengthy and detailed program, but a step-by-step system nonetheless. The three parts of the book were designed to provide easy access to address whichever step you need to work on in your planning.

Recall our definition of an exit strategy plan:

> The written goals for the succession of a business's ownership and control, derived from a well-thought-out and properly timed plan that considers all factors, all interested parties, and the personal goals of the owners in a manner and a time period that accommodates the business, its shareholders, and potential buyers.

Part I of this book highlighted the marketplace of exit strategy planning needs, illustrating the challenges with transferring or converting illiquid wealth to cash. It also discussed your overall readiness for an exit, offering different types of owners and different options for an exit.

Part II discussed each of these options and applied them to a case study so that you could see them in action. Each option has a different value. It is critical to realize that the value that you receive needs to be applied to your personal goals in order for your plan to be successful.

Part III has shown you the most likely hurdles that you will encounter when exiting your business. Taxes, fees, and your advisory team need to be navigated to design an exit that meets your objectives.

The chapters of this book have mirrored the step-by-step process illustrated in the Chapter 1. (See Exhibit 15.1.)

The optimal way to illustrate how the parts of an exit strategy plan come together is to return to our exiting owner, Bill, to see how the step-by-step system assists him in establishing his own written plan to protect the wealth in his privately held business.

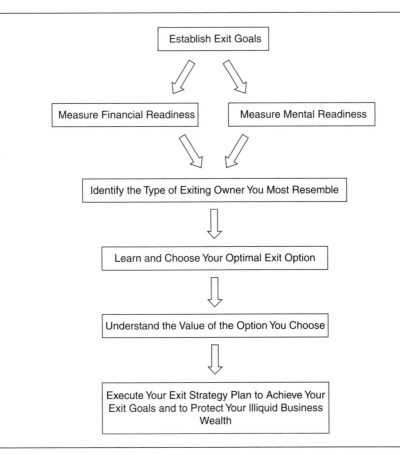

EXHIBIT 15.1   EXIT PROCESS STEPS

STEP 1. PLANNING THE EXIT—BILL WRITES
DOWN HIS EXIT GOALS

Too many exiting owners today are not proactive with their business exit planning. It is hoped that the content and design of this book—and perhaps a caring advisor who shared the information with you—has created an urge to get you started with planning your exit and protecting your wealth.

Step 1—*Stop* what you are doing. Get out a sheet of paper. Write down your goals for your business exit. If you cannot visualize what you want, likely you will remain on the treadmill of running your business, and precious time and opportunities will pass you by as you procrastinate further.

Let's examine the rest of the steps in the process by returning to Bill.

I want to achieve _____ with my exit strategy.

Examples   ☐   Get most money.

☐   Time and money freedom.

☐   Continue running the business but diversify my estate.

☐   Leave a legacy—maintain family harmony.

☐   Pay as little taxes as possible.

☐   Keep control as long as possible, diversify along the way.

☐   Pass on to employees.

The reason that this is most important to me is because

_____ .

I would like to achieve this by _____, _____ .

                              Month / Day   *Year*

I am going to achieve this by:

_____   reading this book.

_____   writing out my goals.

_____   studying whether my goals are achievable.

_____   analyzing my options for liquidity.

_____   making changes in my routine to accommodate this plan.

I will know that I have reached my goal when these outcomes manifest:

The business is owned / run by _____ (insider/outsider).

I have $ _____ in after-fee and after-tax money in my investment account.

After the exit I will engage my mind in these activities:

_____   _____   _____

Exhibit 15.2   Summary Sheet of Personal Goals

Bill begins his exit strategy planning by writing down his exit goals. He uses the form provided in Exhibit 15.2 to help organize his thoughts and begin to focus on what life will be like once he has left the business.

Is this exit something that Bill is excited to step into or does he perceive his business as being reluctantly left behind?

Bill knows that he does not want to continue with the business as it has been run in the past, but he is not certain that he wants to exit right away either. Recognizing that he *is* the business, Bill determines that making a personal assessment of his ability to walk away from it is his next best step.

STEP 2. FINANCIAL AND MENTAL READINESS

Bill's closest advisor suggests that he answer a set of questions that will help him determine both his financial and his mental readiness for his business exit. On the financial readiness side, Bill measures his monthly and annual expenses, many of which are currently run through the business. He assumes the most conservative scenario: that the business will not be able to pay these expenses going forward because someone else owns it. From that assumption, Bill determines the amount of after-fee, after-tax proceeds that will be required to meet his postexit expenses. There is a rather substantial value gap—the difference between what Bill currently has saved and what he needs to satisfy his exit. Bill rates his financial readiness as low and plots a point on the exit quadrant chart.

Bill also does some soul searching, remembering back to when—and more important, why—he started and continued to run his business. Why did he do it? Why the long hours? Why the pressure? Why did he possess that desire to achieve personal financial freedom? And, why is he continuing to wait to enjoy the fruits of his labor? Perhaps work is the main thing that Bill has always known. However, now that he has arrived at a point of substantial financial, albeit illiquid, means, he wonders why he does not act in a manner that protects it. Bill rates his mental readiness as low and plots that point on the exit quadrant chart.

STEP 3. EXIT QUADRANT CHART—IDENTIFY WHAT TYPE OF EXITING OWNER YOU ARE

From the steps detailed in Chapters 2 and 3 Bill determines that he has a rather low mental readiness for an exit and a rather low financial readiness. He plots his point on the chart (Exhibit 15.3) and recognizes that he identifies most strongly with the stay-and-grow exiting owner. Bill reads about this type of exiting owner and resonates with most of what is described. Bill also sees his future and reads about the get-me-out-at-the-highest-price exiting owner. He does not want to end up as that person who is forced to sell the business in order to meet retirement expenses. Instead, Bill resolves to begin his planning today with an eye toward his exit.

Bill now wants to know his options for making such a plan.

Bill has taken some very significant steps so far. He has prepared his mind to focus on learning options from which he can begin to construct his business exit strategy plan even though he is not ready to leave the business today.

The exit quadrant chart is filled with these options (Exhibit 15.4). Bill can review the options and seek the one that most closely aligns with where he currently is with his readiness for his exit.

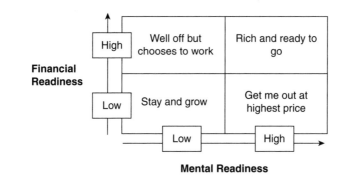

EXHIBIT 15.3 EXIT QUADRANT CHART

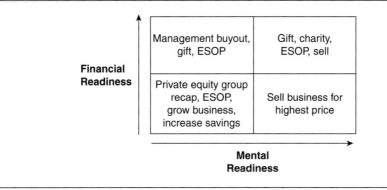

EXHIBIT 15.4 EXIT OPTIONS CHART

STEP 4. LEARN AND CHOOSE YOUR OPTIMAL EXIT OPTION

As Exhibit 15.4 shows, Bill's top three options appear to be an employee stock ownership plan (ESOP), a recapitalization with a private equity group, or simply beginning the process of improving his current savings so that he does not one day become the exiting owner who needs to get top dollar via a sale of his business.

Bill reads about each of these exit options and is impressed with the flexibility that he has either to sell or keep control. Each option has different outcomes associated with it. Therefore, Bill calls on his team of advisors to help him assess the pros and cons of each exit alternative. He is taking definite actions toward getting a written plan to meet his goals.

Bill asks his advisory team to help him measure the net result to him—in terms of control of the business, plus current and future cash flows—from each of the options available so that he can see whether his goals will be achieved. Bill is organizing the resources of his advisory team for designing his optimal exit strategy plan.

STEP 5. UNDERSTAND THE VALUE OF THE OPTIONS YOU CHOOSE

Bill sees that each exit option brings with it a different expected value. For example, the ESOP option measures value under the fair market value standard, while the private equity group recapitalization measures value under the investment value measurement.

Value measurement is only one component of the exit strategy plan; Bill also knows that taxes and fees will reduce what he gets in value. The ESOP, generally speaking, has lower fees and taxes and leaves Bill in control. The recapitalization transaction has a higher value but higher fees and taxes. With a recapitalization Bill sells control but keeps his job. In both cases Bill can retain a stake in the business going forward so that value is delivered to him once again when he monetizes his remaining interest in the future.

Since Bill's value gap is substantial, he consults with his advisory team to help him get estimates of value for discussion purposes only. This initial conversation around value makes Bill realize that his company will likely be worth enough under either scenario to close the value gap and provide for his postexit expenses. This is good news, but the planning is far from over.

STEP 6. EXECUTE YOUR EXIT STRATEGY PLAN

Bill has written down his goals and determined that he is not ready to leave his business today. That being said, his exit strategy planning moves forward because even though he does not want to leave his business right away, he is very interested in protecting his wealth.

Bill decides to make one of his advisors his quarterback for the design and execution of his exit strategy plan. Bill selects his financial advisor, who originally brought the exit strategy planning idea to his attention. This advisor has experience and support systems for developing customized exit strategy plans. Bill wants each member of his advisory team to provide input on the details of the plan. Because most of Bill's wealth is tied up in his business he knows that this process is well worth the investment of time and some advisory fees. Being proactive with this planning increases the potential for Bill to protect his wealth.

Bill's advisory team includes his:

- Accountant, who provides cash flow projections, business analysis, tax consequences of each option, and the financial statements preparations and interpretations.

- Attorney, who provides a legal audit exercise to look at the company through the eyes of a buyer. He also provides an estate planning review to determine Bill's current estate tax exposure and the design of his trusts and the titling of his assets. He will also establish the irrevocable life insurance trust (ILIT) that the insurance advisor recommends.

- Insurance advisor, who assists in transferring Bill's $2 million life insurance policy to the ILIT and makes recommendations for key-person policies, and provides an overview of all records of Bill's insurance coverage and which policies need to be moved out of the business and where additional coverage is required.

- Financial advisor, who aggregates the work from the other advisors and reports back to Bill with the updated written exit strategy plan that organizes all of this data. This exit strategy report should show Bill the cash flows of each transaction and how the net amount of each payment goes toward satisfying his personal goals. The financial advisor runs the projections of income versus expenses to determine how Bill's postexit lifestyle will be maintained.

- M&A advisor, who is consulted on the current market conditions for external as well as internal transfer. The M&A provider also provides a range of values for all of the transfers options being considered to put some numbers behind this level of planning.

When all of this work is done, Bill and his team are ready to execute the plan that best meets his goals. At this point, the execution of the plan is relatively easy. The hard work has been completed.

Bill now has a written plan for the succession of his business's ownership and control. The plan is well thought out. Its execution can be timed in order to accommodate the needs that Bill has identified and incorporated into his plan. Again, for an example of a sample exit strategy plan, go to www.exitingyourbusiness.com.

Bill has followed the six steps. He has studied his exit as intensely as he designed his plan to get into business. Only now the outcomes are more predictable. The main constraint to Bill protecting his wealth and designing an exit strategy plan that meets his goals had been a lack of awareness of what was required to begin and complete this type of planning. That constraint has been removed.

CONCLUSION

Now you too are empowered with valuable information. The aim of this book is to provide written guidance that inspires you to go out and treat your exit strategy planning with the same vigor that you held as you built your own personal empire: your successful privately held business.

I would enjoy hearing from you about how this book has assisted in your exit strategy planning. You can reach me at my Web site: www.exitingyour business.com.

I wish you the very best with your exit strategy planning and the protection of the wealth that you have worked a lifetime to achieve.

And once again, congratulations on all of your success in your private business. May it serve you well in your next phase of life.

INDEX